AF605238

The Jewish Publication Society expresses its gratitude for the generosity of the following sponsors of this book:

In appreciation of this thorough presentation of the long, often troubled yet distinguished history of Jews in Germany. To honor my mother, Frieda Roberg, and my uncle Wilhelm Marx, who enabled my own perilous escape in 1941. And to memorialize our family members who died in the Holocaust.

—Kurt W. Roberg

University of Nebraska Press | Lincoln

JEWS AND GERMANS

Promise, Tragedy, and the Search for Normalcy

GUENTER LEWY

The Jewish Publication Society | Philadelphia

 Published by the University of Nebraska Press as a Jewish Publication Society book. Manufactured in the United States of America. ♾

Library of Congress Cataloging-in-Publication Data
Names: Lewy, Guenter, 1923–, author.
Title: Jews and Germans: promise, tragedy, and the search for normalcy / Guenter Lewy.
Description: Lincoln: University of Nebraska Press, 2020. | Includes bibliographical references and index. | Summary: "'Jews and Germans' is the only book in English to delve into the history and challenges of the German-Jewish relationship from before the Holocaust through today. Were the Weimar Republic years (1918–1933) truly reciprocal for Jews and Germans? Post-Holocaust, how has that complex relationship evolved?"—Provided by publisher.
Identifiers: LCCN 2019053433
ISBN 9780827615038 (hardback)
ISBN 9780827618497 (epub)
ISBN 780827618503 (mobi)
ISBN 9780827618510 (pdf)
Subjects: LCSH: Jews—Germany—History—1800–1933. | Germany—Ethnic relations—History—1800–1933. | Germany—Politics and government—1800–1933. | Jews—Germany—Public opinion—History—1800–1933.
Classification: LCC DS134.25 .L49 2020 | DDC 943/.00492400904—dc23
LC record available at https://lccn.loc.gov/2019053433

Set in Questa by Laura Buis.

In der Fremde

Ich hatte einst ein schönes Vaterland.
Der Eichenbaum Wuchs dort so hoch, die
  Veilchen nickten sanft.
Es war ein Traum.
Das küßte mich auf deutsch, und sprach
  auf deutsch
(Man glaubt es kaum,
Wie gut es klang) das Wort: “Ich liebe dich!”
Es war ein Traum.

....

In a Foreign Land

I once had a beautiful fatherland.
The oak
grew there so high, the violets gently nodded.
It was a dream.
It kissed me in German, it spoke in German
(one can hardly believe it,
it sounded so good)
the phrase: “I love you!”
It was a dream.

HEINRICH HEINE, Paris 1844

Contents

Illustrations

TABLE

Acknowledgments

I want to thank the two readers who evaluated an early version of this work and made valuable suggestions for its improvement. My daughter Barbara helped spot and eliminate her father's occasional relapses into his Germanic style of writing. I am indebted to Rabbi Barry Schwartz, director of the Jewish Publication Society, for his interest in this book and his helpful editorial work. I thank the University of Nebraska Press for copublishing the book.

Most important, I want to express my gratitude to Joy Weinberg, managing editor of the Jewish Publication Society, whose editorial acuity has immensely improved the readability of this book. Joy's eye for clarity of expression and her attention to detail have been exemplary, and I have been most fortunate to benefit from her commitment to this work.

Introduction

The fifteen years of the Weimar Republic—between Germany's defeat in World War I in 1918 and Adolf Hitler's accession in 1933—have been called a time of unparalleled German-Jewish convergence. In language, appearance, and patriotic conviction, German Jews became Germans. Enjoying full civil rights, they became ministers, mayors, civil servants, and full professors at the universities. Even more so, relations between Germans and Jews became more intimate, and more fruitful, than ever before. Jews occupied a significant place in German culture—in literature, music, the theater, journalism, science, and many other fields. Between 1918 and 1933, when German Jews comprised fewer than 1 percent of the German population, twelve German-Jewish personages received the Nobel Prize for their cultural achievements.

The great majority of German Jews considered themselves primarily German, with the Jewish part—religion or ethnicity—playing a subordinate role. Most of them dismissed anti-Semitism as a relic of the past that would soon be overcome. Indeed, assimilation into German society appeared to be well on the way. Interreligious marriage flourished, reaching 40 percent in 1933. Meanwhile, the Zionist ideal of a Jewish homeland in Palestine, promulgated by the Austrian journalist Theodor Herzl with the 1896 pamphlet "The Jewish State," found few adherents.

Nazi rule quickly put an end to what had come to be seen as the German-Jewish symbiosis. The promising dream turned into a nightmare. Jews were dismissed from the civil service, and Jewish businesses were subjected to boycotts. Leading Jewish members of left-wing parties were hauled into concentration camps, and many were murdered. The Nuremberg laws of 1935 deprived Jews of their citizenship and made them pariahs. The events of Kristallnacht—the "night of broken glass" of November 9, 1938, during which the display windows of Jewish businesses were smashed and synagogues burned—marked the beginning of state-sponsored violence against Jews that would eventually culminate in the Holocaust. The shock of this wave of hostility was immense, and a growing number of Jews were leaving their beloved homeland. Had German Jews pursued a delusory dream? Had their celebration of German culture been naïve? Did that optimistic appraisal stand in the way of recognizing the disaster that was to come? Was the Holocaust foreseeable through less expectant lenses?

The concept of "symbiosis" as used in biology describes the mutually dependent and advantageous relationship between two different species. When applied to the human sphere, symbiosis similarly stands for a coexistence in which each community retains its own characteristics and enriches the other through a fruitful merger. Unlike the term "assimilation," which implies abandoning one tradition in favor of another, symbiosis entails a fusion of distinctive features leading to a new synthesis. While clearly there were German–Jewish creative collaborations during the Weimar era—just think of Berthold Brecht and Kurt Weill of *The Threepenny Opera* fame—scholars continue to debate the question of whether a German-Jewish symbiosis was in fact truly achieved. Was there ever a commonality of German and Jewish essential qualities? Did the desire for a German-Jewish merger exist outside of the Jewish community? How significant is the fact that the idea of a German-Jewish symbiosis was first mentioned (in 1927) by an anti-Semitic German, Wilhelm Stapel, who vigorously rejected such a merger of traditions?

This book critically confronts the answers that have been given to these questions. It tells the story of this enduringly important topic historically and carries it forward to the present day. It concomitantly addresses the pitfalls of reading the history of the German-Jewish relationship backward, solely for clues to a crime to come, with Auschwitz standing at the end of an inevitable outcome. And it explores many other critical questions. How could the Holocaust follow on the heels of such a period of German-Jewish togetherness? After the Nazi takeover, why did Jews persist in hoping against hope that relations would return to normal? How did Jews who believed in the Communist ideal reconcile with the Communist reality in postwar East Germany? Today, some seventy-five years after the Shoah, with some two hundred thousand Jews living in the land of the murderers, is there hope for the eventual restoration of German-Jewish collaboration?

The book begins with the history of the German-Jewish struggle for emancipation. From there it portrays Jewish life in Weimar Germany, when assimilation reached its zenith and German Jews sought to be more German than the Germans. During this time the Jewish contribution to German culture became immensely important. It is difficult to think of Weimar's cultural and scientific life without the contributions of Lion Feuchtwanger, Arnold and Stefan Zweig, Arnold Schönberg and Otto Klemperer, Albert Einstein, and many other great figures. Subsequent chapters address the influence and fate of the German-Jewish youth movement and of Jewish patriotic organizations such as the National League of Jewish Combat Soldiers (RJF), in which Jews largely modeled their values and actions on the prized Germanic qualities of the era. A subsequent chapter shows how, given the very—one could say militantly–pro-German environment, the Jewish reaction to the Nazi seizure of power included the attempts of some conservative German Jews to show allegiance to Nazi nationalism and obtain exemption from anti-Jewish legislation, solely for themselves.

The final two chapters discuss the state of German-Jewish relations after the defeat of Nazi Germany. More than three thousand German-Jewish Communists returned to what became the German-Democratic Republic, better known as Communist East Germany, expecting the Jewish question to be resolved through the establishment of a new society of socialist harmony; with the downfall of capitalism, anti-Semitism would disappear, and a new Marxist version of the German-Jewish symbiosis would ensue. This hope, too, would meet with disappointment. Many leading Jewish Communists would pay dearly for their misplaced faith in a Marxist utopia.

By contrast, Jewish life in postwar West Germany was decisively shaped by the large-scale influx of Jews from the former Soviet Union. The relations of these Jews to their German hosts were not burdened by the experience of the Holocaust. With the passage of time, anti-Semitism declined, but has since increased again, partly as a result of the arrival of about one million Muslims from the Middle East and Africa in 2015 and 2016.

Hence—as I show through personal stories—many Jews in Germany today have deeply ambivalent feelings about living in the land of the murderers. Meanwhile, many contemporary Germans believe they shouldn't have to feel guilty on account of crimes committed by an earlier generation. Still other Germans display a philo-Semitism that differently complicates achievement of a normal Jewish–German relationship in the twenty-first century.

I approach the controversies about Jewish life in Germany both as a historian and a witness to the unfolding Holocaust. Born in Breslau, Germany (today the Polish city of Wroclaw), in 1923, I grew up in a typical German-Jewish family. My father had been a volunteer soldier in World War I. Our family's Jewishness consisted of attending religious services on the High Holidays. I lived for six years under Nazi rule, attending German schools and receiving a good education in German culture during most of this time. For about five years I belonged to a German-Jewish youth movement that after 1933 underwent a transition from identifying as primarily German to becoming Zionist in outlook and practice. During Kristallnacht in 1938 I was on the receiving end of storm-trooper violence, and in March 1939 I left Germany for Palestine, after which I lived in a kibbutz for three years. In late 1942, with General Rommel's divisions threatening an imminent assault on the Jewish home in Palestine, I volunteered for the British army. I served for four years in the Palestine Regiment and, later, in the Jewish Brigade, part of General Montgomery's Eighth Army in the battle for Italy. For about a year after the war, I was an interpreter for the British military police in occupied Germany. In 1946 I solved the problem of where a dispossessed German Jew was to live by coming to the United States and reuniting with my parents, whom I had not seen for seven years. More important, I found in the United States a rewarding life and a new home—one I continue to treasure with a genuine sense of pride.

Writing this book has been for me more than creating a work of scholarship. It has made me recall a chapter in my life that I cannot and should not forget. Today the number of those with personal recollections of the Nazi era and the unfolding Holocaust is dwindling rapidly. I am happy to be able to contribute my share to this important literature.

JEWS AND GERMANS

1

The Struggle for Emancipation

The first documentary evidence of a Jewish settlement in what is today Germany dates from the fourth century. A decree of the Emperor Constantine in the year 321 speaks of a well-organized Jewish congregation in Cologne whose members owned houses and were Roman citizens. Other Jewish centers existed at that time, on various trade routes along the Rhine and the Danube—in Mainz, Worms, Trier, Augsburg, and Regensburg.

Harsh Life in the Medieval Ghetto

Jews lived in towns because the feudal order of the time, bolstered by religious rules, prohibited non-Christians from owning land. These urban Jews tended to be merchants, artisans, and physicians, as well as men learned in the Jewish scriptures. They were favorably situated in the world of trade due to their knowledge of languages and links to their fellow Jews, widely dispersed throughout the Mediterranean. Bishops and secular nobles who ruled the towns appreciated the economic importance of the Jews, who served as economic agents and advisors, and they protected the lives and property of Jews with special letters of privilege.

Like other commercial and occupational groups in medieval towns, Jews lived in distinct neighborhoods. A separate residence was also required by ritual rules and especially the observance of the Sabbath. These so-called *Judengassen* (Jewish lanes) were usually close to the marketplace and the castle of the noble rulers.[1]

The separation of the Jewish quarter from the rest of the town by walls and gates was a gradual process that followed the decisions of the Lateran Church Councils of 1179 and 1214. By the fourteenth century German Jews lived in ghettos. The rise of a money economy prompted the Church to forbid Christians to charge interest on loans, so Jews, by default, became the primary moneylenders. Many of them became prosperous as a result, but they were also despised as profiteers and agents of the nobility.

The resulting tensions exploded during the Crusades. Incited by the rabble-rousing sermons of Peter of Amiens in 1096, and ostensibly focused on liberating Jesus's burial place in the Holy Land and avenging his death, the Crusaders undertook to kill Jews who since early Christian times had been accused of having murdered Christ. The inhabitants of entire Jewish communities in Speyer, Worms, Trier, and Cologne would be slaughtered. Many Jews took their own lives, incurring martyrdom by what in Jewish tradition is known as *kiddush hashem* (sanctification of the divine name). Meanwhile, many bishops tried to protect their parish Jews, both because of their important economic functions and because canon law forbade their murder. In some towns, bishops and local burghers tried to force Jews to become baptized, but these efforts to save them largely failed, as the urban rabble was eager for booty. The total loss of German Jewish life during the first Crusade is estimated as at least twelve thousand.

The Fourth Lateran Council of 1215 added the largest number of anti-Jewish rules. Jews had to wear a distinctive badge and a special hat and pay heavy taxes. Another wave of persecutions followed in the middle of the fourteenth century after the outbreak of the Black Death in Europe, which Jews were accused of having caused. In Germany, new ill-treatment of the Jews began even before the onset of the plague. Instigated by rumors coming from France, Jews were charged with desecrating the host (the unleavened bread used in the Christian ritual of the Eucharist) and killing Christian children to obtain blood for secret rituals.

A fresh round of abuse commenced in the fifteenth century. Among other fabrications, it relied on the age-old calumny that the Jews had ordered the crucifixion of Jesus from the Roman governor and therefore were responsible for the death of Christ. Jews were expelled from all major cities—from Konstanz in 1431, from Munich and Upper Bavaria in 1442, from Berlin in 1450, and from Breslau in 1453. The Jewish population of Regensburg, one of the oldest Jewish communities, was driven out in 1519. Before leaving, the Regensburg Jews were forced to tear down their synagogue; their cemetery was also laid waste and the gravestones used for building houses.[2]

Since there was no central authority that could have ordered countrywide banishment (as was the case in England, France, and Spain), German Jews never disappeared entirely from Germany. Often, after being molested or driven from one place, they took refuge in another.[3] A considerable number of Jews who were expelled from the cities were able to move to the countryside, where members of the nobility, recognizing their usefulness, allowed them to start a new existence. Here the Jews made their living as peddlers, pawnbrokers, and traders in corn, wine, and cattle. Their lives were regulated by numerous restrictions: for example, they needed special permission to travel from place to place and to marry, and they paid taxes for births and deaths. While the great majority of German Jews constituted an impoverished class, a very small stratum became wealthy and functioned as bankers and purchase agents for the nobility. Among these court Jews, as they were known, were Jost Liebmann (at the court of Frederick I of Prussia) and Samuel Oppenheimer (for Count Karl Ludwig of Heidelberg; eventually Oppenheimer became a financier for the German emperor Leopold I).

The harsh life of German Jews continued during the fifteenth and sixteenth centuries. Deprived of the right to live in the major German cities, many Jews left the country for the East. They settled in Bohemia (now part of the Czech Republic), Silesia (today a province of Poland), and especially in Poland, where they became an important force in promoting trade and commerce. Once again, some Jews also functioned as financial agents for the nobility. Living in a Slavic environment, these Jews who spoke middle-high

German (the form of German spoken in the High Middle Ages) retained their native tongue, which, incorporated with words from Hebrew as well as Rotwelsch, the cant of vagabonds and tramps, became known as Yiddish.

The flow of migration reversed itself again in the nineteenth century, when large numbers of Jews fleeing the East's wave of anti-Jewish riots known as pogroms either moved to the United States or back to Germany. Their German neighbors regarded the use of the Yiddish language as both comical and unpleasant, making Jews the object of many malicious and hateful comments.[4] Industrialization and the attendant rise of a new middle class beginning in the eighteenth century eventually led to dramatic upward mobility for German Jews. Opportunities in commerce and industry as well as in banking and manufacturing benefited Jews who had a long mercantile tradition and an interest in being self-employed. In 1671 Frederick William of Brandenburg, knows as the Great Elector, had invited some fifty families to settle in his realm. Enlightened absolutism (a benevolent form of absolute monarchy) and the rebellion of the middle class against the feudal order built the foundation for a new worldview that stressed the equality of all men. The age of the Enlightenment greatly aided the Jews.

Assimilation in the Age of the Enlightenment

A powerful force for religious toleration—the Magna Carta of German Jewry, in effect—was Gotthold Ephraim Lessing's play *Nathan the Wise*. Published in 1779 and first performed in Berlin in 1783, the drama, set in Jerusalem during the Third Crusade, described how three individuals—a Muslim, a Christian, and a Jew—overcame their religious differences to connect in friendship and love of their common humanity.[5] Lessing's Jew, Nathan, was modeled on the non-Jewish playwright's close friend Moses Mendelssohn, a Jewish philosopher who had come to Berlin in 1743 and lived there as a result of a special privilege. For both Lessing and Mendelssohn, Jews and Germans were members of the family of mankind. This idea was the beginning of what would later be referred to as the "German-Jewish symbiosis."

Mendelssohn sought to combine Enlightenment ideas and traditional Judaism. He translated the Pentateuch and other parts of the Bible into elegant German and wrote commentaries relying on medieval rabbis. Mendelssohn also aimed to liberate Jews from their cultural isolation with a secular education, hoping that this would allow them to become citizens with equal rights. In recognition of Mendelssohn's original scholarship in Jewish exegesis, the Prussian Academy of the Sciences proposed to make him a member, but the Prussian king Friedrich Wilhelm II objected that the illustrious body should not be soiled by a Jew. Most Jews celebrated Mendelssohn as a second Moses who had liberated his people from the burden of superstition and led them out of the ghetto.[6]

One of Mendelssohn's many German friends was the Prussian state councilor Wilhelm von Dohm, who, in 1781, at Mendelssohn's suggestion, published *Über die bürgerliche Verbesserung der Juden* (On the amelioration of the civic status of the Jews).[7] Dohm defended the equality of all men and proposed extending full civic rights to Jews; at the same time, the beneficent German did not believe in the equality of Jews and Germans. Assimilation was the precondition of emancipation. Reflecting the state of what was then enlightened German public opinion, Dohm envisaged not an encounter between Judaism and Germany, but the dissolution of the former into the latter.[8]

The outbreak of war between Prussia and revolutionary France delayed any action on these proposals. In 1812, however, King Friedrich Wilhelm III finally issued a decree of emancipation that abolished many restrictive practices. Jews were henceforth granted the rights and duties of Prussian citizenship, and, as such, they became subject to military service and had to assume family or last names so they could be taxed and drafted.[9] However, Jews continued to be barred from the civil service and the judiciary, and they could not serve as military officers. The retention of these restrictions reflected the tenacious resistance to full Jewish emancipation within the state bureaucracy as well among the citizenry at large.[10] The decree of 1812 ushered in the emergence of the modern German Jew, optimistic about belonging to his German homeland. The baptized poet Heinrich Heine, living in exile in Paris, noted the "deep affinity" between Jews and Germans: "Fundamentally, the two peoples are alike."[11]

At the same time, emancipation introduced difficult questions of identity, as a result of interacting with a more accepting environment. For the leading Jewish intellectuals of the day it was clear that the Jews' entry into German society required changes in Jewish life, especially in regard to religious ritual and language. Adherence to Jewish dietary laws (*kashrut*) was one of the first rules to be abandoned by many German Jews, who now were willing to eat in the homes of their German friends. As for the language issue, David Friedländer, a close friend of Mendelssohn's, counseled in a letter to an Orthodox Jew the use of German for reading, speaking, and thinking, in order to complete the unity of Christianity and Judaism.[12] In a pamphlet that appeared shortly after the 1812 emancipation decree, Friedländer argued that without reform of the synagogue, the coming generation would not be able to fully exercise the civil rights that had been granted. The language of prayer had to be German rather than Hebrew. To further this assimilationist approach to acceptance, many congregations not only prayed in German but omitted any reference to Zion as the site of the messianic promise. We should not pray for a return to Palestine, some contended, while our heart is linked so strongly to our German fatherland.[13]

The issue of changing Jewish religious observance fomented harsh disputes between reformers and Orthodox Jews. Ultimately, a group of liberals guided by the rabbi and scholar Abraham Geiger—who is considered the founder of modern Reform Judaism, which eventually became widespread in the United States—largely won out.[14]

Assimilation was not merely the attempt to blend into a new cultural environment, but also the dissociation from traditional Jewish foundations. Jews who wanted to fully assimilate into German society changed their names, to the consternation and criticism of their more traditional fellow Jews.[15] The break with tradition also included new behavior. Jewish reformers stressed the importance of manners, politeness, refinement, a new kind of dress, and a modulation of tone—all qualities supposedly lacking in the Jew of the East. Despite or because of the fact that German Jews were themselves products of the ghetto, their distaste for the ghetto and what it symbolized was particularly intense. They harshly judged Orthodox Jews who refused to accept the new ways and derided East European Jews as being *Ostjuden*, essentially deficient in esteemed middle-class gentility. Assimilated German Jews also groused about the continued use of Yiddish jargon. Attainment of *Bildung*—a uniquely German concept encompassing self-education, the striving for a cultured personality through the study of literature and philosophy, and the building of an aesthetic sensibility through the arts and music—was considered possible only through the use of uncorrupted German.[16] Bildung in itself was regarded as the "knighthood of modernity" and the gateway to bourgeois respectability.[17]

Traditional Judaism also ran counter to the rise of individualism that characterized the nineteenth century. The Jewish religion had always been rooted in family and community, but the new bourgeois society emphasized the individual, whether in economic competition or the assertion of liberty and rights against the state. In line with the growing secularism in German society, religion was being relegated from a phenomenon that governed the entirety of life to observances on Sunday or Saturday and holidays. Although prosperous Jewish congregations built impressive synagogues, religious belief declined.[18] In the spirit of the Enlightenment, Bildung and a faith in reason became substitutes for religion. As the philosopher Friedrich Schlegel formulated it, the more Bildung, the less religion. Even as secularization affected all of German society, it had an especially strong impact on the Jews, for whom faith had always ensured their survival as a people. As religious bonds weakened, Jewish identity became endangered.[19]

Bildung advanced Jewish assimilationist aspirations in yet another way. It was seen as a symbol of shared humanity: all individuals, regardless of accidents of birth, nationality, and religion, could attain it. Not surprisingly, German Jews began to pursue Bildung as a quasi-religious value in an effort to achieve their full emancipation. The children and grandchildren of rabbinic scholars and poor peddlers alike now flocked to universities in numbers greatly disproportionate to their representation in the population. Albert Einstein is said to have remarked that the Jews had apparently spent the two thousand years of exile preparing for their entrance examinations. "Doctor is a Jewish forename" was a quip current at the time.[20]

The observance of Bildung and friendship was also the foundation of the Berlin salons organized by the Jewesses Henriette Herz and Rahel Varnhagen. The celebration of German culture—including its promotion of universal human values—in the salons provided the milieu in which it was possible to feel German without being Christian. All the major cultural figures of the day (among them Johann Gottlieb Fichte, Wilhelm von Humboldt, Friedrich Schleiermacher, and the Schlegel brothers) attended the salons.

The German writers and philosophers Friedrich Schiller, Johann Wolfgang von Goethe, Immanuel Kant, and Johann Gottfried Herder were often idealized in conversation; the anti-Jewish sentiments found in their work were ignored.[21] Most of the German luminaries present at the salons belonged to the "Christian-German Dinner-party Society," the statute of which excluded not only Jews but also baptized Jews and their descendants.[22] Herz and Varnhagen had hoped that the essence of the German spirit would eventually overcome parochial differences and solve the Jewish problem. Meanwhile, however, both of them converted to

Christianity, buying what Heine would call the "entrance ticket to European culture."[23]

And they were not alone. Varnhagen commented that half the Jews of Berlin were either baptized or married to Christians. Although this figure was exaggerated, many Jews did indeed choose baptism as the way out of forced membership in the Jewish caste that was still widely regarded with derision.[24] Yet conversion did not always achieve its aim. For most Germans, Jews after baptism did not become Christians but remained "baptized Jews."

Formal Equality but No Social Acceptance

In truth, the emancipation of the Jews had been a grudgingly conceded administrative act. Jews were granted civic equality, but German society continued to refuse them social acceptance.[25] Prejudices against associating with Jews continued. Freemasonry owed its origin to religious toleration, but Jews were not welcome. Even as many German Jews deemed themselves assimilated, their distinctive economic and familial characteristics marked them as a recognizable group. And while the social rapprochement of Jews and Christians in Berlin salons caused a great stir, the bulk of the Jewish population was not affected.[26]

The emancipation of German Jewry met with far more than social and political opposition. During the decades between the Napoleonic Wars (1813–14) and the revolutions of 1848, it also manifested in violence against Jews—physical attacks, the plundering of homes and businesses, burning of synagogues, and vandalizing of cemeteries. In August 1819 the so-called Hep! Hep! riots started in Würzburg in Bavaria. The origin and meaning of the phrase "Hep! Hep!" is unclear, but it rhymed with *Juda verrecke!* (Jews, perish!) and became the battle cry of bands of apprentices and other lower-class discontents who attacked and killed Jews, smashed windows, and burned Jewish property. Riots also broke out in villages. Peasants suffering from the severe economic downturn of 1816–17 found a convenient scapegoat for their impoverishment in the Jews. The old charge that Jews were the murderers of Christ frequently merged with economic grievances.[27] The riots spread to Frankfurt/M and beyond. As an epilogue to the riots, the author Hartwig Hundt von Radowsky proposed in his *Judenspiegel* (Mirror of Jews) of 1819 that the Jews of Germany be sold to the English as slaves for their Indian plantations. The propagation of the Jews could be prevented by castrating the men and consigning the women to brothels. Germany, he concluded, had to be cleansed of this "vermin."[28]

A new wave of riots broke out during the revolutionary upheaval of 1848–49. Its scope and severity exceeded the events of 1819 by far, inciting violence against Jews in some 180 locales, including Silesia, Moravia, Bohemia, and Hungary. Once again, a serious economic downturn in 1846–47 preceded the assaults on Jewish businesses. Jews were charged with profiteering and usury. At times local authorities used the riots to force the Jews to abandon their demand for full emancipation.[29]

Many Jews downplayed the significance of these outbreaks. An Orthodox rabbi called them a *Blutweihe*, a consecration of German freedom by blood. Participation in the revolutionary movement for constitutional government was held to be more important than such disturbances.[30]

A significant number of Jews did indeed join the struggle for a new liberal state, part of the revolutions of 1848 that broke out in many European countries. In Germany unrest began with a series of loosely coordinated protests and rebellions expressing discontent with the traditional autocratic structure of the German Confederation. Only in such a new political order, it was believed, could Jews achieve their sought-after total political, legal, and social integration into German society. Four members of the first national parliament that convened in Frankfurt in May 1848 were Jews, among them the assembly's vice president, Gabriel Riesser, who participated in drafting a new constitution. For Riesser, defending the civil rights of Jews was part of fighting for a democratic Germany—the separation of church and state, equality before the law, and universal human freedom.[31]

Many Jews had high hopes after the 1848 revolution. Indeed, on December 27, 1848, a new law went into effect that guaranteed all German Jews unconditional equality before the law: "Religious belief neither secures not limits the enjoyment of civic rights."[32] But by this point the revolution had already lost much of its strength. During the period of retrenchment that now started in many German states, the Jews' legal status reverted to what it was prior to the partial emancipation. In Prussia, furthermore, the revised constitution of 1850 declared that the Christian religion was the foundation of the state, facilitating all kinds of new discriminations. In several other German states the Jews' enjoyment of civic rights was made conditional on adherence to the Christian faith. Ironically, a converted Jew, the professor of public law and legal philosophy Friedrich Julius Stahl, had provided the ideological underpinning for the idea of a morally superior "Germanic Christianity." The state, he had argued some years earlier, could not be "complete" unless Christianity was the state religion and this religion permeated all aspects of life. What he hadn't realized was that in such an entity Jews would necessarily be a foreign element. Stahl's advocacy of a national consciousness, based on Christianity and a romantic notion of what it meant to be a German, became the foundation of a new Christian anti-Semitism. The new nationalism contained a pronounced anti-Jewish component.[33]

It was not until the 1860s that a revived liberal movement succeeded in doing away with the restored restrictive practices. On July 2, 1869, the North German League, headed by the Prussian king, adopted a law of emancipation abolishing all differences in the legal status of Jews and Christians. After the unification of Germany in 1871, this law became binding for all of Germany.

A New Radical Anti-Semitism

And yet, at the very time that a German nation formally repudiating anti-Jewish provisions finally came into being, there emerged a new, radical anti-Semitism that insisted once again on drawing boundaries against the Jews. The more legal protection the Jews received and the more they assumed the behavior, clothing, and speech of other Germans, the more vehemently anti-Semites rejected them.[34] Indeed, assimilated Jews were considered the most dangerous because they could easily infiltrate German society.[35] One of the many Germans holding this view was Wilhelm Marr, who coined the term "anti-Semite" in 1879.[36]

Some of the contemporary manifestos of hate and persecution read like twentieth-century Nazi anti-Jewish propaganda. While the victory of National Socialism and the devastating destruction of European Jewry in the succeeding century would not be a direct result of these developments, it is clear that the Nazis' murderous anti-Semitism was not a new invention after World War I, but had a long prehistory. The negative image of the Jews in the nineteenth century helped create a climate of opinion in which a state-ordered program of annihilation of the Jews could become acceptable.[37]

Emerging most strongly during Germany's economic depression of 1873–96, the new anti-Semitism represented a secular version of the age-old anti-Judaism. The Jew was no longer the Antichrist, condemned by God, but the person responsible for all the deleterious changes in German society. The Jewish spirit, allegedly anchored in specific racial characteristics, was denounced as a source of decay and a threat to the moral fiber of the nation. Promoted by militant nationalists, the *Völkische*, this secular anti-Semitism fused with more traditional religious and social anti-Jewish prejudice among the nobility, the officer corps, and the bureaucracy. Within the ranks of the educated, hostility toward France tended to discredit Enlightenment ideals, encourage sentiments opposed to equality and liberty, and fan opposition to the Jews who were held to embody these values. Members of the lower classes—peasants, craftsmen, shopkeepers—embraced the argument that their difficulties, the negative social consequences of industrialization and capitalism, were caused by Jews. Meanwhile, among the free professions such as the law and medicine, there was growing resentment of Jewish competitors: their rising standard of living, their influx into commerce and banking, their alleged general domination of the arts, press, and culture.[38] All in all, the new anti-Semitism had become part of the political culture, embraced by a large and diverse segment of the German population.

More than any other person, the Berlin professor of history Heinrich von Treitschke helped to make these anti-Jewish sentiments respectable. In his 1879 article "A Word about Jewry," Treitschke denounced the Jews as an alien force that sought to dominate German life. Jewish businessmen employed falsehood and deceit in pursuit of profit: "In thousands of German villages sits the Jew who sells out his neighbors with usury. . . . Most dangerous . . . is the preponderance of Jewry in the daily press." Unless appropriate measures were taken, "millennia of Germanic morality would be followed by an era of German-Jewish hybrid culture." Treitschke summed up his indictment with *"Die Juden sind unser Unglück"* (The Jews are our misfortune), a slogan that became the rallying cry of much of the German intelligentsia. During the Nazi era, this invective would be featured on the front page of every issue of Julius Streicher's hate rag *Der Stürmer*.[39]

The philosopher and economist Eugen Dühring also launched brutal attacks upon Germany's Jews. His elaborate formulation of racial anti-Semitism was widely disseminated in his 1881 book *The Jewish Question as a Matter of Racial Characteristics and Its Threat to the Existence of the People, Their Morality, and Their Culture*; in later writings he went on to call for the destruction (*Vernichtung*) and extirpation (*Ausrottung*) of the Jews.[40] Like Dühring, the British-born philosopher Stewart Chamberlain—Richard Wagner's son-in-law and a German by choice—denounced the Jews' racial characteristics, although he stressed that subjective factors such as consciousness and will, rather than biological or Darwinian categories, determined membership in a certain race. His two-volume work *The Foundations of the Nineteenth Century*

(1899) sold widely and would later be designated a "classic" of anti-Semitic agitation.[41]

The anti-Jewish vocabulary was even more radical in the writings of the well-known orientalist and theologian Paul de Lagarde. "The Jews," Lagarde wrote in 1887, "are as Jews aliens in every European state, and as such they are nothing but harbingers of decay."[42] Lagarde compared the Jews to bacilli and trichinae, which fostered sickness and death. With such vermin, he argued, one does not negotiate; rather, one must exterminate them as quickly and thoroughly as possible. Meanwhile, in his widely read book *Antisemiten-Katechismus* (1893), later published under the title *Handbook of the Jewish Question*, the writer and publisher Theodor Fritsch proposed that Jews be required to emigrate or engage in agriculture and other productive crafts. In a public debate he pronounced that human life will rise to a higher level of existence only when there is no more room available for the parasitic Hebrews. Fritsch died in early 1933, shortly after the Nazis had come to power. Hitler would undertake to realize Fritsch's dream of a world without Jews.[43]

These authors were only some of the most prominent anti-Jewish writers of the second half of the nineteenth century. Next to their works flourished an entire literature of anti-Semitic polemics. It is estimated that during the reign of Otto von Bismarck (1862–90) alone more than five hundred proclamations were published on the "Jewish Question."

Organizations focused solely on anti-Semitic agitation also arose, the Christian Social party—founded in 1878 by the Prussian court chaplain Adolf Stoecker—being the most prominent. Stoecker claimed that the Jews' rejection of Christianity and conservative values had enabled them to acquire excessive power; finance, banking, commerce, and the press were now under their control. Stoecker found an audience among the people suffering from the economic turbulence of the 1870s. An "Anti-Semitic Petition" he and his friends circulated in 1880–81 demanding the revision of Jewish emancipation and the limiting of Jewish employment (especially in the administration of justice, the teaching professions, and the like) was signed by more than a quarter of a million people.

The first anti-Semitic organization to be inspired by völkische ideas was the Antisemiten Liga (League of anti-Semites) founded by the journalist Wilhelm Marr in 1879. The Alldeutscher Verband (Pan German league), too, established in 1891, gradually came to embrace a biological racism in which Germans were seen as the superior race in need of protection against inferior races such as Jews. Numerous smaller organizations emerged as well, though many of them were plagued by internal fighting. The First International Anti-Jewish Congress convened in Dresden in September 1882 but was unable to overcome differences of opinion on how to solve the Jewish problem. The Day of Anti-Semitism, another attempt at a united anti-Jewish front, was held in Bochum in June 1889 but similarly failed.

A year later the Marburg librarian Otto Böckel founded the Anti-Semitic People's Party, which would be renamed the German Reform Party in 1893. In the elections held that year the three anti-Semitic parties gathered 263,861 votes out of 7.7 million cast and together elected sixteen deputies. This marked the highpoint of anti-Semitic agitation as an instrument of political success during the years prior to World War I.[44]

Germany's organized working class largely resisted the spread of anti-Semitism, though it also did little to fight it. Labor movement leaders believed that Jewish national peculiarities would gradually disappear as a result of inexorable economic developments. Assimilation was therefore seen as a natural and progressive force.[45] The ideological father of modern socialism, Karl Marx (born to Jewish parents and baptized at age six), wrote a series of essays beginning in 1843 identifying Judaism with the hated capitalism. For Marx, the essence of Judaism was the profit motive, focused on money and haggling. Hence, he wrote, "the social emancipation of Jewry is the emancipation of society from Jewry."[46] Only the end of human exploitation and alienation in a new classless society would eliminate the need for religion and achieve the solution of the Jewish Question.

The organizer of Germany's first labor party (in 1863), Ferdinand Lasalle, was, like Marx, a person of Jewish origin who detested Jews and who said, "There are two things in the world I cannot stand: Jews and literati. Unfortunately, I am both."[47] Karl Kautsky, the leading theoretician of the German Social Democratic party, similarly regarded Judaism as something to be discarded. "The sooner it disappears," he wrote, "the better it will be for society and for the Jews themselves."[48]

By the end of the nineteenth century, more than half a million Jews lived in Germany. The imperial state had granted the Jews formal equality, but in daily administrative practice it continued to bar them from service in the state bureaucracy, the judiciary, university faculties, and the officer corps. Since 1885 no Jew in Germany (except in Bavaria) had been promoted to the rank of reserve officer, the essential step toward a respectable career (most notably in state service), and also proof that one was a *"vornehmer Mann"* (gentleman).[49] Hence, large numbers of Jews turned to the free professions, becoming physicians, lawyers, and journalists. In 1910 Jews constituted only 1 percent of the total German population, but represented about 6 percent of doctors, 10 percent of lawyers, and 8 percent of writers and journalists—a situation that encouraged envy and hostility.[50] Many assimilated Jews sought to avoid discrimination by changing their names, but beginning in 1894 a succession of administrative edicts made it difficult to do so. In 1900 the minister of the interior was given exclusive power to decide whether Jews or people of Jewish descent could change their family names, and in 1903 Jews were formally forbidden to change their names upon conversion to the Christian religion. The actions of civil servants and the behavior of the German people had created a web of discrimination from which it was difficult to escape.[51]

The Jewish Defense Organization CV

With antisemitism firmly established in the many professional and social associations of the country, a number of Jewish organizations formed to fight for Jewish rights. The Centralverein deutscher Staatsbürger jüdischen Glaubens (Central association of German citizens of the Jewish faith), known as CV, established in 1893 to help bridge Germandom and Judaism—became the most important on several fronts, including as an instrument of assimilation.

The CV's programmatic declaration sought to confront the anti-Semitic challenge head on by convincing a prejudiced German public that German Jews were true patriots. "We German citizens of Jewish faith stand firmly on the grounds of the German nationality," it stated. "Our community's bonds with Jews of other countries are no different than the ties of the community of German Catholics and Protestants with the Catholics and Protestants of other countries."[52] The declaration also affirmed loyalty to Judaism, but most CV members were ignorant of Jewish values, practiced a Reform style of worship, and felt that being German took clear precedence over being Jewish. They were not Jews living in Germany, but Germans who happened to belong to the Jewish religion. The CV built an elaborate network of cultural, recreational, and sports association and thus came to engage between one-third and one-half of the Jews in Germany.[53]

Non-Jews who undertook to defend Jews against anti-Semitism likewise stressed the importance of assimilation. The Verein zur Abwehr des Antisemitismus (Association for resistance to antisemitism), established in 1890, conducted large meetings and issued a weekly bulletin chronicling anti-Semitic incidents. While its membership of about twelve thousand was mostly Jewish, it did include about five hundred Christians of repute, a cross-section of the liberal upper middle class. The most prominent member of the Abwehrverein was the highly regarded historian Theodor Mommsen (1817–1903). Mommsen's view that the Jews had to abandon their particularistic ways in order to achieve full rights in the German state became paradigmatic for the Abwehrverein. As long as Jews behaved like a distinct social caste, it was believed, their fellow Germans would continue to treat them as one.[54] The well-known sociologist Werner Sombart defended the full legal equality of the Jews in his 1912 book *The Jews and Modern Capitalism*, but counseled them not to make use of these rights in public.[55]

Despite great efforts, the Abwehrverein achieved limited success in stemming the inroads of the new anti-Semitism. Full assimilation, too, remained a lofty goal that was stubbornly pursued but never achieved. Middle-class Jews lived like middle-class Germans, but they rarely became part of that class and had little social contact with non-Jews. As for the economic elite, the Jewish banker Gerson Bleichröder was made Bismarck's financial advisor and ennobled in 1872 (thus being allowed to add *von* to his name), but was respected merely on the basis of his wealth and never accepted into Prussian aristocratic circles.[56] Bleichröder would invite the elite of Germany's capital to his home for sumptuous feasts, but, as the well-informed Count Paul Vasili observed, "Berlin society is divided into two camps: those who go to Bleichröder while mocking him, and those who mock him but do not go."[57]

For some Jews the only way out of this predicament was conversion or a formal declaration of exit from the Jewish community, though these steps were hardly cure-alls.[58] Such apostates were often severely criticized by their fellow Jews while their reception in German society was uncertain. Victor Klemperer, the son of a rabbi and author of a famous diary of life under the Nazis, had himself baptized in 1903 in order to become a reserve officer. He did so unenthusiastically: to be a Christian, he told himself, was part of being a German and having a "decent confession."[59] Still others attempted to resolve the anguish of assimilation by internalizing the prejudices of which they were victims. The Jewish liberal politician Ludwig Bamberger argued that Jewish characteristics comprised "pushiness and tactlessness, greed, insolence, vanity and tittle-chasing, 'intellectual parvenuism,' and servility."[60] In the eyes of the Jew Franz Kafka, Jews were greedy, domineering, and possessive, and the German-Jewish intellectual in particular was "stuck by his little hind legs in his fore-father's faith, and with his front legs groping for, but never finding new ground."[61] More generally, it was offensive to call Jews who wanted to be indistinguishable from Germans "Jewish-looking"; it hurt their self-esteem.[62]

Eastern Jews and Zionism

Many German Jews blamed the prevailing anti-Semitism on the influx of so-called *Ostjuden*, unassimilated ghetto Jews from the East. By 1890 some twenty thousand out of Germany's half a million Jews were foreign born, and their number continued to climb. The Ostjuden were reputed to be dirty, loud, and coarse. German Jews feared that the newcomers' appearance and conduct would endanger their own hard-won respectability and standing as solid citizens. Raphael Löwenfeld, one of the CV's founders, warned his fellow Jews in 1893 that "we have to prove to our enemies that we have nothing in common with [these] bad elements, even if they call themselves Jews."[63] Jewish newspapers and organizations were alarmed enough to appeal to authorities to limit the scope of this emigration from the East. The Jewish physician Max Marcuse declared in 1912 that closing the German borders against the Ostjuden was a "cultural imperative for Germany."[64] In 1904 a CV leader argued that Jews from Russia and Galicia should receive vocational training to make them eventually *exportfähig* (exportable), and German Jews condescendingly provided such charitable support in the hopes that the needy Ostjuden would be mere transient elements in their homeland.[65] Indeed, between 1905 and 1914 some seven hundred thousand eastern European Jews passed through Germany on their way to the United States.[66]

Unlike among eastern European Jewry, Zionism, the movement aimed at establishing a Jewish home in Palestine, had few adherents among German Jews. Moses Hess, Marx's one-time companion, advocated the Jewish people's rebirth in their ancient abode in his book *Rome and Jerusalem: A Study in Jewish Nationalism* (1862), but German Jews largely ignored his early advocacy of the Zionist ideal. (Hess, however, would influence such later Zionist leaders as Ahad Ha'am and Theodor Herzl.) In the years before World War I, the first German Zionist organization, which by then had been renamed Zionistische Vereinigung für Deutschland, or ZVfD (Zionist association for Germany), averaged a meager annual membership of 4,500 to 9,000, many of them university students who suffered from discrimination and found in Zionism both identity and pride. Notably as well, only a small minority of those who even considered themselves committed Zionists expected to actually emigrate to Palestine, an undeveloped country under Turkish rule. A Jewish state was seen as a valid objective for the persecuted Ostjuden, but not for German Jews. Admittedly, in 1912, influenced by a younger generation of German Zionists, the organization did affirm that it was every Zionist's duty to settle in Palestine, but most ZVfD members regarded the resolution as an empty gesture, and indeed it had little credibility.[67]

The Illusion of Assimilation

Some German Jews were fervent German patriots but also adhered to a deeply felt Jewish consciousness. The lyrical writer Berthold Auerbach, whose 1843 work *Schwarzwälder Dorfgeschichten* (Black Forest village stories) was universally hailed as an important contribution to Germany's national culture, was one such example. After another inconclusive debate on the Jewish question in the German Reichstag in 1880, Auerbach expressed his despair in a letter: "I have lived and worked in vain! . . . Who would have thought that there could be so much brutality, mendacity and hate among German men."[68] Other Jews advocated a different approach to the reality of being rejected by German society. Penning the 1912 essay "Deutsch-jüdischer Parnass" ("German-Jewish parnassus") in the literary review *Kunstwart* (Art guardian), the young Jewish writer Moritz Goldstein urged his fellow Jews to stop producing works of German culture: "We Jews are managing the spiritual patrimony of a people that allows us neither the right nor the competency to do so." Instead, Goldstein proposed that Jews develop the specifically Jewish side of their creativity. The provocative article infuriated the assimilationists, delighted the Zionists, and fomented a huge debate. The pedagogue Jakob Loewenberg voiced the liberal Jews' strong opposition to Goldstein's ideas. German Jews had fought too hard to obtain their freedom to return to a kind of neo-Hebraic literature: "Here lie our dead and here is our *Heimat* [homeland]. We are Germans and wish to remain Germans."[69]

In late 1913 the Jewish historian and editor Ludwig Geiger thus summed up the status of assimilated German Jews in their homeland: "For us, the free-thinking German Jews, the question of assimilation does not exist; we are completely assimilated. . . . By assimilation we mean total integration into *Deutschtum* [Germandom], into its nationality, language, and culture; without, however, giving up our religious beliefs. We are Germans according to our *Gesinnung* [mindset] and language, yet we remain Jews. . . . Our assimilation has been completed!"[70] Geiger's assessment was widely shared. By this point in time, the waves of rowdy anti-Semitism appeared to have ebbed. Germany's anti-Semitic parties were defeated in the 1912 elections. Meanwhile, increasingly more Jews were identifying themselves simply as Germans, both as a result of conversions and the formal ending of their religious ties. Whereas only 8.4 percent of Jews married outside their faith in 1901, 29.38 percent did so in 1915.[71]

Jewish Patriotism during World War I

At the outbreak of war in 1914 German Jews shared the general wave of patriotism and expected that this commitment would further their integration into German society. Here, finally, was an opportunity to prove to their German fellow citizens that Germany's Jews considered themselves German above all.[72] The CV issued an appeal to all German Jews to go beyond the call of duty in the service of the fatherland: "Sign up [for military service] voluntarily!" Heeding the CV's call, many thousands of Jews, including my father, volunteered to fight before they were conscripted.

The entire Jewish press, liberal as well as Zionist, engaged in displays of national loyalty, not to say chauvinism. The Jewish poet Ernst Lissauer composed the "Hate Song against England."[73] Sharing in the burst of frenzied patriotism, the highly regarded scholar Hermann Cohen, head of Germany's neo-Kantian school of philosophy, argued in 1915 that it was to be hoped that, through the victory of the fatherland, the God of justice and love would end the barbarism under which the Jews' brethren in Russia had to suffer. The triumph of the German weapons would finally confirm and preserve the unity of Germanness and Judaism also in the consciousness of the German people.[74] Despite Cohen's fervent patriotism, when the Berlin Academy undertook to issue a definitive edition of the works of Immanuel Kant, Cohen, being a Jew, was not invited to participate. The early German-Jewish Zionist Gershom Scholem has called the "capacity for self-deception . . . one of the most important and dismal aspects of the German-Jewish relationship."[75]

During the early days of the war, the longed-for moment of full acceptance seemed to be near realization. The emperor declared that he knew no parties, only Germans. The appointment of the prominent Jewish industrialist Walther Rathenau to the post of organizing Germany's war economy further strengthened the impression that Jews were finally being recognized as full citizens.[76] Soon, however, it became clear that these expectations were fatuous, for anti-Semitism was alive and well. In 1916, Völkische and anti-Semitic organizations unleashed the mounting discontent over the hardships of the war upon a readily recognizable culprit: the Jew. The war ministry found itself swamped with letters accusing the Jews of shirking their military duty and engaging in large-scale profiteering. Hence, on October 11, 1916, the ministry issued an order for a *Judenzählung* (census of Jews) that would ascertain whether Jews indeed had sought to evade their military obligation by obtaining "assignments in administrative or clerical posts far away from the front lines."[77]

The census was a slap in the face of Jewish soldiers. The Jewish community was especially upset over the fact that the census was never published, thus enabling anti-Semitic agitators to continue to propagate their tales of unpatriotic, shirking Jews. Only after the war ended did the National Association of Jewish Combat Soldiers manage to broadcast the true figures. Out of a population of about five hundred thousand Jews, one hundred thousand had served their country, about eighty thousand of them in the front lines. The percentage of Jewish volunteers was higher than in the German population at large. About thirty-five thousand Jews had been decorated and at least twelve thousand had been killed.[78]

In subsequent years, as anti-Semitism continued their campaigns of hatred, Jews cited these figures time and again to prove the Jewish commitment to the fatherland. The results, however, were not encouraging. Jews had suffered for a country that did not appreciate their sacrifice.

2

The Heyday of Assimilation and Cultural Greatness

In November 1918 the German war effort collapsed, the emperor fled the country, and a republic was declared in Berlin. The new political order ushered in the high point of integration for Germany's Jews. The Weimar Constitution, named after the city where it was adopted on August 11, 1919, removed the last remaining discriminatory provisions of the empire and finally established full legal equality.

In the new Socialist government, two Jewish ministers—Hugo Preuss and Otto Landsberg—filled the posts of minister of the interior and minister of justice, respectively. Other Jews served in the governments of states and held leading positions in the civil service. For the first time, prominent Jewish scholars including the sociologists Karl Mannheim and Erich Fromm, philosophers Ernst Cassirer and Edmund Husserl, and political theorists Arthur Rosenberg and Gustav Meyer were able to join the faculties of German universities. While the diplomatic service and the army remained as exclusive as before, this state of affairs constituted an exception to a generally open career path.

And yet these gains were uncertain. The new rights for Jews were contested because they were part of a wider democratization that was also contested. Germany had become a republic, but the forces of the Right, opposed to the new order, were strong and combative. It was a time of violent political clashes marked by assassinations of democratic political figures.[1]

For Germany's Jews, it was easy to overlook these uncertainties. Jewish cultural life and institutions flourished. Jewish communities (*Gemeinden*) supported Jewish libraries and new Jewish schools. In Berlin 20 percent of all Jewish children attended Jewish educational institutions; in Hamburg, Frankfurt am Main, and Cologne, the percentage was almost 50 percent. Before World War I only a few Gemeinden had issued their own news bulletins; by 1932 more than forty local Jewish newspapers had a combined circulation of about 310,000.[2] Two multivolume Jewish encyclopedias spread and redefined knowledge about all things Jewish. Jewish music was performed for attentive concert audiences.[3]

Progenitors of a Jewish Renaissance

A number of high-ranking Jewish leaders were instrumental in creating this cultural richness.

LEO BAECK

In 1919 Leo Baeck helped establish the Academy for the Study of Judaism, reviving what in German academic terminology was called the *Wissenschaft des Judentums* (science of Judaism). Leo Baeck, it has been said, "symbolized the delicate, fertile symbiosis of Jewish and German thought that characterized the years before Hitler's Reich."[4] Born in 1873 in Lissa (now Leszno, Poland) as the son of a rabbi, the young Baeck moved to Breslau (now Wroclaw, Poland) to study at the conservative Jüdisch-Theologische Seminar (Fränckelsche Stiftung) and later to Berlin to enroll at the more liberal Hochschule für die Wissenschaft des Judentums. In 1897 he secured his first position as rabbi in Oppeln (now Opole, Poland), and it was there that he published his important book *Das Wesen des Judentums* (The essence of Judaism), written in response to Adolf von Harnack's *Das Wesen des Christentums* (The essence of Christianity). According to Baeck, the essence of Judaism was not to be found in outmoded rituals and laws, but in the intersection of rational ethics and a personal experience of the divine. Searching the scriptures for ethical principles made Judaism a perpetually modern system of critical thought.

In 1912 Baeck returned to Berlin as rabbi and lecturer at the Hochschule für die Wissenschaft des Judentums. During World War I he served as a chaplain in the German army. In 1922 he became president of the Union of German Rabbis, and, two years later, of the German branch of B'nai Brith. He also was a member of the Central Association of German Citizens of the Jewish Faith (cv) and the Jewish Agency for Palestine. Being a German patriot, committed to the cause of maintaining and protecting Jewish life in Germany, made him the leader of German Jewry par excellence.

In 1933 Baeck was elected president of the new umbrella organization of German Jewish groups, the Reichsvertretung deutscher Staatsbürger jüdischen Glaubens (National agency of German citizens of the Jewish faith). As German Jews were gradually being deprived of their status as German citizens, Baeck sought to uphold their morale, alleviate discriminatory practices, and support emigration. He himself refused to leave his post, reportedly saying that he would depart from Germany only after the last Jews had reached safety abroad. He was incarcerated in the concentration camp Theresienstadt and there continued his teaching of philosophy and religion.

After the liberation of the camp by the Red Army, Baeck settled in England, where he completed his second major work, *The People Israel*. He also traveled extensively, teaching and lecturing in Israel, the United States, and Germany. At a heavily attended lecture in Hamburg in 1948 he posed the question "Is there progress in morality?"—a query he answered in the negative. The Holocaust, he argued, implicated not only the German people, but also the rest of the world, which had failed to prevent this enormous tragedy. In 1955 Baeck and other German-Jewish intellectuals who were meeting in Jerusalem founded there an institute for the study of German Jewish history and culture. Honoring Baeck's preeminent standing in this field, it was named the Leo

Baeck Institute, and he became its first president. Baeck died a year later, on November 2, 1956.[5]

FRANZ ROSENZWEIG

Also known for his nonparochial Judaism was another major figure of German-Jewish learning, Franz Rosenzweig. He was born in 1886 into a well-to-do assimilated family in Kassel. Under the influence of his close friend Eugen Rosenstock, Rosenzweig converted to Christianity in 1913, but this step led him into a major crisis and almost to suicide. After attending a Yom Kippur service that year, he decided to remain a Jew and thereon committed himself to Jewish education.

In 1920 Rosenzweig founded the Freies Jüdisches Lehrhaus (Free Jewish academy) in Frankfurt, an institute of adult education that quickly became an important center of Jewish learning. Among its faculty were Martin Buber and Leo Baeck, as well as many other outstanding Jewish scholars. Similar institutions of adult education soon opened up in other major German cities.[6]

In 1921 Rosenzweig published his main work, *Star of Redemption.* Outlining the equally important roles of both Judaism and Christianity in the spiritual fabric of the world, it would have an important impact on Jewish-Christian dialogue. Together with Buber, Rosenzweig undertook a new translation of the Hebrew Bible in order to acquaint German Jews with the spirituality within it.[7] Rosenzweig died in 1929, leaving behind an extensive body of scholarship in both philosophy and theology.

MARTIN BUBER

The philosopher and theologian Martin Buber was born in Vienna in 1878, but spent much of his adult life in Germany. He is best known for his 1923 book *I and Thou,* which offered a new framework for understanding the different modes of human existence while emphasizing the crucial importance of faith in God. Buber advocated Jewish cultural renewal through the study of Hasidic Judaism. His Hasidic tales, advocacy of a direct relationship to

God, and stress on character education appealed to a segment of the German-Jewish youth movement, for whom he became a spiritual leader. Buber was also an important advocate of Jewish adult education through the creation of Jewish education centers, which stressed the message of religion as "lived presence, to be human in a Jewish way."

Buber propagated a cultural Zionism based primarily not on national identity but on a return to the traditions of Judaism. He criticized the mainstream Zionist movement's neglect of Palestinian Arabs' needs and rights and advocated a binational Israeli-Palestinian state. Despite his ambivalence about Zionism, Buber moved to Palestine in 1938 and became a professor at the Hebrew University in Jerusalem. He died in 1965.

The CV's Quest: Bring Together German Citizens of the Jewish Faith

The strong commitment to Judaism on the part of Baeck, Rosenzweig, and Buber was not typical of German Jewry during the Weimar period. Most German Jews wore their religion lightly. As during the empire, the majority of German Jews considered themselves German citizens of the Jewish faith, with their religious observance limited to attending synagogue during the High Holidays. They believed no contradiction existed between being Jewish and being German any more it did for Protestant or Catholic Germans.

The organization that stood for this outlook continued to be the CV, the Centralverein deutscher Staatsbürger jüdischen Glaubens (Central association of German citizens of the Jewish faith). The CV's central purpose was defined as bringing together the German citizens of the Jewish faith, irrespective of their religious and political outlook, in order to strengthen their willingness to defend their legal and social equality as well as their dedication to their German identity. The quick growth in the CV's membership proved the great need for such a defense organization against the prevailing anti-Semitism. In the year of its founding in 1893 the CV had 1,420 members. By the time of World War I, membership had grown to some 37,000 members; at war's end in 1919 it stood at 45,000; and by 1930 it had reached about 60,000. Many local clubs and organizations were also affiliated with the cv. All together, the cv represented some 300,000 German Jews, more than half of the total Jewish population.[8]

The weekly *cv Zeitung* (cv newspaper) was printed in an edition of 65,000. Some 35,000 issues of the monthly edition were sent free of charge to non-Jewish politicians, journalists, and other influential public figures. A cv monthly magazine, *Der Morgen* (The morning), specialized in scientific articles for the educated public. A cv press service distributed information to the media.[9]

Orthodox Jews stayed apart from the cv. Even some liberal Jews expressed concern about it, but for different reasons. They feared that the existence of a separate Jewish organization would be seen as proof of the failure of emancipation. It might also strengthen the position of the anti-Semites who demanded the exclusion of Jews from German society.

Despite this criticism, the cv prospered and confidently asserted its central message—the synthesis of *Deutschtum und Judentum* (Germandom and Jewishness). In the words of Eugen Fuchs, president of the cv in 1919 and its acknowledged ideological leader: "Our program and motto [was and remains] the reconciliation of Germanness and Jewishness, and finding a synthesis of religion and fatherland, of religious faith and homeland." Being the inheritors of a proud tradition, Fuchs went on to say, "we do not want to abandon the tradition of our fathers." Instead, he explained, the cv sought to revive Judaism and link up with those of other religions "in a kind of higher humanity."[10]

Fuchs insisted that members of the cv wanted to remain "good Jews." They opposed conversion to Christianity as strongly as the Zionists, and it was therefore presumptuous for the Zionists to claim that only they were true Jews. The cv, Fuchs argued, stressed loyalty to the German fatherland at the same time that it stood for loyalty to the Jewish religion. Zionism constituted a nationalistic excess. In common with anti-Semitism, it failed to find the right relationship of citizenship and religion. Just as it made no sense to have a Catholic or Protestant state, it was absurd to seek a Jewish state. The ancient state of Judea, Fuchs maintained, could not be resurrected, nor was it necessary for the preservation of Jewish values.[11]

The cv continued to adhere to this position throughout the twelve years of the Weimar Republic. Jakob Marx, head of the cv in Baden, wrote in 1925 that Zionism had done much damage to German Jewry; it undermined the commitment of German Jews to the German people.[12] Even if Palestine were to flourish, as the Jewish educator Heinemann Stern affirmed in 1926, it could absorb only a fraction of those Jews who needed a new home. Whatever their situation here in Germany, he continued, their fate would be decided here: "If millions of Germans today acknowledge us as Germans, they do so only because they believe in our dedication to Germany." German Jews had demonstrated their affirmation of Germanness; they considered themselves German because of their rootedness in German civilization—the German language, German literature and art. "The land in which I was born and where the graves of my ancestors lie, is for me the most beautiful thing in the world," Stern declared. "This land is my fatherland, my *Heimatland* [native country]." German Jews had made significant contributions to German culture: "Hence the conditions for our acceptance into the German *Volksgemeinschaft* [people's community] have been fulfilled. We have done our share; now it is up to you [the German people] to do yours."[13] At a mass rally in 1930 in front of the Reichstag, protesting the racial agitation of National Socialism, Alfred Wiener, the cv secretary general, declared with pride: "If there were a Nobel prize for German sentiments, the German Jews would win it."[14]

For Franz Rosenzweig too, Jewishness and being German were inseparable. Rosenzweig was critical of the cv for ignoring the tension that underlay the German-Jewish synthesis, yet his commitment to being German was strong. In a letter to a friend written in 1923 he declared that "becoming more Jewish has not made me a worse but rather a better German."[15]

Affirming Jewish Identity

Some well-known German Jews, among them the scientist Albert Einstein and the composer Kurt Weill, stood by their faith amid the assimilationists.

ALBERT EINSTEIN

Albert Einstein, the recipient of the 1921 Nobel Prize for Physics and today considered the most creative scientific genius of modern times, was born in 1879 into a typical assimilated German-Jewish family. His father called Jewish rituals "ancient superstitions," and Einstein shared these sentiments, staying aloof from Judaism for a time. However, unlike most of his coreligionists, Einstein repudiated Germany's nationalistic and militaristic tradition, exemplified by its authoritarian school system. Between 1895 and 1914 he studied and lived in Switzerland, and in 1901 he renounced his German citizenship. In 1914, in order to be able to accept the post of director of the Kaiser Wilhelm Institute of Physics and a professorship in Berlin, Einstein became a German citizen once more, but he made his final break with Germany when, on account of being Jewish, he lost his position in 1933 and subsequently left his homeland for good. His opponents had called his theories "Jewish physics."

In 1933, while Einstein was visiting the United States, Hitler came to power in Germany. Einstein remained in the United States and became a citizen. He was proud to be an American—he admired the country's commitment to individual liberty—but by this point Einstein also considered himself a member of the Jewish people. He was opposed to assimilation, which he called an "undignified mania." A Jew who abandons his faith, he believed, is like a snail that abandons its shell; it remains a snail.[16]

KURT WEILL

The composer and German cultural icon Kurt Weill never denied his Jewish identity. Born in Dessau (Saxony) in 1900, the son of a cantor, Weill revealed an early musical talent. His first composition, in 1913, was a Jewish wedding song. Weill's fame, both in Germany and in the world at large, became linked to *The Threepenny Opera*, which he composed to a text by Bertold Brecht. His *Eternal Road*, first performed in 1934, is a musical pageant of Jewish history. In 1935, together with his wife, the well-known singer Lotte Lenya, Weill came to the United States, where he continued a successful career as a composer. In 1946 he composed a Jewish prayer, "Kiddush," dedicated to his father. He died in 1950.[17]

Downplayers and Deniers

If the supporters of the CV solved their Jewish problem by stressing the synthesis of Germanness and Judaism, another large segment of German Jewry during the Weimar era downplayed or denied entirely their Jewish origins. Many of them were declared atheists. The members of this group considered themselves German intellectuals par excellence, especially intellectuals of the Left. Embracing cosmopolitanism or socialism, they expected that the Jewish problem would solve itself in a truly free European society. Their engagement, if they had an interest in politics at all, was in the fate of the embattled Weimar Republic, though they had few constructive answers. For most of them, the tribulations of their Jewish brethren in Eastern Europe were of no concern.

ERNST TOLLER

The writer Ernst Toller was a typical representative of this outlook. In his 1933 autobiography Toller spoke of Germany as "the country where I was raised, the air I breathe, the language I speak, the spirit that has formed me." In his childhood he had often been called a "dirty Jew," but this experience, he stressed, did not make him adopt the "Jewish deceit." Toller saw himself as a citizen of the world: "If someone had asked me to whom I belong, I should have replied: a Jewish mother brought me into the world, Germany nourished me, Europe formed me, my home is the earth, the world is my country."[18]

And yet Toller soon had to learn that the outside world did not share this characterization. The Nazis' rise to power in 1933 forced Toller into exile. The English translation of his autobiography published in 1934 carried the telling title *I Was a German.* Ousted by the Germans and estranged from his Jewish origins, the homeless Toller fell into despair. On May 22, 1939, he committed suicide. The gifted poet and dramatist was forty-five years old.[19]

LION FEUCHTWANGER

The novelist, playwright, and poet Lion Feuchtwanger, born in 1884 in Munich, as the son of a wealthy Jewish industrialist, was another example of this outlook. Feuchtwanger studied philosophy, literature, and languages and became a distinguished literary figure in Weimar Germany. He discovered the radical playwright Bertolt Brecht, and later collaborated with Brecht on several plays.

Feuchtwanger would go on to write many historical novels with protagonists who happened to be Jewish, but, being a Socialist, Communist sympathizer, and pacifist, he showed no particular interest in things Jewish. The hero of his famous novel *Jud Süss* (Jew Süss) is a court Jew who renounces his Jewish heritage and assimilates into German life and culture. Feuchtwanger found exile in the United States and died there in 1958.[20]

STEFAN ZWEIG

Stefan Zweig was one of Germany's most popular writers. Born in Vienna in 1881 into a wealthy Jewish family, Zweig was able to arrange his existence as he wished, moving around Europe and living independently from personal and professional ties. In his writings Zweig avoided any Jewish themes, characters, or problems. Politically naive, Zweig saw himself as a conciliator of cultural conflicts who would help overcome nationalism and imperialism. His autobiography, written in exile in Brazil and subtitled *Memoirs of a European*, voiced the hope that the "European conscience would not tolerate inhumanity."[21] This optimistic expectation was soon disappointed, and Zweig, who was forced into being a homeless refugee, became increasingly depressed. Fearing that the Nazi war machine was unstoppable, he and his wife committed suicide on November 28, 1942.

MAX REINHARDT

The theater and film director Max Reinhardt was born in Baden in 1873 into an Austrian Orthodox Jewish family named Goldmann. The family soon moved to Vienna, where young Max attended acting school. Seeking to distance himself from his Jewish origins, the aspiring actor assumed the name Max Reinhardt, and by age thirty-two he had become owner and director of the Deutsches Theater (German theater) in Berlin. Eventually he would produce some five hundred plays and become one of the most famous German-language theater directors. Forced into exile by Hitler, Reinhardt came to the United States in 1938. In a memoir that was never finished he reassessed his identity: "I am a Jew. That says a lot and is the proudest thing I can say about myself. . . . and that is why I begin my memoirs with this statement."[22]

ARNOLD ZWEIG

Arnold Zweig (not related to Stefan Zweig), was born in 1887 in Glogau (today Glogow, Poland) as the son of a Jewish saddler. He studied history, philosophy, and literature and, during the Weimar era, received wide recognition as a novelist. Military service during World War I changed Zweig from a Prussian patriot into an eager pacifist, and his 1927 antiwar novel *The Case of Sergeant Grischa* gained him world renown. Zweig's 1933 essay on the German-Jewish relationship, "Bilanz der deutschen Judenheit," published in 1934 in Amsterdam under the title "Insulted and Exiled: The Truth about the German Jews," attributed the flourishing of German culture to the creative symbiosis of Jews and non-Jews.

Zweig flirted with Zionism and spent the war years in Palestine. Abandoning Zionism, in 1948 he accepted an invitation from East

German authorities to return to Germany, where he became an ardent supporter of the Communist regime. He served as president of the German Democratic Republic's Academy of the Arts, as a delegate to the World Peace Congresses, and on the cultural advisory board of the Communist party. The regime rewarded him financially and bestowed on him many medals and prizes. In 1958 Zweig received the Lenin Peace Prize for his antiwar novels. He died in East Berlin in 1968.[23]

Arnold Zweig's embrace of socialism was shared by many German-Jewish intellectuals. In line with Marx's rejection of the Jewish religion, these Jews considered themselves as belonging to the community of mankind and embraced the vision of a classless society in which all racial or religious conflicts would disappear. Putting an end to the exploitation of man by man was in line with the traditional Jewish passion for social justice, but otherwise the secular messianism of Marxian socialism had nothing in common with the Jewish prophetic tradition. The Jewish religion was seen as part of the ideological superstructure of capitalism that would disappear with the coming of a new classless society of peace and harmony.[24]

Some left-leaning Jewish intellectuals regarded the Socialists as insufficiently radical in their opposition to capitalism and joined the Communist movement. The Communist party (KPD), with its militancy and strict discipline, appeared to provide a haven for insecure assimilated Jews who sought ideological cohesion and emotional security.

ROSA LUXEMBURG

Rosa Luxemburg was born in 1871 in Zamos, Poland, the youngest of five children in a lower-class Jewish family. Interested in politics from an early age, she left Poland and the repressive regime of Czar Alexander III and eventually settled in Berlin. Married to a German worker, she attained German citizenship and joined the leftist faction of the German Social Democratic party that eventually broke away and became the German Communist Party.

The Jewish Communists embraced internationalism. They ignored their Jewishness and showed no concern for persecuted Jews. In a letter to a friend, Luxemburg wrote: "Why bring up the special issue of Jewish suffering? I am just as concerned about the poor victims of rubber plantations in Putumayo [South America], the Negroes in Africa. . . . I hear so many voices [of the tortured and dying] that I have no special place in my heart for the ghetto. I feel at home in the world where there are clouds and birds and human tears."[25] Similarly, in his book *The Demise of Judaism*, the Austrian Jewish Communist Otto Heller denounced Zionism as "a tool of world imperialism in its struggle against the liberation movement of the colonial people."[26] Heller, who might have found refuge in the Jewish home he had vilified, died in the Nazi concentration camp Mauthausen in 1945.

WOLFGANG LEONHARD

Susanne Leonhard was a close friend of the Communist leaders Rosa Luxemburg and Karl Liebknecht. Her son Wolfgang, a historian, followed in her ideological footsteps and became a member of increasingly more radical leftist parties—the Independent Social Democratic party of Germany (USPD) in 1918, the German Communist party (KPD) in 1919, and in 1921 the German Communist Workers party (KAPD), which demanded the immediate abolition of bourgeois democracy and the establishment of the dictatorship of the proletariat. During the 1930s Leonhard fought in the Spanish Civil War, spent the World War II years in French detention, and returned to East Berlin following the defeat of Nazi Germany. His first doubts about Stalinism had come in 1936, when his mother was arrested in the Soviet Union; his final disillusionment with Communism occurred after the consolidation of dictatorial rule in Communist East Germany. Eventually he became an acknowledged expert on Communist rule in Eastern Europe, serving as visiting professor at several West German and American universities. His 1955 book *Die Revolution entlässt ihre Kinder* (The revolution abandons its children), published in

English as *Child of the Revolution*, was translated into many languages and became an international bestseller.

A few Jewish Communists went further than displaying indifference to the Jewish problem, they actually employed anti-Semitic slogans that they regarded as politically useful. In 1923 the prominent Jewish Communist Ruth Fischer told a group of nationalistic students in Berlin: "The German Reich can only be saved if you recognize, gentlemen of the populist side, that you must struggle in collaboration with the masses organized by the KPD. Whoever struggles against Jewish capital . . . is already a class fighter, even he does not know it. . . . Shoot down the Jew-capitalists, hang them from the lampposts, crush them!"[27] The Jewish Communists had no problem with the 1933 Communist broadside that shouted "SA and SS! You have shot enough workers. When will you hang the first Jew?"[28] In later years the KPD would reject anti-Jewish violence, but its Jewish members retained an anti-Jewish bias. To be accepted in the Communist movement they had to give up their Jewishness and Jewish traditions. Their vehement repudiations of all things Jewish bordered on Jewish self-hatred.

THEODOR LESSING

The term "Jewish self-hatred" itself was coined by Theodor Lessing, who was born in 1872 in Hanover to an assimilated Jewish middle-class family. His parents did not get along, and the young Lessing came to hate them both. To him, they exhibited many of the traits common among assimilated bourgeois Jews, prominently the courting of money and success. Unable to attain a position as a professor on account of his Jewishness and his leftist views, Lessing was forced to make a living as a substitute teacher and lecturer. In his book, *Der jüdische Selbsthass* (The Jewish self-hatred), published in 1930, he analyzed the phenomenon of Jews sharing the anti-Semitic views of their enemies. He also advocated the return of Jews to their ancient home in Palestine; restoring the Jews as a people of peasants, he believed, was far better than having them continue their decadent lives in

Europe. Still, he also warned against an excess of nationalism.[29] He was murdered by the Nazis while in exile in Czechoslovakia in the summer of 1933.

OTTO WEININGER

The young philosopher Otto Weininger was an example of the self-hating German Jews Lessing wrote about. For Weininger, Judaism was undignified and indeed loathsome. On July 21, 1902, the day he received his doctoral degree, Weininger had himself baptized as a Protestant, a decision taken in order to cut all ties with his hated Jewish origins. And yet this step apparently did not bring peace to his troubled sense of self. In 1903, at age twenty-three, Weininger committed suicide.[30]

KURT TUCHOLSKY

The leftist Jewish intellectual Kurt Tucholsky has been called the most important journalist of the Weimar Republic. He also excelled as a satirist, poet, and composer of cabaret songs. Born in 1890 as the son of a Jewish bank cashier, the assimilated Tucholsky repudiated Judaism, married a non-Jew, and repeatedly declared that the Jewish problem was no concern of his. Between 1923 and 1930 he published a series of monologues by "Herr Wendriner" (Mr. Wendriner), a fictitious Jewish capitalist who is selfish, vulgar, and interested only in money. On account of these sketches, which were extremely popular in Germany, Gershom Scholem called Tucholsky one of the most gifted and repulsive Jewish anti-Semites he had ever encountered.[31] Critics, then and now, have argued that his satirical depictions of businessmen, judges, clergymen, and politicians undermined the fledgling German republic. Tucholsky eventually realized that his attempt to cease being a Jew had failed. In December 1935, a few days before he committed suicide while in exile in Sweden, he wrote to his fellow writer Arnold Zweig: "I have declared my exit from the Jewish faith in 1911, and I know [now] that one cannot do that."[32]

WALTHER RATHENAU

The Jewish industrialist and statesman Walther Rathenau was yet another self-hating German Jew. Born in 1867 into a prosperous Jewish family, Rathenau became a highly successful industrialist, a member of a circle of men known as the *Kaiserjuden* (Imperial Jews). During World War I he played a key role in ensuring the production and distribution of raw materials essential for the war effort. In May 1921 he was made minister of reconstruction, and in January 1922 became Germany's foreign minister. Six months later, on June 24, 1922, Rathenau was assassinated by militant nationalists who hated him as a Jew, an alleged advocate of "creeping Communism," and a symbol of the despised Treaty of Versailles, whose terms Rathenau had honored.[33] His murderers were the kind of blond, blue-eyed young men Rathenau had admired so much.[34]

Being Jewish, Rathenau had failed to attain the coveted title of reserve officer, an emblem of elevated social standing in German society. He also fell short of being fully accepted among the political and economic elite of the day. Yet instead of expressing his repugnance of the German society that rejected him, Rathenau voiced hatred for the Jewish minority whose conduct he held responsible for the discrimination he experienced. In an essay published in 1897, the thirty-year-old Rathenau demanded that Jews who did not fit their social environment change their looks: "You must ensure that, amid a race that is bred to strict military discipline, you do not make yourself a laughing-stock by your slovenly, shambling appearance. Once you have recognized your ill-constructed build, your high shoulders, your clumsy feet, the soft roundness of your forms, as signs of physical decay, you will have to spend a couple of generations on your external rebirth."[35] The Jews, Rathenau went on to say, existed as a "separate, foreign human race" in the midst of German society. This "Asiatic horde" lived on German soil but actually inhabited an invisible ghetto as a "foreign organism."

Rathenau advised his fellow Jews to look in the mirror as a first step toward self-criticism and changed behavior. They had to abandon their "south-eastern appearance" and "wagging subservience and most foul arrogance" *(wedelnde Unterwürfigkeit und schnöde Arroganz)*, traits that could not be washed off. "The end of this process of self-education should be the emergence of a German-mannered and German-educated Jew."[36] Not surprisingly, this provocative article created a sensation among both Jews and non-Jews.

Remaining at all times a proud German, in later years Rathenau somewhat softened his views of his fellow Jews. He was linked to them, he wrote in 1916, by the same elements that linked every German to Judaism—the Bible and the figures of the Old Testament. Rathenau often avowed his belief in the Gospels and the divinity of Jesus, but, while recognizing that conversion might bring some social advantage, he never formally became a Christian. To do so, he stated in 1911, would be to implicitly endorse Prussia's Jewish policy, "which is nothing less than the most grievous insult that a state is capable of directing against a group of its people."[37] Being born Jewish, Rathenau, maintained, did not involve his real essence: "I have and recognize no other blood, no other stock, no other people but those that are German. Even if one were to expel me from my German soil, I would remain German, and nothing would be changed."[38] He further believed that all German Jews had to uphold this standard. Even when Jews were being discriminated against, Rathenau insisted, they needed to continue to improve themselves and "serve their country with redoubled love."[39]

It became the tragedy of German Jewry that their anti-Semitic opponents did not share these views. The German writer Arthur Stapel, for one, was the first to use the term "German-Jewish symbiosis," but he did so only in order to reject decisively the possibility of such a merger. Jews remain Jews, he argued, even if they try to appear German in speech and behavior.[40] For the Nazis, too, a Jew by birth or descent remained a Jew by blood. No matter how effectively German Jews managed to look, behave, speak, and think like Germans, their enemies would not accept them as part of German society and ultimately set out to destroy them physically.

Intra-Jewish Hostility

Overall, assimilated German Jews were hostile toward their eastern brethren, who, in fleeing the pogroms of Eastern Europe, were moving to Germany in increasingly large numbers. By the turn of the century there were 11,000 eastern Jews in Berlin, or 12.6 percent of Berlin's Jewish population. In 1925 eastern Jews constituted almost 20 percent of German Jewry, with 43,000 eastern Jews or 25.4 percent of Jews living in Berlin alone.[41] For many assimilated Jews, their eastern brethren conjured up the old specter of the ghetto. The "German Jews" considered their coreligionists dirty, pushy, and loud. Jakob Marx, a director of the CV, charged that all too many of them were "profiteers, crooks, currency and stock speculators, thieves and dealers in stolen goods."[42] The head of the CV in Upper Silesia, Rabbi Max Kopfstein, declared in 1923 that in view of Germany's economic problems, the immigration of foreigners was "undesirable."[43]

Self-identified "respectable" middle-class German Jews thus regarded eastern Jews with a mixture of fear and repulsion. They worried that they would encourage anti-Semitism and threaten the integration of Jews into German society. Many Jewish women colored their hair blond and straightened it in order not to be taken as eastern Jews.[44] While liberal Jews contributed substantial sums of money to support the destitute refugees, they considered them objects of welfare rather than sons and daughters of the same people. In some Jewish communities eastern Jews were not allowed to be voting members. Much of the money raised was spent to speed up their departure from Germany to the United States. The eastern Jews, in turn, considered the German Jews as lacking in Jewish consciousness. They called them "Yekkes," a term of unclear origin but of definitely negative connotations.[45]

German Jews felt that Palestine eased the burden of Germany as a place of refuge for the unwelcome Ostjuden but rejected it as an option for themselves. Even among declared Zionists, the number of those willing to emigrate to the forbidding Near East remained small. By 1933 fewer than two thousand German Jews had gone to Palestine. As a joke circulating at the time put it, a Zionist is a Jew who seeks with great effort to convince a second Jew to use the money of a third Jew to emigrate to Palestine.[46] While by the early 1920s the author Arnold Zweig, at that point a Socialist Zionist, was urging his fellow German Jews to abandon their exaggerated enthusiasm for all things German and emigrate to Palestine, he himself did not leave Germany until the Nazis assumed power in 1933. He, too, could not cut the umbilical cord that linked him to the venerated German culture. It was in Germany, after all, where he had made his name as a writer.[47]

Gershom Scholem

Among the few German Zionists who went to live in Palestine before 1933 was the famous scholar of the Kabbalah and Jewish mysticism Gershom Scholem, originally named Gerhard Scholem. His assimilated father strongly opposed his early interest in things Jewish, but, thanks to his mother's intervention, he was allowed to study Hebrew and the Talmud with an Orthodox rabbi. Enrolled at the Friedrich Wilhelm University of Berlin, Scholem studied mathematics, philosophy, and Hebrew. He also came into contact with Martin Buber and other Zionist greats such as Hayim Bialik and Ahad Ha'am. In 1923, four years after the University of Munich granted him a doctoral degree in Semitic languages, he emigrated to Palestine, where he eventually became a professor at the new Hebrew University of Jerusalem. There, Scholem established Jewish mysticism as a legitimate academic discipline. He taught that the Kabbalah was an expression of the collective hopes and traumas of the Jewish people over the centuries, and a vital expression of Jewish spirituality. His celebrated work *Major*

Trends in Jewish Mysticism, published in 1941, was dedicated to his close friend Walter Benjamin. In 1977 he published *Sabbatai Sevi: The Mystical Messiah*, a book on the seventeenth-century failed messiah Sabbatai Sevi. Arrested in Constantinople in 1666, Sabbatai Sevi had been given the choice of conversion to Islam or death. He chose to become a Muslim, ending a time of ardent messianic fervor in the Jewish diaspora and creating a deep crisis of faith among his followers. This also led to the emergence, in late eighteenth-century Poland, of a new form of Jewish mysticism: the Hasidic movement. Scholem considered the trauma of the failed messiah's apostasy one of the decisive factors explaining the beginning of modern Jewish history.

Scholem was also strongly engaged in cultural criticism and political activism, which included the dispute with his longtime friend Hannah Arendt over the 1961 Eichmann trial. Arendt, a noted philosopher and political theorist born in 1906 of Jewish parents in Hanover, covered the Eichmann's trial in Jerusalem for the *New Yorker*, and her collected articles appeared as the 1963 book *Eichmann in Jerusalem: A Report on the Banality of Evil*. Her characterization of Eichmann as a mere bureaucrat quickly became controversial, with Scholem among her most severe critics. In his letters of June 23 and August 12, 1963, addressed to her, Scholem rejected Arendt's picture of Eichmann as a "banal gentleman" in SS uniform. Eichmann, Scholem noted, was a committed Nazi ideologue who enjoyed his evil deeds. Arendt's discussion of Jewish behavior under the extreme conditions of the Final Solution, including that of the Jewish councils, badly lacked balanced judgment. Ultimately, Scholem was most upset about the overall tenor of Arendt's book. What divides us above all, he wrote, "is the heartless, the downright malicious tone you employ in dealing with the topic that so profoundly concerns the center of our life." She had no trace of "what the Jews call *ahavath Israel* or love of the Jewish people," he told her, a disagreeable posture also held by many intellectuals of the Left.[48] Scholem died in 1982, leaving behind a rich trove of diaries, letters, and other writings.[49]

No to Zionism, Yes to Germany

Unlike Scholem, most of the German Zionists were content to stress their Jewish ethnic consciousness or to talk of the commonality of two national movements—the Jewish and the German. In an essay published in 1931, the Zionist Gustav Krojanker suggested sympathy for those nationalists who strove for a strong German state and a powerful sense of German identity. The Zionist movement, he argued, had also arisen from similar spiritual and material distress.[50]

Not surprisingly, the CV looked upon this endeavor as damaging the full civic rights of German Jews and creating a conflict of loyalties. It was feared that any affirmation of Jewish national identity would lend credence to the *Völkische*'s charge that the Jews constituted a foreign body. A resolution adopted by the CV board of directors in 1921 opposed any support toward settling Palestine, such as the work of Keren Hayesod, the money-collecting agency of the Zionist movement. Such support would strengthen the goals of Jewish nationalism, which the CV rejected with vehemence. The organization exhorted its members to say "No to Zionism and Yes to Germany."[51] In 1928 the CV General Assembly approved the so-called Mecklenburg Resolution, named after its author Georg Mecklenburg, which criticized "Zionist propaganda" as giving credence to the separation of Germans and Jews. To impede any threat to the achievements of emancipation, the CV resolved to reject any belief in a Jewish nation. Both in national and cultural aspects, the Mecklenburg Resolution affirmed, German Jews "belonged exclusively to the German people."[52]

Jewish Converts

Some assimilated German Jews—among them the famous conductors Otto Klemperer and Bruno Walter, the composer Arnold

Schoenberg, and the chemist Fritz Haber—took the ultimate step: abandoning their ancestral faith.

OTTO KLEMPERER

Born in 1885 in Breslau (today Wroclaw, Poland) to musically inclined parents, Klemperer, the cousin of the diarist Victor Klemperer, had his first piano lesson at age four. While studying music he met and became friends with the composer and conductor Gustav Mahler. On Mahler's recommendation he became conductor of the German opera in Prague. In the following years Klemperer held a number of major appointments in Germany. His renditions of the music of major composers were remarkable for their dramatic strength, and Klemperer quickly became known as one of the great twentieth-century German conductors. In 1933 Klemperer received the Goethe Medal from President Paul von Hindenburg for his contributions to the advancement of German culture, but in 1933 he was discharged from his post as music director of the State Opera in Berlin. His conversion to Christianity in 1919 did not protect him against the Nazi regime, which classified him as non-Aryan. That same year Klemperer emigrated to the United States, where he continued his illustrious career as the leader of major orchestras. He died in 1973.[53]

BRUNO WALTER

The renowned German conductor Bruno Walter was another protégé of Mahler (whose music Walter would later promote enthusiastically). Born in 1876 as Bruno Walter Schlesinger, in 1896 the young musician was offered the post of second conductor at the Breslau opera house, on the condition that he change his obviously Jewish surname. He did so, and several years later he converted to Catholicism in order to be able to accept an appointment as chief conductor of the Riga Opera. We have no information about his religious practices, though he apparently took his new religion seriously. Walter went on to became conductor of several major German orchestras, including the Gewandhaus

Orchestra of Leipzig. Regarded as a Jew by the Nazis, Walter left Germany in 1936, and eventually came to the United States, where he continued a brilliant career. He died in 1962.[54]

ARNOLD SCHOENBERG

The composer Arnold Schoenberg was born in Vienna in 1874 into a middle-class Jewish family, but in 1898 he converted to Christianity. Showing early talent, Schoenberg composed his first musical piece before he was nine years old. A 1909 composition was the first to dispense with traditional tonality and manifested what became known as the twelve-tone method.

Schoenberg was also a gifted painter. In 1923 the painter Wassily Kandinsky invited him to join the faculty of the Bauhaus school of design in Weimar. In his invitation Kandinsky noted that the Bauhaus school generally did not hire Jews, but that an exception would be made for Schoenberg. An angry Schoenberg rejected the invitation. In a letter to Kadinsky he declared: "For I have at last learned the lesson that has been forced upon me during this year. It is that I am not a German, not a European, indeed perhaps scarcely a human being, but I am a Jew."[55]

After Hitler's rise to power in 1933, Schoenberg left for Paris, where he returned to Judaism. He eventually came to the United States, where he continued an illustrious musical career. He died in 1951.

FRITZ HABER

Another German Jew who converted to Christianity was the eminent chemist Fritz Haber, who received the 1918 Nobel Prize for discovering the process of synthesizing ammonia. Born in 1868 in Breslau (now Wroclaw, Poland) into an assimilated Jewish family, Haber adopted the dress, manner, and even the pince-nez of a Prussian gentleman. In 1914 he enthusiastically greeted the outbreak of war, joining ninety-two other German intellectuals in signing the "Appeal to the Cultured World," a manifesto that defended German militarism and the attack on Belgium.

Haber also became known as the "father of chemical warfare"; he invented the deadly chlorine gas and personally supervised its first use in the second battle of Ypres in the spring of 1915. While the employment of gas in warfare was in violation of the Hague Convention of 1907, and chlorine gas in particular caused a painful death by asphyxiation, Haber defended the weapon, saying that death was death, by whatever means. As was to be expected, the National Socialist regime did not recognize Haber's dedicated service to his beloved German fatherland, and he left it in August 1933. In poor health, he traveled in several European countries. Haber died in January 1934 in Basel, Switzerland.[56]

Rise of Anti-Jewish Agitation

Other German Jews married a non-Jewish partner and so gained the opportunity for closer contact with non-Jewish society. While the number of mixed marriages had been increasing for some time, the pace accelerated during the Weimar years. Nearly 13 percent of Jews married outside the faith in 1920, and by 1933 the Jewish intermarriage rate reached 28 percent.[57] In most of the larger cities, the share of interfaith marriages was even higher. In Hamburg, for example, 57 percent of all Jewish weddings in 1933 involved a non-Jewish partner.[58] For some Jews—Tucholsky being a good example—marriage to a non-Jewish partner was a deliberate step to complete assimilation, but, no matter what the reason, the result of intermarriage was a weakening of Jewish cohesion. Only about a quarter of the children in mixed marriages were raised as Jews.[59]

The rate of intermarriage is always dependent in part on the number of eligible spouses, and in Weimar Germany the large number of gentile women willing to marry a Jew may have been affected by the shortage of men after the carnage of World War I. The large figure could signify increased tolerance on the part of the German population toward minorities, but it could also indicate a worsening of anti-Semitism, from which Jews sought to escape by way of a mixed marriage, and, indeed, anti-Semitism did become a steadily more dangerous problem for Germany's Jews in the Weimar era. During the war they had been charged with shirking their responsibility and profiteering; now the Jews stood accused of having caused Germany's defeat by organizing the Communist revolutions of 1918, thus thrusting a knife into the back of the valiant German soldier, the so-called *Dolchstosslegende*. Had not Jews such as Rosa Luxemburg, Paul Levi, Kurt Eisner, Gustav Landauer, Ernst Toller, and Eugen Leviné played a prominent role in the Spartacist revolt in Berlin and the short-lived Bavarian Soviet Republic?! Most of these figures of the Left did not see themselves as Jews, while on the other hand many other Jews were actively involved in putting down the Communist uprisings—but these facts were conveniently ignored. During the following years, Jews were vilified as both Jewish Bolsheviks and as capitalist speculators and monopolists. They became scapegoats for all of the problems afflicting a defeated Germany, including the disastrous inflation of the early 1920s and the growing unemployment that accompanied the Great Depression that began in 1929. The Jew Hugo Preuss had created the republican constitution; hence, militant nationalists denounced the Weimar Republic as a *Judenrepublik* (a Jewish republic).[60] The prominent role of such Jewish Communists as Leon Trotsky and Béla Kun in the Russian and Hungarian revolutions lent further credibility to the charge of a worldwide Jewish revolutionary plot.[61]

Much of this anti-Jewish agitation was not new. The main difference between the anti-Semitism of the pre- and postwar years was not its content, but, in the case of the latter, its success.[62] The most conspicuous sign of an escalating anti-Semitism was the emergence of organizations openly committed to violence against Jews. In comparison with the time of the empire, there now were more persons willing to act against Jews.

The largest and most influential of these organizations was the Deutschvölkischer Schutz-und Trutzbund , or DVSTB (German nationalist league for protection and defiance). Founded during a meeting of the Pan-German League in Bamberg in February

1919, within less than a year the DSTB had about thirty thousand members; by the middle of 1922 membership had reached almost two hundred thousand, with some six hundred active local branches. The majority of members belonged to the lower middle class, but there were also many teachers, civil servants, physicians, and academics. The league's declared purpose was to fight Judaism. Its constitution stated: "The Bund fights for the moral rebirth of the German people. . . . It considers the pernicious and destructive influence of Jewry to be the main cause of the defeat and the removal of this influence to be necessary for the political and economic recovery of Germany, and for the salvation of German culture." Carrying out this program, the DVSTB distributed large numbers of leaflets vilifying the Jews, encouraging violence both at mass meetings and in the pages of its publication *Deutschvölkische Blätter* (German nationalist pages), circulated to about 160,000 Germans. Alfred Roth, the longtime leader of the League, declared at a meeting in Kassel in March 1922 that once the DVSTB had achieved political power, it would put the Jews not only in the pillory but lead them to the gallows. The best known of the league's victims was Foreign Minister Rathenau, who was assassinated in 1922.[63] The DVSTB was banned after this act, and most of its members joined the budding Nazi party.

The novel *Die Sünde wider das Blut* (The sin against the blood), authored by Artur Dinter, a member of the DVSTB's directorate, was one of the most widely read anti-Semitic diatribes. Published in 1917, it had an estimated readership of 1.5 million. Written in a semipornographic style, the book described the life of a Jewish businessman who systematically impregnated blond German virgins. The novel combined old stereotypes of the abnormal sexual prowess of the Jews with new racial beliefs about their corrupt nature. The German people, Dinter declared in a speech, should "never cease fighting and wrestling until this devilish race be made harmless for mankind. Not until they shall be rid of this unsavory race will the German people be able to fulfill the destiny marked out for them by God."[64] Also very popular was *The*

Protocols of the Elders of Zion, a work first published in Russia in 1903 that described an alleged worldwide Jewish conspiracy that planned to wrest control of Christian nations. Altogether, some seven hundred publications and magazines spread the anti-Semitic poison. At a time of severe economic dislocation, writings that blamed every disaster on a convenient scapegoat had a wide appeal.[65]

In the early years of the Weimar Republic, more than one hundred völkische (militant nationalist) organizations were spreading the hatred of Jews, and many of those advocated and practiced outright violence against them. Among the political parties committed to an anti-Semitic platform, the Nazis, the National Socialist Workers party, stood out. They saw Jews as the embodiment of human equality, parliamentary democracy, peace and international brotherhood—all doctrines the Nazis had sworn to destroy. The party program of 1920, known as the "Twenty-Five Points," demanded that Jews be denied citizenship, civil rights, and the ability to hold public office. In 1931 a statement of aims added the removal of Jews from the economic and cultural life of the nation and making mixed marriages between Jews and gentiles a major crime. In a party composed of various social elements, anti-Semitism served as an important unifying element.[66]

Hitler's hatred of Jews was extreme even by Nazi standards. By his own account, anti-Semitism was the main reason for his going into politics. Hitler blamed the Jews for Germany's defeat in the world war, the punitive Treaty of Versailles, and the disastrous inflation of the early 1920s. In his book *Mein Kampf* he expressed regret that during the war Germany had missed the chance to liberate the country from "the pestilential disease" of Jewish Marxism. "If the best were killed at the front," he wrote, "then one could at least destroy the vermin at home." In the final chapter, ominous words portended future events: "If, at the beginning of the war and during the war, ten or fifteen thousand of these Hebrew corrupters of the nation had been subjected to poison gas, such as had to be endured on the front by hundreds of thousands of our very best German workers of all classes and professions, then the sacrifice of millions on the front would not have been in vain."[67] At other times Hitler compared the Jews to "the maggots in a putrefying body," "the spider that slowly sucks the blood of the people," "the typical parasite," "a band of rats who fight bloody battles with each other," and the like.[68] At still other times, for tactical reasons, Hitler omitted the Jewish issue from his inflammatory speeches.

The vilification of the Jew was a regular feature in Nazi propaganda. "Whoever spares the Jew," Joseph Goebbels declared in 1929 in *Der Angriff* (The attack) the newspaper of the Nazi party of Berlin, "commits a sin against his own people. One can only be a servant of the Jews or their enemy. Enmity to Jews is a matter of personal hygiene."[69] Agitation at lower levels frequently encouraged outright violence. Jews were compared to fleas that sucked the blood of its victims and were to be treated like fleas. A speaker at a meeting in Nüdlingen, Bavaria, in April 1932 declared bluntly: "When we have the power, the gentlemen [Jews] will have a shovel pressed into their hands so that they can dig a hole that is long or broad or deep, depending on whether they prefer to sit or stand or lie in it. Then one of us will step up, take the shovel, hit him on the head so that it splits right down the middle. Into the hole, earth on top. That's all—the end."[70] Parading storm troopers regularly chanted in the streets *Juda verrecke!* (Jews, perish!) and *Wenn das Judenblut vom Messer spritzt, dann geht's noch mal so gut* (When Jewish blood spurts from the knife, than all goes doubly well). The Nazi hate rag *Der Stürmer* pronounced with every issue *"Die Juden sind unser Unglück"* (The Jews are our misfortune).[71]

Jews in Weimar Culture

This time of aggressive and ominous anti-Semitic agitation was simultaneously an era of cultural distinction in which Jews had a significant share. Several outstanding Jewish figures such as Leo Baeck, Franz Rosenzweig, and Martin Buber helped create a renaissance of Jewish education and learning. At the same time, other Jews made outstanding contributions to Weimar's artistic, literary, and scientific life. For the most part, they did so not as Jews but, at best, as Germans of Jewish descent, yet the non-Jewish world considered them Jews just the same.

A tension always existed between what Germany's Jewish intellectuals sought and what they achieved in terms of integration and acceptance into German society. Anti-Semites charged that German culture had become *verjudet* (dominated by Jews), and, given the large number of Jews contributing to that culture, it is easy to see how this accusation came to be accepted.

All in all, the Weimar years marked the high point of Jewish emancipation and assimilation in Germany. Jews were largely convinced that they belonged to a society in which one's religious or ethnic background was irrelevant. The onset of Nazi rule in 1933 showed this belief to have been an illusion, but it was an illusion productive of excellence. Weimar was concomitantly a time of artistic innovation and notable creativity in all fields of endeavor, and Jews played a crucial role in this cultural flourishing. The question of the sources of Jewish creativity continues to be debated. The Jewish religion is said to encourage questioning and independent thinking, but most German-Jewish intellectuals were not religious. The status of Jews as outsiders in a Christian society and the sense of alienation produced thereby is often mentioned as well. Whatever the answer to the question, there is general agreement that the encounter between Jews and Germans during the Weimar era produced true greatness.[72]

3

Jewish Patriots

Even as most German Jews considered themselves German citizens of the Jewish faith, several organizations went beyond this outlook and can legitimately be described as specifically patriotic.

The RJF

The largest of these associations was the Reichsbund jüdischer Frontsoldaten, or RJF (National league of Jewish frontline soldiers) founded by the retired Jewish major of the reserves and ardent German nationalist Leo Löwenstein. Linked to the RJF were youth and sports clubs that aimed at making Jewish youngsters more hardy and organizations dedicated to the welfare of Jewish war victims, the care of war memorials, and the graves of the fallen.

In its first public pronouncement, issued in January 1919, just before its official founding on February 8, 1919, the RJF called upon all Jewish combat veterans to join the new organization in order to defend their good name in the face of ugly attacks upon their record. Jewish soldiers, together with their gentile *Volksgenossen* (national comrades), had spent their blood. Thousands had died, been wounded, or emerged from the war as cripples. All of these sacrifices, the RJF declared, now appeared to have been in vain. Unconscionable slanderers were calling them "cowardly shirkers" and vilifying their fallen Jewish comrades. The very existence of the RJF, the appeal continued, will help affirm the truth about us. Every German Jew, irrespective of political allegiance or religious orientation, should join the effort to fight those who incite religious and racial hatred and defile our honor as Germans and Jews.[1]

The new wave of anti-Semitism as well as the memory of the humiliating Jewish census of 1916 induced large numbers of Jews to join the RJF. Like most other Jewish frontline veterans, my father became a member, and as his son I participated in the activities of one of its affiliated sports clubs. By 1926 the combined membership of all of these organizations reached forty thousand.[2]

The RJF's leaders were right-of-center nationalistic Jews, but the rank-and-file membership adhered to a more diverse political outlook and even included Zionists such as Felix Theilhaber, who authored a book on Jewish pilots in the Great War. The continued attacks on the record of Jewish soldiers in World War I, it was widely realized, were but a means to question the Jews' political commitment to Germany and to contest their political rights. In response, time and again the RJF distributed statistics about the outstanding record of Jewish soldiers in the war and stressed the defining experience of combat service. In addition, seeking to refute the racial slurs of the anti-Semites, RJF leaders argued that membership in the German *Volksgemeinschaft* (people's community)—a concept used by German nationalists and especially the Nazis—should not be determined by race but by the existence of a common language and culture. Using these criteria, German Jews were Germans as good as any Nordic gentile.[3]

All the while concerned about Jewish behavior that might encourage anti-Semitic attacks, in 1920 the RJF founder Löwenstein organized a "self-discipline committee" that carried the motto "Back to simplicity and serious living!" This advice was directed especially to Jewish women, who were encouraged to avoid ostentatious clothing and jewelry.[4] Sharing this solicitude, the Berlin attorney Adolf Asch, a founding member of the RJF, impugned Jewish parvenus who had profited from the postwar inflation and now ostentatiously displayed their wealth. His *Selbstzuchtorganisation* (self-discipline organization), created in 1922, issued warnings to Jews to conduct themselves with dignity, especially before and after religious services, and similarly advised Jewish women to avoid showy clothing and jewelry.[5] Some CV leaders considered these efforts demeaning and viewed them with a mixture of amusement and condescension. But to the chairman of the CV, Ludwig Holländer, these concerns made sense. As he put it: "Stepchildren must be doubly good."[6]

The search for a modest external appearance was in line with the RJF's endeavor to reform the social structure of German Jewry, especially by creating Jewish farmers. Like the promotion of sport, agricultural life was to prove that Jews were not unduly intellectualized.[7] The health of Jews, it was believed, would benefit from toiling the land and becoming rooted in the German soil. Hence the RJF established a Jewish farm at Gross Gaglow near Cottbus, but only twenty-five families accepted the offer of land.[8] It would require the idealistic and pioneering spirit of the Zionists in Palestine to effect real change in the occupational configuration of the Jewish people.

The struggle against anti-Semitism also included the formation of self-defense units in various German cities. When a mob attacked the Jews of the Scheunenviertel section of Berlin in 1923, a group of RJF members armed themselves and came to the aid of the vulnerable *Ostjuden*. An RJF member shot and killed a Nazi. Tried for murder and the illegal possession of a weapon, the RJF man was acquitted on the grounds that, in view of the failure of the police to stem the riot, he had been justified in coming to the aid of his brethren. For some days after the riot, RJF members, armed with rubber truncheons, set up guard posts at synagogues in various parts of Berlin and sent out patrols at regular intervals. In 1927 outnumbered RJF men stood their ground during anti-Semitic disturbances in Chemnitz and Wiesbaden. On April 29, 1927, the Berlin branch of the RJF organized two mass demonstrations against Nazi violence that were attended by 2,600 persons.[9]

Many RJF members had long-standing personal relations with gentile comrades and were members of local veterans' associations. Until the mid-twenties the RJF also worked with the largest national veterans' organization, the *Stahlhelm* (Steel helmet), in organizing commemorative events remembering the war dead. But in May 1926 the Stahlhelm decided to restrict its membership to "men of German descent," and Jews were increasingly excluded from local remembrance events.[10] At the national Stahlhelm convention in Berlin in May 1927, swastikas appeared on the flags of several local groups. At the 1929 Volkstrauertag (People's day of mourning), the traditional commemoration of the victims of war and oppression, a delegation of veterans wearing Nazi uniforms and carrying swastika flags was conspicuously present. An article in the RJF's magazine *Der Schild* (The shield) reacted with consternation, asking, "Did those who admitted this deputation consider what an affront its presence would constitute for the Jewish participants in the service? Did they know that under this symbol the greatest outrages are continually being inflicted upon Jews?"[11]

In the national elections of May 1928, Theodor Duesterberg, deputy head of the Stahlhelm, openly supported "the fight for German racial purity." Sometime later Duesterberg would learn that one of his grandfathers had been a Jewish physician who had converted to Christianity, and during the election of 1932 the Nazis taunted him on account of his Jewish ancestry. With his own racial purity compromised, Duesterberg came close to a nervous breakdown and decided to withdraw from public life.[12]

To bolster the patriotic contribution of Jewish soldiers in the Great War, in the fall of 1932 the RJF published a new list of those who had given their lives for the fatherland.[13] Much to the gratification of the RJF leadership, the ceremonious presentation of this memorial volume to the public on November 17 was attended by high-ranking officers of the Reichswehr (German Army) as well as representatives of various veterans' organizations, including the Stahlhelm. A copy of the book was also presented to the country's president, Paul von Hindenburg, a war hero whom the RJF regarded with great respect and had supported in the presidential elections.[14]

The patriotic sentiments voiced by the RJF reflected the sincere convictions of large numbers of German Jews. The Jewish record in the Great War, they were convinced, had established their right to be equal and full citizens of Germany. And yet, in the eyes of the Right, the Jews were a foreign element. Soon after

Hitler and his National Socialists assumed power in 1933, the Jewish veterans became pariahs in the very fatherland they had venerated. In 1941, while being deported to the East, some of them wore their war medals, but this last show of patriotism did not save them. They perished in the Holocaust like all other Jews, for their enemies knew no other defining element but membership in a purportedly cursed race.

The VNJ

Even more radical than the RJF, in its espousal of German nationalism was the Verband nationaldeutscher Juden, or VNJ (Association of national-German Jews). Established in March 1921 by Max Naumann, a Berlin lawyer who had served as a captain in the Great War and received the medal of the Iron Cross of the First and Second Class, the VNJ aimed to bring together Jewish and non-Jewish *Volksgenossen* (national comrades, another term dear to German nationalists) to work cooperatively in revitalizing the strength, uprightness, and self-confidence of the German people. As the organization's bylaws elucidated, the VNJ would also fight all ideas and activities that might endanger Germany's return to an honored position in the world. In June 1921 the VNJ publicized its first call for public support, signed by eighty-three persons, most of them professionals, such as editors, teachers, and lawyers. Throughout the Weimar era, VNJ membership would remain small—estimated at between 3,500 and 5,000—but its activities would draw considerable attention.[15]

Half of the members lived in Berlin. They were Jews who considered themselves fully integrated into German society. The organization to which they belonged offered their personal approach to the Jewish question as a general prescription for all German Jews. As Naumann explained in his writings, Jews constituted a German tribe (*Stamm*) just as Bavarians or Saxons did, but being one of Germany's tribes did not diminish German national consciousness. Germans of the Jewish tribe were proud of being Germans: "We are German in our hearts and German in our intellects." A person's race, Naumann insisted, was irrelevant to his Germanness. Whether someone was a German did not depend on one's religion or hair color or shape of nose. The sole decisive issue was the strength of feeling for Germany, the strong conviction and identification with all things German. And national-German Jews were linked indissolubly to German culture and German essence. "We are Germans, and nothing but Germans."[16] Together with well-meaning non-Jews, first deputy chairman Alfred Peyser declared in 1926, the VNJ would fight to free Germany "from the chains of internationalism and racial fanaticism."[17]

Not surprisingly, in view of their strong embrace of all things German, most VNJ members belonged to Reform congregations, in which services were conducted in German. In the Reform Temple of Berlin, the chief Reform synagogue in the city, Sabbath services took place on Sunday, in line with gentile German church services held on Sundays. Most VNJ members viewed Zionists and Ostjuden as disloyal elements in German society. The Zionists had assumed a national Jewish identity and therefore made themselves foreigners in Germany, Naumann argued. As a result, the enemies of the Jews had been able to say that the Jews had a different nationality. By contrast, national-German Jews were one with their German brethren, linked by a shared fervent love for their common fatherland.[18]

Naumann was critical of those who had themselves baptized in order to not be regarded as Jews. At the same time, he was hostile toward the Ostjuden, who, he charged, were proud of their alien status in German society and looked upon the German people "with repulsion and contempt." His article in the *Kölnische Zeitung* (Cologne newspaper), an important publication with a right-of-center orientation, vilified the Ostjuden as having "strange eyes" and excited conversations: "In the railway carriages they crouch and draw numbers in their greasy pocket books. In the cafés they go in gesticulating groups, they proceed shouting, wallet in hand, from table to door to the next notary to buy a house. . . . Entire areas of Berlin are falling into their hands. . . . They have contempt for everyone."[19] Since, the VJN also alleged, the Ostjuden had entered Germany in swarms, the organization supported the *Völkische* demand for a closure of the border for Ostjuden. Naumann also considered it desirable to achieve their exit from Germany, though he added that unnecessary hardships in implementing this policy should be avoided.[20]

Other German Jewish organizations sharply criticized the VNJ's view that Zionists and Ostjuden constituted disloyal elements in German society. The CV considered membership in the VNJ superfluous, since the CV was already fully defending the "German ideal." Perhaps more to the point, Jakob Marx, the head of the CV in Baden and a member of its national board of directors, protested against the Naumann organization's ceaseless slander of the CV. We German Jews, Marx proclaimed, reject as groundless the accusation that we are not sufficiently German and consider it an insult to our honor.[21] The RJF, too, was displeased, because the VNJ regarded the majority of German Jews, including the RJF's own frontline veterans, as insufficiently patriotic. Relations became tense in November 1923, when RJF members defended the Ostjuden of the Scheunenviertel against anti-Semitic rioters while Naumann verbally attacked the victims of this pogrom as parasites whose presence in Germany had hurt the German people.[22]

The VNJ reacted to Jewish institutional criticism of its views with legal action for libel. Their main target was the CV, which Naumann castigated for obfuscating the borders between Germans and Jews. Between 1922 and 1927 the VNJ brought at least fifteen suits against leading CV members, charging them with having distorted the true ideas of the VNJ. The CV, in turn, sharply criticized Naumann's litigation which, leaders felt, had inappropriately exposed internal disputes within German Jewry to the wider public. In the fall of 1924 the Lower Silesia section of the CV demanded that all of its members who were also members of the VNJ be expelled. Relations between the two organizations would remain strained throughout the Weimar era.[23]

During the final years of the Weimar Republic, VNJ leaders increasingly shifted the organization's ideology in the direction of absolving the Germans and criticizing their own people, the Jews. They regarded anti-Semitism as the result of Jewish conduct, especially on the part of the despised Ostjuden. This was also the position held by the various anti-Jewish organizations, and a few of their members therefore came to view the VNJ as acceptable partners. Ernst Joerges, for example, a leading member of the Alldeutscher Verband, an organization with impeccable Völkische anti-Semitic credentials, took a benevolent view of the VJN, giving lectures for the organization and publishing articles in its bulletin of information. Naumann took this response to constitute a confirmation of his outlook. In every case where a national-German Jew had come into close contact with an honest German, the latter had eventually acknowledged: "Yes, if only all Jews were like you!"[24]

The nationalistic convictions of Naumann and his followers were probably sincere. They were not just strategizing to ingratiate themselves with the Völkische. Yet these ideas represented wishful thinking. The great majority of the Völkische failed to distinguish between the members of the VNJ and other Jews. In their eyes, the idea of a national-German Jew was an absurdity and impossibility; it was a trick to mislead the German people. As the Nazi leader Julius Streicher declared in the Bavarian parliament in 1928: "There exist no national-German Jews, only Jews."[25] Streicher's view soon became reality. The anti-Jewish measures adopted and implemented by the Nazis from 1933 on showed they had no use for any Jew, no matter how devoted to Germandom.

During the last elections of the Weimar era, the VNJ issued the slogan *"Wählt deutsch!"* (Elect German). Naumann objected to the other Jewish organizations' approach, especially the CV's policy to vote only for those parties that opposed anti-Semitism. Since anti-Semites were present in all the parties, the VNJ contended there was no reason to decide the vote of a Jew according to such a criterion. German Jews, they argued, should not be guided by "special Jewish interests," but only by what was good for Germany.[26] This posture would turn out to be one of many political misconceptions that paved the way for the Nazis' rise to power.

4

The German-Jewish Youth Movement

Young German Jews, no less than their elders, saw themselves as Germans. Hence, as a matter of course, they became members of the German youth movement that emerged at the turn of the twentieth century. It was only after World War I, when this movement began to assume anti-Semitic attitudes and excluded Jews, that an independent German-Jewish youth movement with its own characteristics would develop.

The German Youth Movement

The German youth movement was born in late 1901 in Steglitz, a suburb of Berlin, when a group of middle-class youths aged twelve to sixteen formed an organization they named Wander-Vogel (Wandering bird). Similar groups developed independently in other cities. These young people resented the materialism and social conservatism of the empire. Wandering in the countryside, they believed, provided the opportunity to get close to nature and achieve a more genuine and honest way of life. As Frank Fischer, a leader of the early Wandervogel, put it: "That which is formed in tune with nature, which has lasted of man's creations and which, through its form, still exemplifies that creativity, speaks to everyone who learns to listen. Not only churches and castles speak in this fashion, but also [small] towns, paths, landscapes . . . woods and even rivers." The Wandervogel was in revolt against a conservative society, as well as against schools and parents with their rigid discipline. It was the rebellion of youth who wanted to lead their own lives as integrated human beings.[1]

The search for a new kind of society could have led the Wandervogel into the camp of social revolution, and some members eventually chose that path. During the years before World War I, however, their dissatisfaction with the society of their day largely expressed itself in a romantic return to nature, the rejection of "bourgeois values," and a stress on the simple life. They made the experience of youth into an ideology, translated into a glorification of the past—especially the Middle Ages, a period of German history seen as free from the convolutions of modernity—and the revival of old folk songs and folklore.

Furthermore, like the Burschenschaft, the organization of German students in the first half of the nineteenth century, the Wandervogel affirmed patriotism and national consciousness. In his introduction to the *Zupfgeigenhansel*, the Wandervogel songbook, the editor Hans Breuer wrote: "We should become ever more German. Rambling [*wandern*] is the most German of all innate instincts, it is our basic existence, the mirror of our national character."[2] In essence, the Wandervogel saw a vital connection between rambling and their roots in the German *Volk* (people). Some of these ideas would later became part of National Socialist ideology, but this does not mean that the Wandervogel was a precursor of Nazism. The German youths organized in the Wandervogel were nonpolitical. They had no coherent political program, and even when they lauded the life of the German people, they primarily intended immersion in the Volk to be a personal experience.[3]

Wandervogel organizations consisted of small groups of eight to ten members. Strong cohesion, inner discipline, and comradeship were emphasized. Membership was selective and involved a trial period. Each group was led by a youth just a few years older, who was regarded as the *Führer* (leader) and whose authority was unquestioned. The young people of the Wandervogel sought to differentiate themselves from the current modes in dress and custom. They would ramble in the countryside bare-headed, dressed in shorts, and carrying a rucksack on their backs. To prevent selfishness, they shared the food they brought along. On longer hikes, meals would be cooked outdoors using simple utensils, and tents erected for overnight sleeping. Singing was accompanied by a guitar or lute, and ball and field games pitted groups against each other. Members would also meet in their homes in the evenings to discuss such topics as the consumption of alcohol, relations between boys and girls, and similar issues of personal conduct.[4]

In later years this style of life became known as *bündisch*, the essence of what it meant to be a member of a *Bund*. The literal translation of Bund is "league," but no English equivalent for the word exists because it involved a uniquely German phenomenon. To be bündisch meant being part of an intoxicating experience of togetherness, having allegiance to a group of young people who hiked in nature, appreciating music and poetry, engaging in stimulating intellectual discussions, and committing oneself to a larger cause.

As nature wills it, the young eventually outgrew the youth group. They became students at the universities or practiced professions and occupations. And yet they wanted to continue the idealistic life of the youth movement. The Wandervogel took the initiative to unite these older youths. The result was an organization named Freideutsche Jugend (Free German youth), which included not only the elders of the Wandervogel, but also Socialists and academic associations and organizations devoted to such diverse programs as the advocacy of abstinence, progressive education, feminism and antifeminism, and *Völkische*. A meeting on the Hohe Meissner, a mountain near Cassel, on the evening of October 11, 1913, would prove to be one of the most important events in the history of the German youth movement. There was much communal singing and folk dancing, but also heated exchanges about the adoption of a statement of principles. The Wandervogel saw its main purpose in rambling, while others were dedicated to various educational, political, or social reforms. Finally, the youths agreed to a short formula: "Nach eigener Bestimmung, vor eigener Verantwortung, in innerer Wahrhaftigkeit" (The Free German Youth wants to shape their own lives at their own initiative, on their own responsibility, and with deep sincerity).[5] This formula was vague enough to satisfy most of the contending elements. The unifying spirit was the commitment to a life of honesty and meaning, opposed to the philistinism of the society of the day. Beyond that, each group could pursue its own special aims. There was no clear ideological profile but, in the words of the historian Peter Gay, only "high idealism, unremitting search, and incurable confusion."[6]

As much as the young people wanted to separate themselves from the ideas of the adult world around them, they were not unaffected by it, and this included the inroads of anti-Semitism. Consequently, the Austrian Wandervogel proposed that racial purity be a condition of membership. Jews and those of Slavic and Franco-Italian blood were to be excluded. Similar demands cropped up in other groups.

The Jewish issue became a widely discussed topic in 1912. That year, the Wandervogel of Zittau (a city in southeast Saxony) denied admission to a thirteen-year-old Jewish girl, the daughter of a rich Jewish industrialist who had successfully passed all the candidate tests but was then rejected on the grounds that the Wandervogel was a German movement and therefore had no place for Jews. Others had been rejected elsewhere, but never before with an openly acknowledged anti-Semitic motive. A public debate would ensue, both in the general press and in various local Wandervogel branches.

Anti-Jewish sentiment within the organization reached its high point in October 1913, when the *Wandervogel Führerzeitung* (Newspaper for the guidance of Wandervogel leaders) published its first explicitly anti-Jewish issue. The Jews were charged with exploiting the people of Germany, corrupting its culture, and seducing its virgins. The Wandervogel branches were advised to get rid of their Jews because they were not of German origin and because, in view of their blood, they could never become true German patriots. The tone of these articles was so hateful, they would later be compared to the Nazi Julius Streicher's hate rag *Der Stürmer*.[7]

The regional branches of the Wandervogel reacted in different ways, depending upon their leaders' perspectives. Saxony, northern Thuringia, and several other Wandervogel branches excluded all Jews from membership. The leader of the Berlin-Lichterfelde branch made the acceptance of Jews dependent on whether one could "digest" them and instill them with "Germanic feelings and thinking." He added that, in his experience, few Jews had passed this test.[8] Other Berlin groups, as well as the Silesian and Rhineland groups, protested against the anti-Semitic agitation. In April 1914 the Jewish issue was debated at the national meeting of the Wandervogel, held in Frankfurt.

Its start was not very auspicious. Several Jewish boys and girls in attendance were physically attacked by a group of Bavarian members led by Friedrich Weber, a veterinary surgeon who would later become one of Hitler's closest associates. The meeting itself revealed once again the very different perspectives of the Jewish issue. Some members wanted a complete expulsion of Jews, while others were prepared to accept them in the Wandervogel. The resolution they finally adopted would be described as a compromise. The Wandervogel was declared to be neutral with regard to politics and religion, and the national leadership was asked to enforce this provision. It also had to make sure that no branch excluded Jews as a matter of principle or defamed them. At the same time, local branches were allowed to reject specific Jewish candidates if they concluded that the racial characteristics of these individuals were incompatible with the German essence and past.[9]

The compromise resolution was criticized in many quarters. "Please spare us the sentimental phrases about the friend, the noble Jew, who is not to blame that he was born a Jew," one of the Völkische argued. "It is not a question of one single Jew; the danger for the Germanic race is so great that the question of the individual does not come into it at all."[10] Hans Blüher, the leading intellectual of the Wandervogel, noted that many Jews revered Germany with great intensity, but this was irrelevant. Even the Jew who loves Germany remains a Jew.[11] Jewish reactions varied.

Some Jewish members rejected the case-by-case principle and advised young Jews to join the Zionist movement instead. The assimilationists suggested that Jews stay in those branches of the Wandervogel where they were wanted and fight anti-Semitism. Others sought a new Jewish youth movement. Thus a parting of ways took place. By 1914, an estimated ninety percent of the Wandervogel branches in Germany no longer had Jewish members.[12]

The Blau-Weiss

The Jüdischer Wanderbund Blau-Weiss (Jewish rambling organization blue-white) was the first German-Jewish youth organization. Zionist from its beginning and named after the colors of the Zionist flag, it came into being in 1912 at the initiative of the Zionistische Vereinigung für Deutschland, or ZVfD (Zionist Vereinigung for Germany). By the early 1920s, the Blau-Weiss—as the new organization became known—reached a membership of more than three thousand.

The Blau-Weiss considered rambling essential for overcoming the physical degeneration of the Jewish people. Jewish youth, it was said, suffered more than other youths from the damaging influence of urban life. Max Nordau, the co-founder with Theodor Herzl of the World Zionist Organization, called rambling in nature "the symbol of the new Judaism that enjoyed and affirmed life, demanded its share of the earth and a place in the sun, and was prepared to make the necessary efforts to achieve these goals."[13] The Wandervogel provided a model of a revitalized community, free of nationalistic excess, though in place of the German Volk, the Blau-Weiss put the Jewish people. It developed outdoor celebrations of Jewish holidays and advocated study of the Hebrew language as well as Jewish songs, folklore, and folk dances. Like the Wandervogel, the Blau-Weiss held intimate gatherings promoting cohesion and dedication—but to the Zionist ideal.

The Blau-Weiss followed the teachings of Martin Buber, who advocated a Jewish renaissance and a cultural Zionism based not on national identity, but on a return to neglected Jewish traditions.[14] For Buber, youth was "the great stroke of luck" of humanity, for each new generation rejected selfishness and sought a life of idealism. The Blau-Weiss leadership put pressure on the membership to emigrate to Palestine.

The Blau-Weiss organized occupational retraining, especially in agriculture, as preparation for life in Palestine. The aim was to create a new Jew, the *chalutz* (pioneer), who would build the new Jewish homeland. To this end, the Blau-Weiss established several farms in Germany where young Jews were instructed in crafts and in tilling the soil—all preparations for a new life in Palestine characterized by manual occupations rather than the intellectual pursuits of the Diaspora. These farms were called *Hachscharah* (preparation). Yet the total number of those who made the leap of leaving Germany for Palestine was modest, and the total number who stayed far more. Between 1919 and 1930 about 490 Jewish youths—among them my father's brother and sister, early members of the Blau-Weiss—immigrated to their new Jewish home, though only about one-half of them would remain. Life in the primitive Near East was much harder than the middle-class youngsters had imagined.

In 1927, just fifteen years after it had begun, the Blau-Weiss dissolved. It had failed to develop a large following and shown itself unable to reach an agreement with the Zionist leadership about how to remedy this. This earliest of all German-Jewish youth organizations had steered some young people back to their Jewish heritage, but it did not make a significant contribution to the building of Israel.[15] Large-scale migration from Germany to Palestine would not begin until the onset of Nazi rule and the resulting anti-Jewish legislation.

The Kameradan

The outbreak of the Great War in 1914 temporarily put a stop to the discussion of the Jewish question in the Wandervogel, and in 1918 the organization issued another statement affirming again that membership was to be determined "solely by the criterion of personality" rather than race and blood.[16] But the anti-Semites had never abandoned their attacks, and the year 1916 saw the founding in Breslau of the all-Jewish rambling organization Kameraden (Comrades). The Kameraden, declaring their commitment to the principles of the Hohe Meissner, upheld as ideals the development of self-discipline and the strengthening of one's body through rambling, sport, and a healthy way of life. Developing a social conscience was also important.[17]

The Kameraden described themselves as *Deutsch-jüdisch* (German-Jewish). They were committed to the German fatherland, but they also were proud to be Jews. This concept of German-Jewish papered over internal differences. German-Jewish could mean Germans of the Jewish faith or Jews living in Germany. Some German Jews, like most of the CV, identified themselves with Reform Judaism at the most and had a relatively weak religious consciousness. They also rejected Zionism as a mistaken solution to the Jewish question. Within the context of the Kameraden, this group of young Jews constituted itself as the *Ring* (ring). They read Johann Wolfgang von Goethe and Friedrich Schiller, who were considered the greatest literary figures of the modern German era. They were impressed by Stefan George's poetry, commitment to an aristocratic and pure German sensibility, and advocacy of a life of human nobility, greatness, and beauty. Others in the Kameraden, known as the *Kreis* (circle), sought a stronger Jewish commitment in daily life as well as the acquisition of Jewish knowledge. They admired Buber's Hasidic tales and his advocacy of a direct relationship with God, though there was little understanding of his more philosophical teachings.[18] Those critical of Buber's influence coined the derisive rhyme "*Von der Pubertät in die Bubertät*" (From puberty to Buberty).[19] During the years 1925 to 1928 the Ring would dominate the Kameraden.

By 1920, four years after the organization began, the Kameraden had some three thousand members and about thirty-five local branches. Most of the members were boys of high school age, but there were also groups of girls, and some groups had both male and female members. In 1921 these organizations combined formally in the Deutsch-jüdische Wanderbund Kameraden (German-Jewish rambling organization comrades). Yet the unstable character of the dual loyalty to Germany and Judaism would soon splinter this larger group. Throughout the 1920s various groups left the Kameraden and established rival organizations with similar names.[20] Within the Kameraden, new, smaller groups emerged and pursued their own special aims. One of these was the Schwarzer Haufen (Black lot), led by two dedicated young Communists, Hans Litten and Max Fürst, who argued that a youth movement that took itself seriously had to ally itself with the radical German Left. Furthermore, the Schwarzer Haufen occasionally accepted non-Jews who were Communists as members.[21] The majority of the Kameraden did not share these views, and in 1927 the Schwarzer Haufen was expelled from the parent organization. It dissolved in 1928.[22] Another Marxist group, the Radikal-Sozialistischer Kreis (Circle of radical Socialists), led by the Königsberg Communist Siegfried Adler, managed to stay in the Kameraden (how is unknown).[23]

In 1932 the ideological differences straining the Kameraden reached the breaking point, and at its national convention in May the organization dissolved. Some four hundred members of the German-oriented Ring established the Schwarzes Fähnlein (Black banner), a highly selective group of elite Jewish youth (membership would never exceed one thousand) that lauded German military virtues. A smaller faction of about two hundred Socialists formed the Freie deutsch-jüdische Jugend (Free German-Jewish youth), but the life of this group was cut short in early 1933 after Hitler's ascension, as its members were arrested, had to go underground, or were forced into emigration.

The Werkleute

The largest group derived from the Kameraden was the Werkleute (Workmen), led by Hermann Gerson, which would boast about 1,600 members in 1932. Whereas the Jewish youth movements saw themselves as elitist, wanting only the best of Jewish youth, the Werkleute regarded themselves as the elite of the elite.[24] They were in direct competition with several small outright Zionist youth organizations, including Habonim, Hechalutz, Makkabi Hatzair, Betar, and Hashomer Hatzair, and regarded themselves as superior to them all.

At this point in time, less than a year before the Nazis came to power, the Werkleute adhered to a contradictory ideology. They called themselves Bund deutsch-jüdischer Jugend (League of German-Jewish youth) in order to express their commitment to the German homeland, but soon dropped the German in their name and became a Bund jüdischer Jugend, an association of Jewish youth. They propagated a revolutionary socialism, but were unwilling to make common cause with the German Communist party because the Communists were hostile to religion and sometimes assailed Jewish capitalists. They sought a Jewish personality, one different from what they considered the corrupted Jew of the diaspora. They stressed Jewish learning and Zionism, but decided that for the time being they would stay in Germany since, it was argued, Palestine by itself could not solve the Jewish problem. To the question of how the Jewish problem could be solved, they had no answer.[25]

In June 1933, six months after the Nazis' accession to power, the Werkleute still argued that members unable or unwilling to go to Palestine should not be regarded as less valuable, since Germany would continue to play a role in the lives of young Jews. Even though Germany was now led by a new ideological movement, the Werkleute did not want that the connection of their members with German culture be dissolved. After the first wave of anti-Jewish legislation, however, the Werkleute adopted a full commitment to *aliyah* (moving to the Jewish homeland). In April 1934 a Werkleute group founded Kibbutz Hasorea near Haifa, the first kibbutz (collective settlement) to be established by young German Jews; thereafter, most of the Werkleute, including Gerson, went to Palestine. Gerson changed his first name to Menachem, which is derived from a Hebrew word meaning "consoler" or "comforter," but otherwise the kibbutz soon abandoned any interest in things Jewish. To the Werkleute, living in the Jewish homeland made the entire search for Jewishness irrelevant. Eventually, Kibbutz Hasorea joined the larger kibbutz movement Hashomer Hatzair (Young guard) that, like the Werkleute, adhered to an uneasy mix of Marxism and Zionism and advocated Jewish-Arab understanding.[26]

In Palestine Gerson remained the undisputed leader of the organization. He regarded the Werkleute as a typical Bund, a community of youth committed to the special mission of striving for greatness and a morally superior life. By linking the experience of the Bund to the building of a kibbutz, Gerson solved one of the most difficult problems of the youth movement: how to stay bündisch while its members grew into adulthood and no longer had time for hiking and leisurely evening meetings. By living in a kibbutz, the Werkleute could continue an idealistic life different from that of the average philistine who cared only for material rewards. Kibbutz living meant being a chalutz (and participating in the great task of building the Jewish homeland). Thus Jews could finally overcome the travail of the *galuth* (diaspora), the nemesis of assimilation.[27]

The Greifen

In the middle of the 1930s, a Jewish Bund in Breslau called Greifen–Deutsch-jüdischer Pfadfinderbund (Griffins–German-Jewish scout Bund), previously affiliated with the Kameraden, joined the Werkleute.

The lifestyle of the Greifen, as that of the Kameraden, was bündisch. As someone who became a Greifen member around 1934, I can say that language cannot do justice to what this collective experience meant for its members. For impressionable young people, membership in the Bund created a set of powerful sensations combining mythical, esoteric, and rational elements. Walking at night, singing around the campfire, reading the lyric poetry and prose of Stefan George, Hermann Hesse, and Rainer Maria Rilke, listening to classical music in a darkened room, feeling commitment to a cause and romantic exaltation—these were some of the experiences that struck deep emotional chords in us.[28] For me, membership in the Greifen instilled the conviction that life had to have a special meaning. It encouraged me to become a scholar, devoted to the pursuit of truth and knowledge.

Greifen ideology was eclectic, a combination of boy-scouting and rebelling against parents and school.[29] The Greifen were strictly German, but we also idolized the military heroes of various European countries—the Dutch William of Orange, the Austrian field marshal Josef Radetzky, and the Russian general Alexander Kolchak. We sang newly revived songs of the German *Landsknechte* (mercenaries) and admired their heroic acts. The Greifen theme song had the refrain "Die weisse Möwe weht im Wind / Und lockt zu neuen Taten" (The white gull waves in the wind / And beckons us to new deeds). Another song (the hymn of the German Social Democrats, although we did not know this) proclaimed:

Wenn wir schreiten Seit an Seit
und die alten Lieder klingen,
und die Wälder wiederklingen:
Mit uns zieht die neue Zeit.
Mit uns zieht die neue Zeit.
(When we walk next to each other,
and sing the old songs,
and hear the echo of the forest:
With us moves a new age.
With us moves a new age.)

As against the prosaic bourgeois life of our parents we sought a life of special exploits, though we had no idea what the desired brave deeds or the new age we were singing about would consist of. But then appeared Zionism with its ideal of the chalutz building the Jewish homeland, and our problem was solved. Life in a kibbutz, a communitarian collective that rejected private property even in the case of clothing, practiced the equality of all its members and dedicated itself to building the Land of Israel, represented the kind of service to a cause we had only been dreaming about.

Of course, the adjustment from being a German to becoming a Jew did not come easy. Before we left for Palestine, we had to study the Hebrew language and learn the culture of our soon soon-to-be-home kibbutz. Instead of *Heil* we were now expected to say *Shalom*. In the place of German folk dances came the Hora. Rather than singing the songs of the militant Landsknechte and the heroic sixteenth-century peasant rebellion, we now had to sing the placid songs of the kibbutz—a situation exacerbated by the fact that at first we did not know any Hebrew. Some of these songs did not even have words, but consisted of nothing but "la la la la la la," a musical style we found incomprehensible. All of this resulted in what the fellow ex-assimilant Arnold Paucker has called "a very soft Zionism."[30]

Being young and wanting to adjust, we eventually made the transition and became ready for the kibbutz. In the fall of 1938 I spent several months on a farm in southern Germany to receive training in agriculture (and to partake of my Hachscharah). By 1935 these centers were training some 5,000 youths yearly, and in early 1938 more than 23,000 had passed through them on the way to Palestine.[31] On the day of Kristallnacht—when Jewish shops were looted, synagogues were burned, and adult Jews, including my father, were dragged off to concentration camps—our farm was attacked by Nazi storm troopers. We had hidden ourselves in the attic of the main building, but the Nazis soon found us and roughed us up. One of our members incurred a serious concussion, but what happened to us was not typical. In some instances, being in places of Hachscharah protected young Jews from arrest; some of these instruction sites continued to function as quasi-sanctuaries.[32] Until the onset of the Final Solution, the Nazi authorities were benevolently disposed toward any effort to prepare Jews for emigration.

In March 1939 I, along with a group of other Jewish youngsters, left for Palestine. Jugend Aliyah (Youth Aliyah), instituted in 1932 Germany by Recha Freier, the wife of a Berlin rabbi, arranged our migration; later, this effort would be run out of an office in Jerusalem under the direction of the American Zionist Henrietta Szold. At the border with Italy our train was stopped for several hours. Hitler had swallowed up the rest of Czechoslovakia, and we did not know whether armed hostilities would ensue. And yet the Western nations continued their policy of appeasement, war was averted for a while, and we were able to proceed to Trieste. From there a ship took us to Palestine and a new life in a kibbutz.

Legacy of the German-Jewish Youth Movement

At the time of the Nazi accession to power in 1933, membership in the various German-Jewish youth organizations is estimated to have included only about one-quarter of Jewish youth, but in many ways the Jews who belonged represented the most sensitive and most articulate of their generation.[33] Their early commitment to a meaningful life strengthened their desire for intellectual accomplishment. Many of those who managed to emigrate after 1933 would achieve prominence in their new abodes as natural and social scientists, artists, and historians. Best-known among the latter are the historian and journalist Walter Laqueur, the historian and editor Arnold Paucker, and Jehuda Reinharz, president of Brandeis University from 1994 to 2010. Günter Holzmann made a fortune as a wood trader in South America and became a generous benefactor of important intellectual enterprises such as the publication of *Monde diplomatique* in France. Many of the bündische young German Jews who made aliyah to the Jewish homeland made vital contributions to the State of Israel as diplomats, judges, and other professionals.

1. Jewish soldiers celebrate Passover at the front in World War I. German Jews were highly patriotic; the percentage of Jews who volunteered for military service before being drafted was higher than in the German population at large. Courtesy of the Leo Baeck Institute, New York.

2. (*above*) A youth group of the Reichsbund Jüdisher Frontsoldaten-RJF (National league of Jewish frontline soldiers). Founded in 1919, the RJF was a patriotic organization of Jewish veterans of World War I who regarded anti-Semitism as an attack on their honor as Germans and Jews. Courtesy of the Leo Baeck Institute, New York.

3. (*top right*) A Jewish wedding in 1921. German Jews were largely assimilated, but they observed Jewish rites of passage such as bar mitzvah and religious weddings. Courtesy of the United States Holocaust Memorial Museum.

4. (*bottom right*) Three generations of a Jewish family in Stettin in 1930. In January 1939 the young girl was sent on a Kindertransport to Belgium. Three months later her parents left for Shanghai, a place where desperate Jews seeking a place of refuge were allowed to enter. Courtesy of the United States Holocaust Memorial Museum.

Ich habe
ein
Christenmädchen
geschandet!

5. (*top left*) In August 1933 a Jewish student is paraded in Marburg, forced to carry a sign that reads: "I have defiled a Christian maiden." Public humiliations of Jews accused of *Rassenschande* (defilement of the race) were common in the early years of Nazi rule. Courtesy of the United States Holocaust Memorial Museum.

6. (*bottom left*) A man who has made a purchase in a Jewish store in violation of the boycott of Jewish stores announced on April 1, 1933, is shown holding a sign he has been compelled to display: "I am a slave of the Jews." Courtesy of the United States Holocaust Memorial Museum.

7. (*above*) A youth group of the Central Association of German Citizens of the Jewish Faith (CV). The CV represented some three hundred thousand German Jews and dedicated itself to defending their legal and social rights. Courtesy of the Leo Baeck Institute, New York.

8. (*above*) Jewish youth at a Hachschara, holding farming tools. A Hachschara was a farm in Germany where young people prepared themselves for agricultural work in Palestine. Courtesy of the United States Holocaust Memorial Museum.

9. (*top right*) The passport of Jewish girl in Karlsruhe. The passports of all German Jews were invalidated on October 5, 1938, and reissued with the stamp "J" (Jude). Courtesy of the United States Holocaust Memorial Museum.

10. (*bottom right*) Jewish DPs are married in a ceremony in Heidelberg in November 1948. Thousands of surviving and homeless Jewish victims of the Nazi regime lived for several years in displaced persons camps all over Germany. Courtesy of the United States Holocaust Memorial Museum.

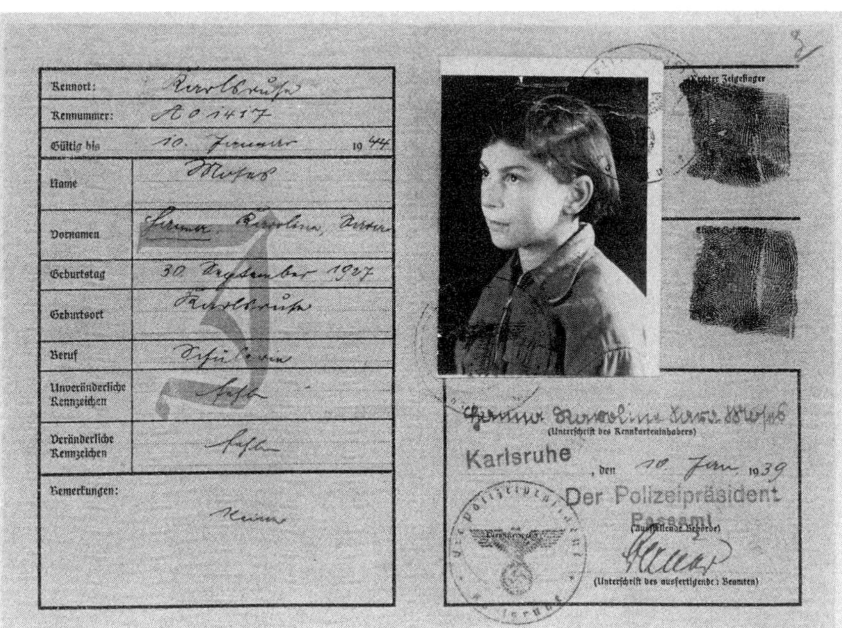

Kennort:	Karlsruhe
Kennummer:	A 01417
Gültig bis	10. Januar 1944
Name	[illegible]
Vornamen	[illegible] Karoline, [illegible]
Geburtstag	30. Dezember 1927
Geburtsort	Karlsruhe
Beruf	Schülerin
Unveränderliche Kennzeichen	fehlt
Veränderliche Kennzeichen	fehlt
Bemerkungen:	keine

Rechter Zeigefinger

Linker Zeigefinger

(Unterschrift des Kennkarteninhabers)

Karlsruhe, den 10. Juni 1939

Der Polizeipräsident
Passamt
(Ausstellende Behörde)

(Unterschrift des ausfertigenden Beamten)

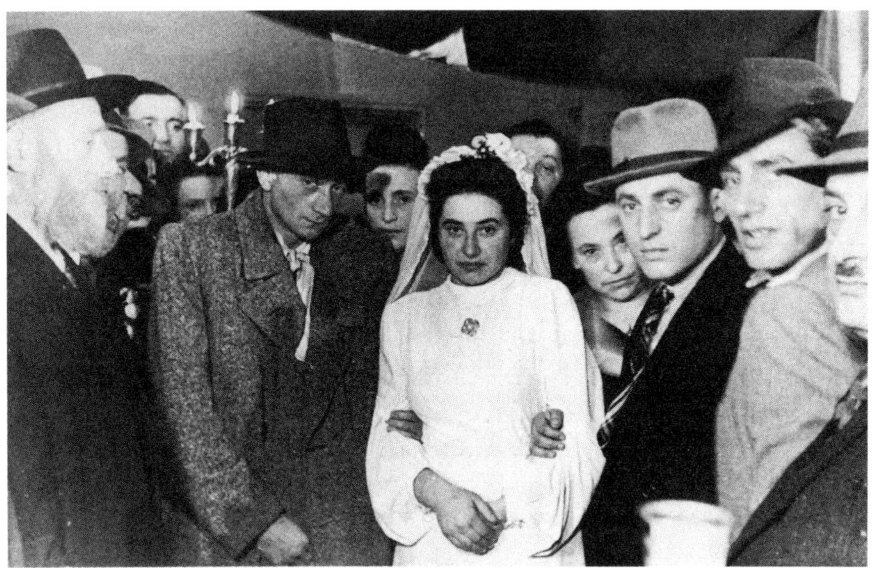

11. (*above*) Commemoration of Kristallnacht in the Roonstrasse synagogue of Cologne, November 1988. On the right is the mayor of Cologne, Norbert Burger. The Jewish community of Cologne was one of the oldest in Germany, and one of the first to be reorganized after World War II. Courtesy of Edward Serotta / Centropa, https://www.centropa.org.

12. (*top right*) Irony in action: Markus Wolf, the former East German spymaster on whom John Le Carré based his character Karla, at a Hanukkah party in Berlin in 1995. Mordechai Levy, Israel's consul general, is lighting his cigarette. Courtesy of Edward Serotta / Centropa, https://www.centropa.org.

13. (*bottom right*) In the Jewish community center of Munich, 1992. Courtesy of Edward Serotta / Centropa, https://www.centropa.org.

JENNY
GEB. BRANDOROWITSC
JG. 1908
DEPORTIERT 1943
AUSCHWITZ
ERMORDET
HIER WOHNTE
DEPORTIERT
AUSCHWITZ
ERMORDET
HIER WOHNTE
VICTOR
SCHNEEBAUM
JG. 1941
DEPORTIERT 1943
AUSCHWITZ
ERMORDET
HIER WOHNTE
THEA
SCHNEEBAUM
JG. 1931
DEPORTIERT 1943
AUSCHWITZ
ERMORDET

14. (*top left*) In the community center on Fasanenstrasse, Berlin, in 1995. Today a large percentage of Jews in Germany are from the former Soviet Union. Courtesy of Edward Serotta / Centropa, https://www.centropa.org.

15. (*bottom left*) *Stolpersteine* (tripping stones) in Berlin. The German artist Gunter Demnig installed these on the sidewalks where Jewish victims of the Nazi regime lived. As of 2019, there are 48,000 such memorials, primarily in Germany but also in other European countries. Courtesy of Dale Lazar.

16. (*above*) Teens from the former Soviet Union at a Havdalah service at a Jewish youth center in Berlin, 1996. Courtesy of Edward Serotta / Centropa, https://www.centropa.org.

17. German stamp issued in 2000, commemorating the hundredth anniversary of the birth of the German-Jewish composer Kurt Weill. Known for his collaboration with Bertolt Brecht, Weill was one of the most popular German composers in Weimar Germany. Courtesy of PJR Stamps / Alamy Stock Photo.

18. Cantor Isaac Sheffer holds a Torah at the reopening of the Rykestrasse synagogue, August 31, 2007. The Rykestrasse synagogue, completed in 1904, is the largest and best-preserved prewar synagogue in Berlin. Courtesy of Reuters.

19. Protesters at the Berlin Wears Kippah demonstration on April 25, 2018, wearing *kippot* in solidarity with the man wearing a *kippah* who had been attacked for being Jewish. Rallies also took place in other German cities. Courtesy of DPA / Alamy Stock Photo.

5

Seeking a Place under Nazi Rule

On January 30, 1933, Hitler became chancellor of Germany, and anti-Jewish violence erupted almost immediately. When Socialist and Communist leaders were seized, the Jews among them were often singled out for particularly brutal treatment. Jewish professors were assaulted. Storm troopers forced their way into courthouses and attacked Jewish judges and lawyers. In Königsberg a synagogue was set on fire, and a Jewish businessman was kidnapped and beaten so badly that he later died in a hospital. In Wiesbaden, young Nazis broke the windows of Jewish shops and beat up their owners. In many places the boycott of Jewish shops on April 1 was accompanied by more violence. Those who attacked or even killed Jews, destroyed their homes or places of business, no longer had to fear punishment.[1]

The terror from below was accompanied by official anti-Jewish measures. On April 11 the new government promulgated a law that purged Jews from the civil service. Even those with merely one Jewish grandfather were declared non-Aryan and therefore ineligible for government service. In Germany the universities were state institutions, and the introduction of the Aryan stipulation therefore affected large numbers of Jews. Only those who had been office holders on August 1, 1914, were themselves soldiers who had fought in the Great War, or who had fathers or sons who were killed in the war for a time were exempted from these provisions.[2]

German Jews reacted to these developments with shock. The painter Max Liebermann wrote to friends in Palestine: "Like a horrible nightmare the abrogation of equal rights weighs upon us all. But especially upon those Jews who, like me, had surrendered themselves to the dream of assimilation. . . . As difficult as it has been for me, I have awakened from the dream that I dreamed my whole life long."[3]

"My Home Is Germany"

Some 25,000 Jews left Germany during the first weeks of the Nazi regime, most of them leftist intellectuals and members of the Socialist and Communist parties who knew their lives were endangered. The majority of German Jews, however, believed the anti-Semitic outbursts were only temporary, and they saw no reason to reevaluate their commitment to Germany. The reaction of the highly esteemed Nobel laureate chemist Richard Willstätter was typical. When the Zionist leader Chaim Weizmann asked him to move to Palestine, he replied: "I know that Germany has gone berserk. But when a mother has become sick, this is no reason for a child to abandon her. My home is Germany."[4]

Most Jews continued to dream of German-Jewish cooperation and affirm with pride their place in Germany's intellectual life. Shortly after Hitler's accession to power, Leopold Ullstein, the Protestant scion of a famous Jewish publishing family, initiated a project to document German Jewry's important contributions to German culture, and the resulting *Juden im deutschen Kulturbereich* (Jews in German culture) was a monumental synopsis—forty essays, extending over more than one thousand pages, describing the Jews' central role in the arts, the sciences, film, theater, politics, the economy, and many other areas of learning. Not surprisingly, the Nazis took a dim view of this work. The Gestapo forbade publication "in the interest of public safety and order," and the book did not see the light of day until 1959.[5]

The great majority of German Jews expected to be able to continue to live in Germany, even if under discriminatory provisions. This expectation was not completely unreasonable. The boycott of Jewish stores in April 1933 had not been fully observed. For a time, the regime did not interfere with Jewish religious and cultural life, including Jewish schools and newspapers. Moreover, Nazi leaders sometimes expressed views that appeared to promise a more moderate course. In an interview with the Turin newspaper *Gazzetta del Populo* in May 1932, Hermann Göring, one of Hitler's closest confidants, had affirmed that once in power the National Socialists would remove Jews from leading positions in schools, universities, and the government. However, he added: "The decent Jewish businessman, who wants to stay in Germany as a foreigner, will be protected by the law regarding aliens. He will be able to continue his business activities undisturbed and will suffer no harm."[6]

Today, with the Nazis' Final Solution to the Jewish Question—the Nazis' euphemism for their attempted destruction of the Jews of Europe—culminating in the horror of the Holocaust being history, it is difficult to understand the sentiments of German Jews in 1933 who hoped for achieving some modus vivendi with the new rulers. But I believe we must be wary of hindsight. The systematic campaign of annihilation of the Jews that lay ahead was almost inconceivable not only to Germany's assimilated Jews but to almost anyone else as well. In retrospect, Hitler's anti-Jewish measures appear to exhibit a consistent pattern of increasing severity, but, in point of fact, as the historian Karl Schleunes argues convincingly in his 1970 book *The Twisted Road to Auschwitz*, there exists no direct line connecting the boycott of April 1, 1933, and the extermination camps that murdered Jews in factory-like precision. What eventually took place did not have to happen, and it could not be foreseen. For this reason, I believe, we must look with empathy rather than righteousness at the fumbling steps taken by organized German Jewry as its leaders tried to cope with an utterly new reality.[7]

The Reichsvertretung

In 1933 some 1,300 synagogues were affiliated in state associations (*Landesverbände*), but there existed no national organization representing all of German Jewry. In view of the growing Nazi movement, in the summer of 1932 seven prominent Jews met in Berlin to discuss such a body. The result of these deliberations was the Reichsvertretung der Deutschen Juden (National representative agency of German Jews), to be led by two cochairmen, the highly regarded Berlin rabbi Leo Baeck and the jurist Otto Hirsch. The agency began functioning in the spring of 1933. After the Nazi government called for a boycott of Jewish stores and department stores for April 1, causing widespread consternation among the Jewish population, the planned Reichsvertretung and the governing body of the Jewish congregation of Berlin sent a joint statement to Reich-Chancellor Hitler on March 29.

> German Jews are deeply shocked by the boycott call of the National Socialist Workers party.
>
> On account of the misdeeds of a few, for whom we carry no responsibility, all German Jews, who with all the fibers of their hearts feel linked to the German homeland, are to be exposed to economic ruin.
>
> In all the patriotic wars and due to this link, German Jews have offered sacrifices of blood. In the Great War 12,000 out of 500,000 German Jews have given up their lives. In times of peace, mustering all our strength, we have done our duty.
>
> The Jewish organizations have fought strenuously and successfully the atrocity and boycott campaign carried out abroad. They have done all in their power and will continue to do so.
>
> Even so, German Jews, as the alleged guilty ones, are now to be ruined.
>
> We direct this call to the German people, to whom justice has always been its highest virtue:
>
> Our honor has been deeply hurt by the charge that we have done harm to our people. For the sake of truth and our honor we protest against this accusation. We have confidence in the president and the government of the Reich, that they will not

allow taking away our rights and the possibility of living in our German fatherland. We repeat at this hour the avowal of our belonging to the German people. To participate in the renewal of Germany is our holiest duty, our right, and our most profound wish.[8]

Predictably, this plea to be allowed to work for the new Germany failed. On June 6, the Reichsvertretung requested a meeting with Hitler to discuss the "possibility of [German Jews] being outlawed in their German fatherland." German Jews, the letter declared, "always have demonstrated, and now are ready to demonstrate, their willingness to adjust to every order of the state, willingly, if one leaves them their decency, work, and freedom." They expected that "the German-Jewish question will be solved on a legal basis."[9] This letter, too, remained unanswered, and the meeting with Hitler never took place.

"The Atrocity Propaganda Is a Propaganda of Lies"

On March 25, Göring, minister of the interior in Prussia, met with several Jewish leaders, including the CV president Julius Brodnitz, the head of the Berlin Jewish community Heinrich Stahl, the leader of the German Zionists Kurt Blumenfeld, and the VNJ's Max Naumann. He urged them to send a delegation to London to put a stop to the "atrocity stories" foreign Jews were spreading about the new Germany. In hopes of securing some political capital, the leadership of the Zionistische Vereinigung für Deutschland (ZVfD-Zionist Association for Germany) indeed dispatched such a delegation to London.[10] Meanwhile, other German Jewish communities and organizations issued similar declarations of protest against the alleged foreign "atrocity campaign"—reports of anti-Jewish violence in the international press and mass meetings of protest. The neoorthodox rabbi Elie Munk had declared in 1930 that racism was not an essential part of the Nazi movement: "Without anti-Semitism, National Socialism would find its most faithful adherents among Jews committed to the Jewish tradition."[11] Now, speaking in the name of the neoorthodox communities of Berlin, Munk sent a telegram to rabbi Leo Jung, a leader of American Orthodox Jews in New York, asking him to see to it that the American press reject as untrue the false and reprehensible stories of atrocities against German Jews. For its part, the Jewish community of Königsberg declared that ever since some individual acts of violence in the first days of the new regime, no further attacks against Jews had taken place: "We reject most resolutely untrue sensationalist news and reports of atrocities." In addition, the official German-Jewish Zionist organization protested the foreign media's alleged attempt to use the situation of Germany's Jews for anti-German propaganda, asserting that the defense of Jewish rights should not be linked to politically motivated attacks against Germany and its foreign policy. A collection of these declarations of loyalty was published in Berlin later that year as a book, *The German Jews Themselves Say that the Atrocity Propaganda is a Propaganda of Lies*.[12]

Among the many petitions sent to the Nazi government during this first fateful year, an appeal to Hitler by the Orthodox community stands out on account of its pessimistic, but ultimately realistic, appraisal of the situation of German Jewry: "If you, Reich-Chancellor, the national government led by you, and the responsible leadership of the NSDAP have decided on the elimination [*Ausmerzung*] of Germany's Jews from the German people, we would like to hear the bitter truth in order to avoid illusions."[13] This statement—to which, again, there was no official response—was in itself very atypical. For the next few years, most Jewish organizations adhered to positions characterized by far more wishful thinking.

Jewish Elders Uphold Morale

Difficult as life was for Germany's Jews following the Nazis' rise to power, it would have been infinitely harder without the guiding role of several outstanding Jewish rabbis and theologians. With Jewish organizations gradually being dissolved, rabbis in many places became the only Jews still able to function as community leaders.

Leo Baeck was a committed German as well as a devoted Jew and probably should be considered the leader of German Jewry par excellence. In 1933 Baeck became president of the new umbrella organization of German Jewish groups, the Reichsvertretung deutscher Staatsbürger jüdischen Glaubens (National agency of German citizens of the Jewish faith). As German Jews were being deprived of their status as German citizens, Baeck sought to uphold their self-confidence, alleviate the discriminatory practices by negotiations with the Nazi government, and support emigration. He himself refused to leave his post, reportedly saying that he would leave Germany only after the last Jews had reached safety abroad. In 1939 he accompanied a trainload of Jewish children to England, but he himself returned to Germany to resume his leadership role.

Following the November 1938 pogrom, the government dissolved the Reichsvertretung and established in its place the Reichsvereinigung der Juden in Deutschland (National association of Jews in Germany). The new organization retained the leadership of the Reichsvertretung, including Baeck, but was closely supervised by Himmler's ministry of the interior. Its duties included promoting Jewish emigration from Germany and supporting the Jewish school system and Jewish welfare. The Nazis used the Reichsvereinigung as an instrument of control, much like the Jewish councils they later formed in the ghettos. It enabled them to implement many of their deadliest ordinances without much publicity, and to play off the Jewish leadership against the Jewish population, who came to blame their own leaders rather than their enemies. The Reichsvereinigung had to fill the quotas of Jewish deportees and to care for them during the roundups.

On January 27, 1943, Baeck was arrested and sent to Theresienstadt, a hybrid concentration camp, ghetto, and transit camp, to the killing centers of the East. Theresienstadt, located in the fortress town of Terezin in the German protectorate of Bohemia and

Moravia, also came to harbor outstanding Jewish personalities, the disappearance of whom would have attracted notice by the outside world and caused unfavorable publicity. Baeck helped organize the rich cultural life of the camp and gave well-attended lectures on religion and philosophy. Survivors of Theresienstadt would later say that these lectures helped them survive the hardships of the camp; they gave them the conviction that life had a purpose.

Baeck also became the honorary head of the Ältestenrat (Council of elders) that governed with the help of an elaborate Jewish bureaucracy. The system of Jewish self-administration included selecting inmates for deportation, and some postwar authors, including Hannah Arendt in her book *Eichmann in Jerusalem*, would later criticize Baeck and other elders for withholding from their charges the true purpose of the deportations. A more balanced assessment would acknowledge the impossible situation into which these men had been unwillingly cast, confronted with moral dilemmas for which there were no good solutions. Later in his life, Baeck would deliver a heavily attended lecture in Hamburg in which he posed the question "Is there progress in morality?"—a query he answered in the negative. The Holocaust, he argued, implicated not only the German people, but also the rest of the world which had failed to prevent this enormous tragedy.[14]

Another important leader of German Jewry during the trying 1930s was rabbi Joachim Prinz. Born in 1902 in a village in Silesia, the gifted Prinz obtained a degree in philosophy from the University of Giessen at the age of twenty-one. In 1926, after his ordination as a rabbi at the Jewish Theological Seminary of Breslau, Prinz obtained a pulpit in Berlin. A gifted orator, he often preached before standing-room-only congregations.

From early on Prinz was a convinced Zionist. In *Wir Juden* (We Jews), written in October 1933 and published in 1934, Prinz declared: "The theory of assimilation has collapsed." Using then-popular terminology, he argued: "In place of assimilation we now have to set the affirmation of the Jewish nation and the Jewish race." During the long years of struggling for emancipation, Prinz maintained, German Jews had come to embrace the values of German culture, and, no matter where fate would now propel them, they would continue to adhere to what had become a piece of themselves. German Jews, he wrote, would never forget the German forests and cathedrals as well as the music of Mozart and Bach and the poetry of Goethe, Hölderlin, Kleist, and Hebbel: "Our love of Germany and of all that it has created is not invoked in order to ask for anything. It simply exists." At the same time, Prinz continued, we must be allowed to educate self-confident and proud Jews. We must stress our Jewishness, which most basically means the creation of a Jewish nation in its old habitat. The reestablishment of a Jewish homeland, as first proclaimed at the 1897 Basel Congress of the Zionist movement, was the only solution.[15] Prinz's affirmation of the Zionist ideal, linked to his continuing love of Germany, probably helped many German Jews make the difficult, but ultimately life-saving, decision to abandon the land of their ancestors for an uncertain future in Palestine.

Martin Buber, too, saw the deprivation of the civil rights of German Jews as a test of their spiritual and moral resilience. To him, the most appropriate response to Nazi persecution was Jewish adult education, which would nourish German Jewry's inner resources and sustain the morale of a tormented people. Buber's language was not always easily understood, but its essence was clear. In their past, Buber maintained, Jews could find God speaking directly to them, whether at the time of the prophets or in the teachings of the Hasidic rabbis. In this way, God could be a close presence for God's people and help them in their hour of need.[16]

In 1937 Buber appointed the young Polish-born Abraham Joshua Heschel as his successor at the Freie Jüdische Lehrhaus (Free Jewish academy) in Frankfurt, founded in 1920 by Franz Rosenzweig. The academy sought to acquaint assimilated Jews with the religious foundations of their faith; it constituted the most important center of Jewish adult education in Germany. But, in October 1938, Heschel, together with other Polish Jews, was deported to Poland, and by the end of the year the academy had ceased functioning.

The CV Affirms Its German Allegiance

The head of the CV, Ludwig Holländer, reacted to the Nazis' accession to power with an appeal for calmness. Even when the SA, the Nazi party's paramilitary organization, searched the CV's Berlin office in late February, the CV did not change its policy of accommodation, proclaiming: "German Jews will not let their attitude to Germany be influenced by attacks which they consider unjustified. Too strong is the recognition of what their German home means to them. This conviction and the awareness of what they have done for Germany provides the German Jews with strength and support."[17] The official newspaper *CV Zeitung* declared on March 5 that the CV would continue to foster German thinking: "Germany will remain Germany, and nobody will be able to deprive us of our native soil and fatherland." On March 16 the paper predicted that "the more [the new government] will recognize the inner dignity and the true moral substance of Judaism, the more Jews will be able to contribute to the building of our nation."[18] In its plebiscite of November 12 the CV advised its members to approve Germany's exit from the League of Nations. In this way, Germany's Jews would prove they had a "German historical consciousness" and stood by their fatherland.[19]

In 1932 the CV had sixty thousand members, but, taking into account the collective membership of all the Jewish communities affiliated with it, the CV represented more than half of Germany's Jews. A November 9, 1933, article in the *CV Zeitung*, written by its editor Alfred Hirschberg, articulated the main elements of the CV's position. Members of the CV felt themselves to be Jews as well as Germans. The strength of German soil and its sun "are our life; the structure created by Germany's poets and thinkers are the house in which we feel at home." While the use of racial criteria undermined Jewish emancipation and German Jewry's sense of belonging, Judaism was indestructible, and Germany would eventually come to uphold "justice, honor, and humanity for all." The day would arrive that "will end the rift between the history of German Jews and German history."[20]

Letters addressed to the CV *Zeitung* show that CV members held varied ideas regarding what was to come next. The CV functionary Heinz Kellermann opined that there existed the possibility of a "fusion [*Einschmelzung*] between German Jews and the constructive work of the national revolution." Some in the CV wanted an even more active collaboration with the new regime. A member in Saxony suggested a meeting with Hitler to propose the creation of a "national socialist Jewish party." Many Jews had fought for Germany, and there was no reason they should have to stay on the political sidelines just because they adhered to the Jewish religion. Hirschberg, however, rejected this idea as unnecessary and liable to lead to misunderstanding. A quite different position was articulated by a businessman from Merseburg, who questioned whether it still made sense for Jews to continue to stress their being German. All around us, he pointed out, Jews are described as Germany's greatest enemies, and hate songs demand our annihilation. By reciting all the wonderful things we have done for Germany, "we preach to deaf ears."[21] Clearly, the CV membership was not monolithic.

The diary of Willy Cohn, a Jewish teacher in Breslau, reveals the dilemmas the regimen's anti-Jewish policies created for Germany's assimilated Jews. "I love Germany so much that this love cannot be shaken by the unpleasantries that we are now experiencing," Cohn wrote in September 1933. Five years later, after the Nuremberg Laws had made Jews into pariahs, Cohn still expressed his sympathy for Germany's resurrection as a major power, a result with which he believed "any nationalistic person will feel a certain kinship." By the time of his entry of November 30, 1938, more than two hundred thousand Jews, almost one-half of Germany's total Jewish population, had left the country, but Cohn continued to affirm his "allegiance to Germany where I have lived for 50 years." On October 9, 1939, after Hitler had invaded Poland and given a belligerent oration before the Reichstag, Cohn called the Führer's speech "measured and sensible. . . . We must recognize the greatness of this man, who has given the world a new look."[22] Cohn paid for his allegiance to a Germany that could do no wrong with his life. On November 21, 1941, he was deported to Lithuania and, together with other Breslau Jews, shot there a few days later.

The Nazis showed no appreciation for declarations of loyalty expressed by Cohn and other assimilated German Jews. On the contrary, such ideas were unwelcome; they ran counter to the Nazi government policy of ridding of the Jews by way of emigration. At a meeting of security officials on November 1, 1937, SS captain Theodor Dannecker, an associate of Adolf Eichmann, proposed that the CV be dissolved because it was the main Jewish organization upholding assimilation. The CV claimed to do no more than defend the economic and legal rights of German Jews, but in fact its chief aim was to perpetuate their existence in Germany.[23]

After a year of Nazi rule, some CV leaders became uneasy in their conviction that because they were Germans, they would be treated as such. The CV's cultural and political expert Eva Reichmann, for one, had a change of heart between 1933 and 1934. In 1933, when she took on the editorship of the organization's influential magazine *Der Morgen* (The morning), she still affirmed the need to continue the fight for Jewish rights, but by the subsequent year she acknowledged that "the era of emancipation had ended." Perhaps, she added, we were too sure of our German destiny and therefore did not believe in the possibility that it could ever end. And yet, she insisted, this outcome should not call into question the worth of emancipation. She wrote, "The opening of the gates of the ghetto and the granting of liberty that came with the emancipation of German Jews was fate, danger and hope." German Jews should remain proud of the Jewish-German synthesis that had evolved: "It would amount to denying the German aspect of our nature if we did not hope that a time will come when the [German] people themselves will demand a different treatment of our rights in Germany."[24] As it turned out, this expectation, too, was to be disappointed. Germany would not be liberated from the Nazis' oppressive rule by its own people. The German Jews' right to be equal citizens would be restored by a military occupation that guided Germany toward becoming a democracy.

After the war Eva Reichmann's husband, Hans Reichmann, who had served for a long time as CV legal counsel, praised the CV's struggle for the rights of German Jews. But he was also aware of the fateful results of CV policy:

> The men of the Centralverein [CV] bear a tragic debt. Because they were Jews, they believed in eternal and inviolable values. They had confidence in the victory of justice; they hoped that humanity and the striving for liberty would prove stronger than the force of terror. . . . The Centralverein and German Jewry paid for this belief with their doom. But their leaders are subject to the verdict of history, whether, relying on this conviction, it was overconfident to stay in the posts on which fate had put them.[2]

The verdict of history, invoked by both Reichmanns, has not been kind to the CV's strong German allegiance. While the CV's identification with Germany was genuine and sincere—its leaders did not embrace these sentiments in order to ingratiate themselves with the new Germany—much of the CV's strong belief in a good Germany was, tragically, overly optimistic.

The RJF Feels Entitled to Preferred Treatment

For its part, the RJF, Reichsbund jüdischer Frontsoldaten (National league of Jewish front line soldiers), a nearly forty-thousand-member organization of Jewish war veterans, argued that, despite many new problems, the future of Jewish veterans remained in Germany. Certainly, the favorable consideration accorded Jewish combat veterans in the law of April 11, 1933, that excluded other Jews from the civil service strengthened this view. A few days earlier, on April 4, RJF leader Leo Löwenstein had asked for this preferred treatment in a letter to Hitler. In the Great War, he pointed out, German Jews had sacrificed their blood for the fatherland. Now, too, they had "the ardent wish to marshal all their efforts . . . for the peaceful rebuilding of Germany as well as for its defense." To make this possible, Löwenstein requested that Jewish veterans and their families not be subjected to "professional and economic discriminatory treatment." He was aware that amid the Jewish population there were some "elements who sought to damage the people" (*volksschädigende Elemente*), and Löwenstein promised that the RJF would fight these individuals as they had always done. German Jewry, he pleaded, should not have to suffer because of some bad persons in their own ranks.[26] (Whether the change in the civil service law was indeed the result of Löwenstein's appeal to Hitler remains unclear. We do know that President Hindenburg intervened with Hitler in favor of the Jewish veterans.[27])

The special treatment for veterans led to criticism from within the Jewish camp, then and later. Löwenstein, it was said, "was willing to sacrifice the interests of some members of the Jewish community, political leftists and Ostjuden, to secure a place for Jewish war veterans and long-established German Jews in Hitler's new Germany."[28] The RJF justified its intervention with the argument that it had saved thousands of positions and jobs.[29] To the RJF the privileged position had been earned by its members' service to the fatherland in the Great War. RJF chairman Ludwig Freund stressed the veterans' political reliability (for only politically trustworthy Jews had a chance of being listened to by the new regime). National Socialism, he said, similar to Italian Fascism, would have drawn the support of many Jews, had it not been for the Nazis' anti-Semitism. In closing, he posed the question: "How long will leading and clear-thinking National Socialist men continue to adhere to this position [of anti-Semitism]?"[30]

This view was widely shared, including by the highly regarded history professor Hans Herzfeld, who had been decorated in World War I, belonged to the largest German veterans organization, the Stahlhelm (Steel helmet), but was classified as "non-Aryan" because of his Jewish grandparents. Herzfeld stressed the importance of fighting *Schädlinge* (pests) in the Jewish ranks who were "both un-German and un-Jewish." His July 1933 piece, printed in the RJF's official magazine *Der Schild* (The shield), advocated getting rid of the *Gauner* (crooks) and other parasites. Jews also had to abandon their support of the "exaggerated individualism" of Weimar liberalism. Only thus would they be able to achieve a recognition of their status as equal German citizens "despite their non-Aryan race."[31]

In the spirit of the times, and in line with other veterans organizations, in June 1933 the RJF adopted the new "leadership principle" of the National Socialist Party, which in this context gave its head, Löwenstein, the right to exercise the powers of both the RJF's directorate and plenary assembly. Just because the leadership principle was an achievement of the national revolution, the Jewish officer argued, Jews should not reject it for that reason. The new organizational principle would prevent the efforts of "parliamentary groups" to restrain the strength and determination of the leader.[32] RJF member Rabbi Ignaz Maybaum of Frankfurt voiced his opposition to this decision. Authoritarian leadership, he stressed, has no place in a Jewish organization. Moreover, the organization had made itself ridiculous by its preoccupation with copying and imitating the protocols and vocabulary of the new regime.[33] Maybaum was not the only dissenter; many RJF members did not share the highly conservative views and suppliant conduct of their leader Löwenstein.[34]

In March 1933 the RJF joined other Jewish bodies, such as the Zionists, in protesting "foreign atrocity propaganda." A telegraph to the US embassy in Berlin asserted that "irresponsible elements" had instigated the anti-Jewish incidents in Germany, and German authorities had forcefully acted only to prevent future occurrences. It was high time to disown "so-called Jewish intellectuals" abroad who carried out an unrestrained smear campaign against Germany. These individuals, who had abandoned their brethren by fleeing abroad, had forfeited the right to speak about German-Jewish matters.[35]

The RJF also continued sending appeals to the new rulers. Between April 1933 and August 1934 it dispatched no fewer than twenty-eight communications to various government offices, most of which remained unanswered.[36] Among the exceptions was Löwenstein's letter of April 16, 1933, signed *"mit deutschem Gruss"* (with German greeting), asking for a meeting with state secretary Hans Lammers. This was approved, and, at the April 28 meeting, also attended by the much-decorated Jewish air force ace Fritz Beckhardt, who had shot down seventeen enemy planes in the Great War, it was agreed that Löwenstein would submit a memorandum to Hitler.

Löwenstein's May 6 memo to Hitler acknowledged that now, as in the past, there existed within the Jewish population some individuals who were indifferent to both state and religion. To protect the core of German Jews against these "un-German elements," Löwenstein proposed that the existing national organization of German Jewry, the Reichsvertretung der Deutschen Juden, be replaced by a new body that "would vouch for the categorical loyalty of Germany's Jews and all of their institutions to the government." Löwenstein went on to assure Hitler that there existed no contradiction between the stress on race and the RJF's demand for full equality for Germany's Jews. Mussolini's Fascist state also valued *völkische* principles while simultaneously granting Italian Jews full citizenship. A large number of them constituted "the most loyal supporters of the fascist state."[37]

Jewish youth, like German youth, Löwenstein affirmed, "must be educated in the spirit of today's state." It was thus imperative that Jewish young people participate in physical strength training and the Arbeitsdienst, the compulsory labor service required of all German youths. He recommended the creation of special Jewish sections for these activities; the RJF's sports organizations could be enlisted for this purpose. After completing their terms of service, he said, young Jews should be allowed to enlist in the

Reichswehr, the German army, in proportion to their share in the German population.[38] The existing Jewish youth movement should be dissolved and replaced by a new unified youth organization pledged to the ideals of the new state. Löwenstein also proposed extending the existing farms at which Jews were being trained for agricultural pursuits. It was desirable that Jews move from work in the press and theater to new occupations, though this change should be voluntary, not enforced. Jewish inventiveness had made important contributions to Germany and should continue to do so in the future.[39] Like many others, Löwenstein's letter of May 6 remained unanswered. The Nazi regime had no use for Jews who wanted to be Germans.

Early in 1933, German veterans organizations continued to invite the RJF to participate in commemorations for the fallen of the Great War. In a few instances, gentile veterans attended such observances in synagogues. However, the veterans organizations soon fell in line with the regime's anti-Jewish policy and cut their ties to the RJF. Good relations between regimental comrades often continued on a person-to-person basis.[40]

For November 12, 1933, Hitler had ordered elections to the Reichstag, though only one party, the NSDAP, was on the ballot. This vote was accompanied by a plebiscite on Germany's exit from the League of Nations that had taken place on October 19. In a letter dated October 19, Löwenstein asked Lammers to inform the chancellor that the RJF gave its "joyful consent to this forceful step which will pave the way for Germany's equal standing [in the family of nations]." The organization's members stood ready, if the hour demanded it and just as nineteen years ago, to deploy all of their personal strength in the service of the fatherland.[41] A response to this offer came a few weeks later, on February 28, 1934, when the 1933 law excluding Jews from the civil service was also applied to the Reichswehr. Some seventy Jewish soldiers had to resign from the armed forces.[42]

The exclusion of German Jews from serving in the Reichswehr was a serious blow to RJF members' self-esteem. On March 23,

1934, Löwenstein conveyed to President Hindenburg the RJF's great unhappiness at being denied the right to bear arms for the fatherland. German Jews, deeply rooted there, had always accepted the call for military service; they had fulfilled their duties. Now this should be recognized by "an honorable inclusion in the national socialist German state."[43] Hindenburg did not respond.

A year later, on March 16, 1935, Hitler ordered general conscription, a step in clear violation of the Versailles Treaty. The RJF issued a March 23 declaration welcoming the introduction of compulsory military service. On March 27, speaking in the name of about one thousand former Jewish officers who had seen combat in the Great War, the organization informed the minister of defense that these officers felt greatly offended by their exclusion from military service and asked that they be allowed to serve.[44] In a meeting with an assistant to Lammers on June 1, Löwenstein repeated this appeal. He was convinced, he stated, "that the goals of the Reichsbund jüdischer Frontsoldaten could be achieved far better in the present state than in the Marxist state dominated by Jews *[in dem marxistischen Staat der Judenherschaft]*. The Reichsbund jüdischer Frontsoldaten had always resolutely rejected this kind of state." Lammers noted in the minutes of this meeting that Löwenstein's denunciation of the Weimar Republic as a Marxist state ruled by Jews demonstrated the extent to which Löwenstein had accepted the prevailing ideology.[45]

The Nazis did not welcome such support. In the spring and summer of 1935, they unleashed a second wave of anti-Jewish violence. Owners and customers of Jewish shops and firms were terrorized. Physical attacks on Jews and their property reached a new high. The regime also tightened its anti-Jewish legislation. The Nuremberg Laws of September 1935 stipulated that Jews constituted a race defined by birth and blood, which excluded them from German citizenship. Even Jews whose parents or grandparents had converted to Christianity were thus declared to be pariahs. This was followed by a November 14 decree that revoked the exemption of Jewish combat soldiers and their families from anti-Semitic legislation.

From here on, the RJF became increasingly irrelevant. On November 25 the Gestapo forbade Hans Wollenberg, editor of the RJF's magazine *Der Schild*, to speak in public, on the grounds that he supported the continued stay of Jews in Germany.[46] In the fall of 1936 the RJF was ordered to limit its activities to the care of war victims. After Kristallnacht, on November 9–10, 1938, RJF members were among the adult male Jews taken to concentration camps. On December 2 combat veterans were granted early release; this would be the last preferred treatment granted to them.

Together with other Jewish organizations, the RJF now dissolved. Forthwith, the regime treated all Jews, no matter their political attitude or background, in the same destructive way.[47] Löwenstein would survive the war but, perhaps embarrassed by his conduct during the early years of the Nazi regime, he refused all requests for an oral history interview. He died in 1956; obituaries written by his erstwhile comrades celebrated his leadership of the RJF.[48] In 2014 the military barracks in Aachen were named "Leo Löwenstein Kaserne" (Leo Löwenstein barracks).[49]

The Schwarzes Fähnlein: Partner of the New Regime

After the Nazis' rise to power, the Schwarzes Fähnlein (Black banner), a relatively small youth organization with an ideological orientation similar to that of the RJF—it glorified German military virtues, wore uniforms, and marched in phalanx formations—sought to convince the new rulers that it itself was a worthy partner in the task of national resurrection. Schwarzes Fähnlein leaders requested the right to participate in the compulsory labor service, promising that the group would serve in the army if the occasion arose. When these efforts did not bear fruit, Günter Holzmann, a leading figure in the organization, declared that its members would nonetheless continue to "see in every SA man [Nazi storm trooper] our Volksgenosse [national comrade]."[50] Some members, Holzmann among them, advocated formally leaving the Jewish community. In this way, Holzmann stated, members would establish "the inalienable right to belong to the country in which we and our fathers were born." Holzmann traveled to Berlin to discuss these issues with Baldur von Schirach, head of the Hitler Youth, but he failed to be admitted.[51]

In July 1934 the Schwarzes Fähnlein held its first national meeting. It was characterized by strife. A faction led by the outstanding athlete, sports journalist, and teacher Paul "Yogi" Mayer argued that a more Jewish orientation was warranted. The RJF supported this group. Together with these young people, the RJF stated, Jewish veterans would recover the civic standing they had been deprived: "For the sake of our honor, as Germans, as Jews!"[52]

But, just six months later, on December 8, the Gestapo dissolved the organization. The Nazis had no use for Jewish patriots who wanted to stay in Germany.[53]

The VNJ Supports the National Renewal

Naumann's Verband nationaldeutscher Juden (VNJ) was another Jewish organization that voiced its sympathy for the regime of national renewal and asked for preferential treatment. Back in August 1932, Naumann had endorsed the Nazi Party as the only political organization capable of bringing about a "rebirth of Germany."[54] On March 3, 1933, the day of the Reichstag elections, Naumann again appealed to "Jews who feel themselves to be Germans" to cast their vote for the national movement. Meeting about two months later with State Secretary Lammers, Naumann protested that the VNJ had done all it could to help the national movement gain power and yet was being treated no differently than Communist and Marxist Jews.[55] He also sought a meeting with Hitler, but was told that the chancellor could not spare the time.[56] Meanwhile, the Nazi press ridiculed the idea of a dialogue with Jews. The SS organ Schwarze Korps (Black corps), declared: "With Jews we do not discuss." Germany's Jews will have to live with "inferior rights." A provincial paper expressed doubt that any "nationaldeutsche Juden" actually existed. In any event, "there was no place for hermaphrodites in the new Reich."[57]

Naumann, though, was not easily rebuffed. Even after large numbers of left-leaning Jews had ended up in concentration camps, and many Jews had been killed because they were Jews, he continued to declare his solidarity with the "regime of national renewal." On March 20, 1935, acting in the name of the VNJ, Naumann sent a memorandum to Hitler. The immediate occasion was the reintroduction of conscription on March 16 from which Jews were excluded: "We national-German Jews, who have welcomed the announcement of conscription with enthusiasm, cannot believe that we will not be allowed to have the honor of defending our fatherland with weapons." He explained that those who really know Jews realize that not every Jew is alike. In order to solve Germany's Jewish problem it was essential to distinguish between national-German Jews and foreign Jews, including those who thought like foreigners. Naumann assured the Führer and Reich chancellor that he would be happy to make specific suggestions on how this sorting out could be accomplished.[58]

Not surprisingly, Hitler did not reply to this memo, but Naumann was not deterred. On September 23 he sent the government the brochure "Legal Provisions for Overcoming the Jewish Question," which distinguished between "German Jews" and "Foreign Jews." German Jews were those who had fought in the Great War or those whose ancestors had lived in Germany since 1868. These Jews should have the same rights and duties as Aryans. No one who was hostile to the state, such as Communists and Zionists, or who held a leading position in the CV, could be a German Jew.[59]

Naumann's attempt to promote VNJ interests at the expense of the other Jewish organizations failed. The Nazis had their own ideas about how to solve the Jewish problem. In September 1935 they issued the Blutschutzgesetz (Law for the protection of German blood), generally known as the Nuremberg Laws. All German Jews, irrespective of their religious beliefs (including those who had converted or whose parents or grandparents had converted) were declared to be non-Aryan and deprived of their citizenship. Two months later, on November 18, the Gestapo dissolved the

VNJ. Naumann himself was arrested, and he tried unsuccessfully to commit suicide. He was released on December 14 and died of natural causes, a broken man, in May 1939.[60]

In April 1933, on Naumann's initiative, the VNJ, together with the RJF, the Schwarzes Fähnlein, and several other smaller pro-German groups, had formed the Aktions-Ausschuss der jüdischen Deutschen (Action committee for Jewish Germans). This body was meant to be a counterpart to the CV, which these nationalistic Jews considered insufficiently committed to a strong Germany. The new organization proclaimed: "We are prepared to work with all our strength for assisting in building the new German Reich." The self-centered Naumann, however, proved an impossible partner, and after two months the organization dissolved itself.[61] A rival grouping, Erneuerungsbewegung jüdischer Deutscher (Movement of renewal of Jewish Germans), came into being in November 1933 and fared no better. The different players advocating a partnership with the new regime were unable to cooperate, and, for their part, the Nazis actively discouraged any organization advocating a stay of Jews in Germany.[62]

The Vortrupp Seeks an Elite in the Service of the New Germany

Still another organization affirming its loyalty to the new Germany was the Deutscher Vortrupp: Gefolgschaft Deutscher Juden (German vanguard: fellowship of German Jews). Its twenty-four-year-old founder Hans Joachim Schoeps wanted to create "a third faction among German Jews rejecting both assimilation and Zionism." Back in 1929, as a student of theology, Schoeps had formed the Jewish fraternity Freideutsche Kameradschaft (Free-German camaraderie), which adhered to an antiliberal and nationalistic ideology, and Hitler's accession to power in 1933 did not change his political outlook. In February of that year he founded the Vortrupp, with its motto *Bereit für Deutschland* (Be prepared for Germany). Even if today others doubt our being German, Schoeps insisted, we do not doubt Germany. No power in the world can tear Germany from our hearts. Our task, Schoeps declared in early 1934, is to "create a Jewish elite in the service of Germany."[63]

Schoeps insisted that there was no contradiction between being Jewish and being German. Addressing himself to the *bündische* Jewish youth in particular, Schoeps wrote in 1934: "We are Germans, and we are Jews, and we should get rid of the 'fatal hyphen' [in] German-Jewish." Not only that: Schoeps stressed the link between the German fatherland and Judaism. Although he was not an observant Jew (and, in fact, was indebted to two non-Jews, the theologian Martin Luther and the philosopher Søren Kierkegaard, for his belief in a personal relationship with God), he believed that the Jewish revelation at Mount Sinai had enabled Jews to understand the course and meaning of history. Until the coming of the messiah, Jews had to stay in whatever country of the diaspora they found themselves. Schoeps insisted that Germany was more than a community of blood—it was also a realm of fate and history—and for this reason Germans of the Jewish faith belonged to Germany: "Those who today do not leave Germany and who as Germans and Jews bear their suffering for the sake of Germany without grudge and resentment, prove thereby in the most compelling and valid manner that they are indeed German."[64]

In the spring of 1933, Schoeps composed a memorandum that summarized his political program, submitted it to the Reich chancellery, and requested a meeting with Hitler. When this request was denied, he sent his memo to several conservative politicians, including Franz von Papen and Hjalmar Schacht. When word of these contacts reached the foreign press, the *Pariser Tageblatt*, a German-language newspaper published by exiled German journalists in Paris, wrote that Schoeps had proposed the formation of Jewish units in the SA. Schoeps learned of this article years later, when the Gestapo interrogated him in the fall of 1936. In January 1933 Schoeps had called the SA a secular version of the bündische youth, but he vehemently denied that he had ever favored the idea of Jewish SA units.[65]

In Schoeps's eyes Hitler deserved the gratitude of all of Europe for destroying the German Communist party.[66] Moreover, Hitler had succeeded in drawing the Germans out of their private isolation and binding them again to the nation. Even the proletarian who was out of work could now bear his fate with dignity, by proclaiming his faith in the Führer with *Heil Hitler*.

Like other conservative Jewish organizations, the Vortrupp denounced the anti-Nazi protest demonstrations abroad. "Ostjuden and alleged German Jews belonging to the parties of the Left who have fled Germany dare to carry on a boundless agitation against Germany," read one Vortrupp statement. Neither the *Ostjuden* nor the leftist politicians had the right to interfere in German affairs.[67] The Nazis' anti-Semitism, Schoeps maintained, was the "fault of the Jews" who for the longest time had made common cause with liberalism and Marxism.[68] At the Vortrupp's second national gathering in August 1933, Schoeps asserted that it was not the new Germany and its policies, including the treatment of its Jews, that had to change, but the Jews themselves. They had to recognize "their own mistakes and their own guilt" and in this way "find their way to the new Germany."[69]

In placing responsibility for the Nazis' anti-Semitism on his fellow Jews, Schoeps utterly failed to understand the central place anti-Jewish hatred played in Hitler's thinking. While Schoeps was far from the only Jew (or gentile) misjudging Hitler's intentions in 1933, it could be claimed that Schoeps's illusions were in a grotesque class in and of themselves. The national Socialist revolution, he argued, was unique in the history of European revolutions in representing "a truly internal revolution without any interest in the outside world." The new Germany "wants to be autarkic, it has no plans for conquest, it wants to live in peace with . . . the other European nations." National Socialism represented the first truly racial revolution, one that sought to heal the diseased body politic by falling back on "the basic elements of blood and race." The new state's claim for total control carried threats to the autonomy of art, jurisprudence, and science, but

Schoeps expressed confidence that this was a temporary problem; a healthy relationship would reemerge in due course. Once the state had established itself on a secure foundation, it would be able to abandon its totalitarian demands and, forsaking its racism, find room also for Jews without the old mistakes—Jews who were "proud and conscious of their essence *[stolz und artbewusst]*."[70]

In his postwar memoirs Schoeps would later recall his 1934 encounter with the head of the SA, Ernst Röhm, at the Kempinski Restaurant in Berlin. While dining, he noticed Röhm sitting at a nearby table and introduced himself as a Jew who wanted to ask Röhm an important question. Röhm appeared to be angry, but finally said, "You have five minutes." Schoeps now inquired: "What do you actually have against the Jews?" Röhm replied that he himself was completely indifferent on this issue, which was the special prerogative of the Führer. Personally, he could well imagine a national revolution without anti-Semitism. After all, Mussolini managed to get along with his Jews. Schoeps asked next whether one could discuss this matter with Hitler, and Röhm answered that, according to his experience, the Führer was "not approachable with regard to this subject." He added that, nevertheless, Schoeps might try it.

Schoeps now began to conceive the following plan: groups of Hitler Youth were regularly received by Hitler. Schoeps, together with several other Jewish youths who, like himself, looked Aryan would try to join such a group. Once in the presence of Hitler, he would pose the question: "What do you have against these young German Jews whose fathers have lived in Germany for centuries? Please give them space to live [*Lebensraum*]!" Friends talked him out of this venture, but years later he expressed regret that this or a similar attempt had not been undertaken.[71]

On June 30, 1934, during events that have entered history as "the night of the long knives," Hitler carried out a bloody purge of his followers. The butchery marked a high point in the substitution of violence and summary justice for legal norms. In his postwar memoirs Schoeps would write that at this point it became clear to him that the National Socialist government "constituted a band of criminals."[72] At the time, however, he continued to advocate for the Nazi regime. After the government had introduced general conscription on March 22, 1935, Schoeps, speaking for the Vortrupp, let it be known that its members were eager to participate in the new army: "Just as our fathers of 1914–1918 fulfilled their self-evident duty for the fatherland, we declare ourselves today prepared for military service, true to our motto *'Bereit für Deutschland!'*"[73]

In early 1935 Schoeps still believed that, despite various tribulations, German Jews would be able to continue to live on "their native soil."[74] It was only after the Gestapo had dissolved the Vortrupp and repeatedly interrogated him in December 1935, on the heels of the Kristallnacht pogrom, that he finally gave up on the Nazi regime. Schoeps left Germany for Sweden on December 24, 1938.

After learning of the systematic murder of Europe's Jews, Schoeps confessed to his son that he felt terribly guilty for not having advocated German Jewry's flight from Germany in time to save many lives. However, he continued to believe that the German people were basically good and being forced to be Nazis. In a letter of August 1939 addressed to his former comrades, he wrote: "Hitler is not Germany. Germany is occupied by a brown army of occupation."[75]

In 1946 Schoeps returned to Germany. From 1947 he held a chair in the history of religion and ideas at the University of Erlangen. He acknowledged that in 1933/34 he had made some political mistakes, but he continued to propagate his conservative views. He advocated the recreation of Prussia, abolished by the victorious allies, and talked about the restoration of the monarchy. In 1970 Schoeps stated: "I have always been a conservative, a Prussian and Jew."[76] He died on July 8, 1980.

The Vortrupp had never had a large membership, but it attracted attention from both Jews and Nazis on account of its attacks on the other Jewish organizations and its unusual ideology. The majority of German Jews, especially German intellectuals, shared Schoeps's love for Germany, but the Germany they identified with was the Germany of Schiller and Goethe, Beethoven and Thomas Mann, a country of liberty and the rule of law, upholding political freedom. By contrast, Schoeps's Germany was völkisch and authoritarian at best. Tragically, Schoeps tried to fuse his German and Jewish identities and ended up being excluded from both.

The Zionists Advocate Emigration

The Zionists were the only ones who realized from the very beginning that only emigration to Palestine would adequately address the new situation of German Jewry. But, for a short time in 1933, even the Zionists thought a mutually acceptable relationship between a Nazi state and Germany's Jews would be possible, and so they tried to stay in the regime's good graces—such as in March 1933, when the ZVfD endeavored to assure Jewish leaders abroad that the foreign-press reports of widespread atrocities against German Jews were false.[77] At times Zionist pronouncements used very similar terminology to National Socialist vocabulary, a tactical device designed to enable the Zionist leadership to function as an effective negotiator with the new government. On June 21, 1933, the ZVfD addressed a declaration to Hitler expressing its desire to work for the resolution of the Jewish problem in a manner that would serve the interests of both the German and Jewish people. The statement rejected assimilation, stating that the Zionists, too, were against racially mixed marriages. The stress on ancestry, community of fate, and confidence in national essence promoted by National Socialism were also the foundations of Zionism and the national rebirth of the Jewish people. The Zionists, the statement continued, worked for Jewish emigration to Palestine, but they also wanted to assure a protected status for the Jewish community still existing in Germany.[78]

A notable success of this initiative was the so-called Haavara Agreement (*haavara* being the Hebrew word for "transfer") between the Jewish Agency for Palestine (established in 1929 to solicit non-Jewish support for a Jewish national home and to represent Jewish interests in negotiations with the British mandate government and the League of Nations) and the ZVfD on the one hand, and the German government on the other. By this agreement, signed in August 1933, German Jews emigrating to Palestine would have to take with them the equivalent of 1,000 pounds sterling (about $2,500 US dollars in 1933) and thereby promote the export of German goods to Palestine.[79] My father-in-law was one of many German Jews who benefited from this arrangement. An active member of the CV and ardently pro-German, he had served for several years on the governing council of the small town of Vacha (Thuringia). However, Thuringia was an early stronghold of the Nazis, and he was twice assaulted and severely beaten. Realizing that his life was in danger, he purchased what became known as the Kapitalisten-Zertifikat (Capitalist certificate) for permission of entry to the Jewish homeland and took his family to Palestine. While Nazi propaganda described the Zionist movement as an arm of the international Jewish conspiracy, on a practical level the Zionist ideology and the Haavara Agreement were in fact useful tools to help make Germany *judenrein* (free of Jews).[80]

The Zionist cause benefited as well. The Zionist leadership saw in the Nazis' anti-Jewish policies a force that would make German Jews return to Jewish values—including Zionism—and avail themselves of emigration to Palestine. As Martin Buber counseled, the German-Jewish coexistence had entered a crisis, and it was best to make a virtue out of necessity.[81] Writing after the boycott action in April 1933, Robert Weltsch, editor of the Zionist weekly *Jüdische Rundschau*, pointed out that the boycott had defined the Jews as a distinct, ineluctable group. No longer could the Jews harbor the illusion that they were anything but Jews. The Nazis had become their salvation.[82]

These observations were largely correct. More effectively than the Jews themselves, their persecutors were about to create a significant revival of interest in Judaism and a return to the Jewish homeland. During the 1920s the Zionist movement had been small.

In 1933 it had no more than 7,500 members nationwide. Prior to 1933 no more than two thousand Jews had emigrated to Palestine, and almost half of them returned to Germany. From now on the Zionist organization would end up growing in direct proportion to the increase in anti-Semitic agitation.[83] Some pro-German Jewish intellectuals such as the writer Alfred Döblin would come to acknowledge the failure of assimilation and concede that Palestine had become the only real home for Germany's Jews.[84]

Relations between the CV and the RJF on one side and the ZVfD on the other had been tense for many years. The RJF in particular had expressed hostile views of the Zionist movement. RJF general secretary Ludwig Freund had advocated "a distinct fighting position against Zionism," for only by demonstrating an unequivocal German conviction would it be possible to achieve results when negotiating with German authorities. In August 1933 RJF head Löwenstein suggested to State Secretary Lammers the creation of a new Jewish umbrella organization without the Zionists, a proposal that of course did not go anywhere.[85] In June 1934 the RJF forbade simultaneous membership in the RJF and the ZVfD; the Zionists reciprocated by not allowing their members to join the RJF.[86]

Victor Klemperer was one of many German Jews who fully supported this hostile view of the Zionists. Even after being dismissed from his academic post as a non-Aryan, Klemperer wrote in his diary entry of June 13, 1934: "To me the Zionists . . . are as disgusting as the Nazis."[87] As the situation of German Jewry worsened, however, the RJF gradually changed its attitude toward Zionism and began to show an interest in emigration. In April 1937 the RJF and ZVfD finally made peace and established friendly cooperation. The Zionists withdrew their decision on the incompatibility of membership in both organizations. The RJF agreed to support the two Zionist fundraising drives Keren Hayesod and Keren Kayemeth.[88]

Between 1933 and 1940 some 260,000 German Jews out of a total population of about 500,000 in 1933 left Germany for an uncertain future abroad. About 57,000 emigrated to Palestine.[89]

Last Chance to Emigrate

For most of the emigrants, the decision to leave their homeland did not come easy, and some Jews preferred a voluntary death. A Jewish woman in Berlin who committed suicide on November 29, 1938, explained in a note: "I am leaving life as someone whose family has had German citizenship for over 100 years and has always remained loyal to Germany. . . . I don't want to live without a Fatherland, without a homeland, without an apartment, without citizenship rights, ostracized and reviled."[90]

After the November 1938 pogrom and intensifying Nazi pressure on Jews, the tempo of emigration accelerated. Some thirty thousand Jewish men who had been taken to concentrations camps were released once they had successfully arranged for their emigration from Germany. My father was one of those who had to spend almost four months in the concentration camp Buchenwald. He returned emaciated and a shadow of his former self. Jewish places of business were forced to close or sell their ownership. Jewish pupils had to leave German schools. Still existing Jewish organizations were dissolved. The Hechalutz, engaged in training Jewish young people for life in Israel, was allowed to continue operating until September 1939 when it, too, finally had to shut down. Georg Karesky's Staatszionistische Organisation (Jewish state organization), part of the militant Zionist Alliance Vladimir Jabotinsky had founded in 1925, expected preferred treatment on account of its strong support of emigration, but it was liquidated as well, on August 31, 1938, several months before the other Jewish organizations.[91] Early in 1939 Jews were concentrated in so-called *Judenhäusern* (Jewish houses). On September 19, 1941, Jews were ordered to wear a yellow Star of David with the word *Jude* (Jew) on the left side of their outer garment.

When Jewish emigration was finally forbidden in October 1941, about 160,000 Jews remained in Germany, caught up in the Final Solution of the Jewish Question.[92] Soon thereafter, the deportations began.

Abandoned by the World and German Compatriots

More Jews would have saved their lives had they had fewer misconceptions about Nazi rule. Most believed that Hitler could not last, and later they did not take the threats against them seriously enough. Certainly more Jews would be alive today had the outside world shown more concern. Jews remained stranded in Nazi Germany because in the 1930s hardly any country was willing to accept Jewish immigrants, especially penniless Jews from Germany.

Some 10,000 Jews went underground in Germany to escape transportation to the killing machine in the East. Approximately half of them sought refuge in the more cosmopolitan capital city of Berlin, and indeed a dedicated number of non-Jewish inhabitants there did provide shelter. As a result, Jews hiding in Berlin were much more likely to escape death. In other centers of Jewish life, far fewer Jews found help and refuge. When the deportations got underway in Munich in the fall of 1941, no more than 100 Jews out of a population of 3,200 were able to hide successfully. Overall, only a tiny minority of Germans were involved in the rescue of Jews, and in the majority of cases the rescuers were friends or acquaintances. Personal ties were more important than humanitarian motives.[93] In all, about 3,000 of the 10,000 Jews who went into hiding would survive.[94]

The great majority of German Jews considered themselves German citizens and had been deeply attached to their homeland; they had considered themselves part of German society. Yet in their hour of need their German compatriots failed them. The only public protest against the deportation of Jews took place in Berlin in February and March 1943, when several hundred women, married to Jewish men who had been arrested prior to being shipped east, congregated before a collection center in the Rosenstrasse. The Nuremberg Laws had forbidden future intermarriages but had not nullified existing ones. Despite great Nazi pressure on such women to divorce their Jewish spouses, they had stuck by their husbands. For seven days in wintry weather the women now loudly demanded their release. The authorities, afraid of the public commotion, gave in and released the men.[95]

The onslaught on the Jews took place in full public view, but no social group openly opposed it. Many Germans privately disapproved of the burning of synagogues during Kristallnacht, but hardly any voices were raised against this pogrom. The closing down of Jewish places of business was regarded as draconian and liable to damage the German economy, yet the measure was accepted because it was legal. After years of agitation, anti-Semitism may have gone no further than the belief that German Jews were not really German and that a reduction of the Jewish influence was desirable. But even such muted prejudice was enough for Germans to do nothing as their Jewish neighbors were deported and murdered: the Jews were out of sight and out of mind. As Hitler's biographer Ian Kershaw has pointed out, "This was not a neutral stance. It was a deliberate turning away from any personal responsibility."[96] It left the Jews at the mercy of a state that had no mercy.

6

Living in the Land of the Murderers

At the end of World War II, some 170,000 Jewish victims of the Nazi regime were scattered in camps and towns all over Germany. Most of them had been camp inmates and forced laborers; some had survived in hiding. These Holocaust survivors, known as "displaced persons" (DPs), hailed from various European countries, the majority from Eastern Europe. Nearly two years later, by the summer of 1947, about 182,000 Jewish DPs were still living in Germany. About 80 percent came from Poland, where anti-Semitism had become rampant and where the Communist-controlled regime offered little encouragement to would-be returnees. At this point in time, some 15,000 of the Jews in Germany were German Jews, about half of them survivors, the other half returnees.[1]

An Uncertain Future

The first years of the postwar period saw acute tensions between the Jewish DPs and the German population. It was a time of severe shortages, and because the DPs had easier access to food and articles for daily use, many of them were active in the black market. According to official statistics maintained by the military government, the rate of such illegal activities was no higher among the DPs than among the urban population as a whole, but still the situation fed anti-Semitic stereotypes of Jewish crooks and speculators. Jewish-run cafés and bars drew the enmity of local storekeepers because allegedly they were protected by the Allied authorities and thus said to be able to disregard building permits and opening-hours regulations with impunity. Some of these enterprises were also said to be catering to prostitution. The requisition of German houses and apartments to Jewish survivors further magnified resentment of the "foreign Jews."[2] Walter Kolb, the mayor of Frankfurt, called on the city's Jews to go back to the countries they had come from.[3]

At times the German police staged raids on DP camps to root out black market activities. The mere fact that uniformed German police accompanied by German shepherds issued orders over loudspeakers inevitably reminded survivors of previous such encounters during the Holocaust. The police, for their part, shared the public's hostility toward the DPs. On February 27, 1950, a force of forty police officers entered a DP camp in Hannover on the ostensible grounds of rooting out black market activity, swinging their rubber truncheons and assaulting the Jews. The worst of these incidents took place in Stuttgart in March 1946. The camp inmates resisted the search of their premises for contraband, and, in the resulting clash, Schmul Danziger, a survivor of Auschwitz and Mauthausen, was shot and killed. The raid otherwise resulted in the confiscation of several illegally raised chickens.[4]

Most of the Jewish DPs did not stay in Germany; they moved on to Israel and the United States. By September 1948 their numbers had declined by more than one hundred thousand to about eighty thousand. The great majority of those who remained were old and infirm, and among them relations were not always smooth. As before 1933 German and eastern European Jews did not get along well. At this juncture the German Jews, in the minority, resented the fact that Yiddish had become the lingua franca of the Jewish remnant in Germany.[5] They further worried that they would not be able to maintain their Reform traditions, as they would be outvoted in the synagogues. For this reason they tried to reserve full temple membership to those who held German citizenship. In several locations court interventions were required to reverse such discriminatory practices.[6]

By 1948 more than one hundred Jewish congregations had been reestablished in Germany, most of them numbering fewer than fifty members. One of the oldest, Cologne, had restarted activities even before the end of the war, in April 1945. Two years later the

Zentralrat der Juden in Deutschland (Central council of the Jews in Germany) came into being as the representative body of Jews in Germany. In contrast to the Zentralverein Deutscher Juden in the pre-Hitler years, this new authority did not call itself an association of German Jews, but a council of Jews *in* Germany. Its first president was Heinz Galinski, a jurist who had survived Auschwitz. A pivotal figure in reestablishing Jewish life in postwar Germany, Galinski would serve as chairman of the Jewish community of Berlin from 1949 until 1992 and lead the Zentralrat both between 1954 and 1963 and again from 1988 to 1992. Galinski was a sharp-spoken man, and he made enemies due to his relentless crusade to keep the memory of the Holocaust alive. But his personal determination was also a great asset, appreciated by many political leaders of the new Germany, with whom he developed strong contacts. In these early years in particular, the Zentralrat was criticized for its concentration on developing good relations with the German government at the expense of other problems facing German Jews. The Zentralrat's emphasis on "diplomacy" was probably the result of German Jewry's feelings of insecurity and the perceived need to obtain the support of the German state against anti-Semitic enemies.[7]

During the first two decades after the war, the outside Jewish world criticized the very fact that Jews took up residence again in Germany. At its first postwar assembly in July 1948, the World Jewish Congress warned Jews worldwide to never again settle on the "blood-soaked German soil."[8] In 1951 the German Zionists were not invited to the World Zionist Congress. After the State of Israel and the German Federal Republic (GFR) established diplomatic relations in 1965, the World Council of Jews, under its president Nahum Goldmann, organized a conference on Jewish-German relations, but no member of the Zentralrat was invited to speak. In subsequent years, as the Jewish communities in Germany expanded, a more grudging acceptance of Jewish life in Germany developed.[9]

Some Germans saw the need to rebuild a positive relationship between Germans and Jews. On November 9, 1949, the eleventh anniversary of the Kristallnacht pogrom, a new German organization, Deutscher Koordinatsrat der Gesellschaften für Christlich-Jüdische Zusammenarbeit (German coordinating council of societies for Christian-Jewish cooperation), came into being, serving as a coordinating body for what eventually became some eighty local societies working toward this same goal.[10] As an acknowledgment of German guilt, the organization Aktion Sühnezeichen (Service for reconciliation) sent German volunteers to work in Israel.

In the early postwar years, quite a few Germans also converted to Judaism. Some converted out of conviction; for others, converting was a way of showing solidarity with the victims. For still others, it was opportunism, to get CARE packages—food parcels sent to needy people from America by the humanitarian organization CARE (Cooperative for American Relief Everywhere). Many converts were German women whose Jewish DP husbands insisted on their conversion. In Berlin a committee of the Jewish community screened the applications. Those who had been in the German army or were children of Nazis were rejected automatically.[11] Conversions to Judaism continued during the years to follow. When the American film *Holocaust* was shown on German television in 1979, it had a powerful impact on many Germans, who identified with the Jewish middle-class family portrayed in the film. The German-Jewish historian Yasha Mounk recalls how a friend of his felt absolutely "devastated" after seeing the film and did not know what to do, so he converted to Judaism.[12]

Conversations and confrontations about Jews in the new Germany reached a high point in 1951, with the prosecution in Munich of Bavaria's most prominent survivor, Philipp Auerbach, the state commissioner for persecuted persons. On account of his energetic pursuit of reparations, the German press had dubbed Auerbach the "Caesar for Reparations." Accused of corruption and fraud in regard to reparations payments, Auerbach was tried in a court of five judges, three of whom where former members of the Nazi party. He was found guilty and given a two-and-a-half-year prison term. Two days later Auerbach committed suicide. In 1956, four years later, a commission of inquiry of the Bavarian parliament posthumously cleared Auerbach of all charges.[13]

Relations between Germans and Jews continued to be fragile. Many Jews, it was said, kept their suitcases packed. One of the bones of contention was the issue of *Wiedergutmachung* (restitution). The Allies had made it known that the building of German-Allied relations required a satisfactory disposition of Jewish claims, but German public opinion was divided. A 1951 survey showed that 96 percent of Germans favored supporting war widows and war orphans, but only 68 percent approved of aid payments to Jews.[14] The extreme right organized an Interessengemeinschaft der Entnazifizierungsgeschädigen (Association of individuals harmed by denazification) and demanded restitution for those affected by denazification.[15] It wasn't until November 1949 that chancellor Konrad Adenauer first addressed the issue of Jewish restitution, and it would take three more years, until September 1952, before an agreement with Israel was finally signed. Furthermore, the West German parliament's subsequent 1953 ratification of the accord became possible only with votes from the Social Democratic (SPD) party. Adenauer was unable to secure enough support from his own party, the Christian Democratic Union (CDU/CSU), for this act of reconciliation.[16]

Anti-Semitism and Philo-Semitism

Open expressions of anti-Jewish sentiments were taboo in the German Federal Republic, which came into being in 1949. Learning from the Weimar experience, the new Germany did not tolerate the open advocacy of National Socialist or anti-Jewish views. In 1952 the German Constitutional Court outlawed the Neo-Nazi Sozialistische Reichspartei (Socialist-National party). Germany also undertook to prosecute Nazi criminals. A key figure in this endeavor was the German-Jewish jurist Fritz Bauer, who organized the trial of twenty individuals who had served in the Auschwitz death camp. Germany's longest jury trial—lasting from

December 20, 1963, to August 20, 1965—resulted in long prison terms, including life imprisonment, the highest penalty under German law, for six of the defendants.[17]

In the early postwar years, many Germans voiced philo-Semitic sentiments, a convenient way of presenting oneself as anti-Nazi. Others remembered that they had had Jewish friends or even had helped Jews. Yet anti-Semitic sentiments remained high among the populace. The first survey measuring popular beliefs about Jews, held in the American zone of occupation in December 1946, classified 18 percent of Germans as "hard-set anti-Semites" and 22 percent as racists. Three years later, in 1952, the results were similar. 34 percent of the population was "demonstratively anti-Semitic," while another 34 percent "felt hostile toward Jews."[18]

But, with the passage of time, anti-Semitic sentiments began to decline. The emigration of the DPs—and, with their disappearance, German resentments concerning their privileges—was one factor explaining this trend. Rising prosperity, known as the *Wirtschaftswunder* (economic miracle), helped people forget the Nazi era and its ideology of hate. Finally, there was the matter of age. As the generation indoctrinated with Nazi anti-Semitism started to die off, anti-Jewish attitudes weakened. The younger generations who were socialized after 1945 showed less anti-Semitic sentiments. Their answers to the question "Would it be better if Germany had no Jews?" manifest the change in attitude:

Table 1. Would it be better if Germany had no Jews? (1952–87)

	1952	1956	1958	1963	1965	1983	1987
Yes, better	37%	26%	22%	18%	19%	9%	13%
No, worse	19%	24%	38%	40%	34%	43%	67%
Undecided/Indifferent	44%	50%	40%	42%	47%	48%	20%

Source: Bergmann and Erb, "Wie antisemitisch sind die Deutschen," 52.

Anti-Semitic sentiments continued to decrease in subsequent years. Between 2002 and 2010 the percentage of German respondents who thought that Jews had too much influence dropped from 22 to 16 percent.[19] Solely from 2014 to 2015, the percentage of Germans holding negative views of Jews fell from 27 to 16 percent.[20] Whereas, during the Nazi era, the educated and elite groups had shared in the prevailing anti-Semitism, in postwar Germany, in general the higher the level of education, the less anti-Semitism was to be found. An advanced education appeared to encourage an acceptance of socially prescribed norms.

But, starting in the late 1990s, a kind of secondary anti-Jewish sentiment emerged. A 2000–2001 survey of university students in Essen found that, even as the students decisively opposed anti-Semitic prejudice—huge majorities rejected assertions such as "Jews care about nothing but business"; "It is bad to have Jewish neighbors"; and "Jews have too much influence"—more than half of the students agreed with the statements "The Jews know how to exploit the bad conscience of the Germans" and "Many Jews attempt to derive an advantage from their experience in the Third Reich and make the Germans pay for it." Almost fifty years after the collapse of the Hitler regime, it seemed that many young Germans had tired of being confronted with their Nazi history and blamed the Jews for reminding them of this stain on Germany's past.[21]

The Issue of German Guilt

During the early years of the postwar period, the responsibility of the German people for the horrors of the Nazi regime could not be openly contested. The trials of Nazi war criminals had laid out in overwhelming detail the participation of thousands of ordinary Germans, including the best and the brightest, in Nazi crimes. Reeducation imposed by the Allied occupation authorities further reinforced the verdict of German guilt. But the German population was not happy with this state of affairs. Large numbers of Germans saw themselves as a nation of victims, helpless in the face of totalitarian terror. The belief in German victimhood found expression in the black joke that "the Germans will never forgive the Jews for Auschwitz."

The subject of German guilt toward Jews received wide attention in 1974, with the play *Garbage, the City and Death*, by the non-Jewish playwright Rainer Werner Fassbinder. Its main character, a Jewish real estate mogul in Frankfurt, wreaks his lust for revenge by exacting huge profits from his German clients and celebrates the fact that no German can resist him because he is a Jew. Eventually he strangles a prostitute. The protagonist bears a striking resemblance to Ignatz Bubis, a leader of the Jewish community of Frankfurt who had become unpopular with the Left after having squatters evicted from houses he owned. The play's shocking diatribes include this declaration by a German character: "And it is the Jew who is guilty because he makes us guilty, for he is here. Had he stayed where he came from, or had they gassed him, I could sleep better today. They forgot to gas him. This is no joke, that's what I think, deep inside of me."[22] Reviewers agreed that the play was anti-Semitic, the publisher stopped selling copies, and planned performances were canceled.

Some ten years later, Günther Rühle, the director of Frankfurt's publicly funded theater, decided that the political atmosphere had changed sufficiently so that allowing criticism of Jews to appear onstage would be a step toward possible normality. In 1969 the Bavarian politician Ludwig Strauss had been roundly criticized for stating that a people who had achieved so much in rebuilding their country had a right to hear no more about Auschwitz. Decades later the desire to feel good about their country had become widespread among Germans of all levels of education. Being reminded of the crimes of the Nazi era stood in the way of this wish for a positive national identity.[23] Rehearsals for the play proceeded. Yet when *Garbage, the City and Death* finally premiered in October 1985, a thousand Jews picketed the performance, a near-riot ensued, and the performance had to be canceled.

The controversy revealed the changed political atmosphere of the 1980. A critic wrote in the *Frankfurter Rundschau*, a respected national magazine, that criticism of the Jews should once again be acceptable in order to expose the "membership of several representatives of Jewish capital in a right-wing cartel." The Frankfurt theater director Rühle declared in a public discussion of the controversial play that "the *Schonzeit* (closed hunting season) is over."[24] On the other hand, to this day, leading German politicians continue to stress that the historical responsibility for the horrors of Third Reich knows no limits for those who were born later, and there is no exception for immigrants. One of the most outspoken figures in this regard has been Richard von Weizsäcker, GFR president from 1984 to 1994. In a speech before the German parliament on May 8, 1985, Weizsäcker told the deputies that their forefathers had left them a grave legacy: "All of us, whether guilty or not, whether young or old, must accept the past."[25] However, much of the population did not share this view. Large numbers of Germans felt that enough was enough. How long must we feel guilty?! was the question raised.

A survey by the weekly newspaper *Die Woche* (The week) in May 2000 showed that the desire to draw a final line under the Nazi past was particularly strong among youth. 81 percent of those between the ages of fifteen and seventeen asked for an end to talk about Auschwitz.[26] Many Germans acknowledged the crimes of the Nazis, but suggested that Germany's glorious past as the country of Goethe and Schiller and the good record of the GFR should not be ignored. Auschwitz should not be forgotten, but the positive side of German history should be given more weight. [27]

The question of the appropriate attitude to the crimes of the Nazi era on the part of the new Germany became a topic of heated debate in the fall of 1998. The well-known writer Martin Walser had been granted the Peace Prize of the German Book Trade, and in his October 11 acceptance speech in the auditorium of the former Church of St. Paul in Frankfurt/M he declared: "Not a day passes on which we are not reminded of our historical debt, our everlasting disgrace. . . . It is inappropriate to turn Auschwitz into a routine threat, a tool for browbeating people at any occasion."[28] The audience gave Walser a standing ovation, and he subsequently received thousands of letters from Germans of all classes voicing their agreement with his sentiments. A Protestant minister from the Rhineland, for one, had found it liberating that a man of such elevated standing had articulated his protest "against political correctness and the manipulation of conscience."[29] Meanwhile, demonstratively keeping his seat in the auditorium was the Holocaust survivor Ignatz Bubis, head of the Central Council of Jews in Germany, who would call the speech "intellectual arson." On November 9, commemorating Kristallnacht of 1938, Bubis commented: "It is unacceptable that the struggle against antisemitism, racism, and xenophobia is ceded to the Jews while [another] part of the society feels rather harassed thereby."[30]

Bubis was not the only one in Germany to voice criticism. Peter Steinbach, the head of a memorial for the German resistance to Hitler in Berlin, argued against the "attempt to escape from history." Others pointed out that Walser had given respectability to views generally expressed only by the extreme right. The average German now could hide behind Walser's speech and demand an end to remembrance without fear of censure. Rudolf Augstein, publisher of the mass-circulation magazine *Der Spiegel* (The mirror), wrote in the November 30, 1998, issue that the planned Berlin memorial for the murdered Jews was directed against Berlin and Germany. "One cannot dictate to us how we remember the past in our new capital." Many viewed the statement as a warning that such coerced remembrance would encourage anti-Semitism. On December 19 a bomb exploded at the grave of Heinz Galinski, an earlier head of the Central Council of Jews. Many drew a parallel between this anti-Jewish plot and Walser's attempt to free the German people from responsibility for their past.[31]

New Critical Attitudes toward Israel

The desire of most Germans to forget the horrors of the Nazi regime coincided with a new willingness to criticize the State of Israel. In Germany, as elsewhere, the Six-Day War of 1967 and the Yom Kippur War of 1973 had been seen as the successful struggle of the Jewish David vanquishing the Arab Goliath. But, after

Israel's invasion of Lebanon in 1982, the widespread solidarity with Israel and concern for the Jewish state's survival weakened. The radical left accused Israel of being a new Fascist *Herrenvolk* (master race)—the vocabulary resembling both Soviet and Arab propaganda that labeled Israel a Nazi state that should be destroyed. Jürgen Möllemann, a member of the Bundestag (German parliament) and deputy chairman of the liberal Free Democratic party (FDP), voiced his sympathy for Palestinian suicide bombers, who, he argued in 2002, were acting in self-defense against the occupation of their country.[32] He also mailed anti-Semitic fliers to would-be voters. Möllemann had to resign his party post, and, on June 5, 2003, as the Bundestag was about to lift his parliamentary immunity, he committed suicide.[33]

The mainstream media used less incendiary wording, but for the most part were also strongly critical of the Jewish state. They singled out Israel, the only democracy in the Middle East, without ever criticizing the autocratic Arab states—such double standards revealing that more than anti-Zionism was at stake. Within German Jewry, too, some voices questioned uncritical support for Israel. In 1980 the Jewish Group of Frankfurt—newly organized by the historian Dan Diner, the University of Frankfurt education professor Micha Brumlik, and the Jewish Museum of Frankfurt educational programs director Cilly Kugelmann—called for building a strong Jewish community in Germany that would include critics of Israeli policy toward the Palestinians. In the same year, a new magazine, *Cheshbon* (Accounting), initiated by Jewish students in Munich, argued (in the words of editorial board member Micha Brumlik) for the study of the Jewish scriptures and traditions as the foundation of Jewish life in Germany. The issue of Israel was relegated to the sidelines.[34]

Important politicians, however, remained solidly in Israel's camp. Chancellor Angela Merkel, for one, paid a three-day visit to Israel in March 2008 to mark the Jewish state's sixtieth anniversary. On March 18, in an unprecedented speech to the Knesset (Israeli parliament), Merkel spoke of her resolute support of Israel. On May 17, 2019, the German parliament was the first government in the European Union to condemn the Boycott, Divestment and Sanctions (BDS) movement targeting the State of Israel. The resolution, brought to the Bundestag by Chancellor Merkel's Christian Democratic Union (CDU) party, as well as by its coalition party, the Social Democratic party (SPD), and the liberal Free Democrats (FDP) and the Greens, read as follows:

> The arguments and methods of the BDS movement are anti-Semitic. The campaign calls for a boycott of Israeli artists as well as stickers on Israeli merchandise that deter their purchase, which is reminiscent of the most terrible phase of German history. "Do Not Buy" stickers of the BDS movement on Israeli products awaken associations to the Nazi slogan *"Kauft nicht bei Juden!"* ("Do not buy from Jews!") and corresponding graffiti on facades and shop windows.
>
> The German Bundestag condemns and resolutely opposes all anti-Semitic statements and abuses that are formulated as alleged criticisms of the State of Israel's policies, but are in fact expressions of hatred of Jewish people and their religion.[35]

Anti-Jewish Violence

The changed German political climate brought with it anti-Jewish agitation and violence. Ever since the end of the war in 1945, neo-Nazi and right-wing extremists had denied the Holocaust or had argued that the Final Solution was no worse than the bombing of Germany in World War II, the mass murder of Armenians in Ottoman Turkey, or the extermination of the Native Americans in the United States. There had been instances of swastikas and anti-Jewish slogans being painted on Jewish installations, and cemeteries had been vandalized.[36] But the new wave of anti-Jewish outrages was far more vicious. It was part of a Europe-wide increase in populist attitudes that stressed national identity, vilified immigrants, and brought with it new outbursts of anti-Semitism.

In 1994 the synagogue of Lübeck was set on fire, the first time since 1938's Kristallnacht that a Jewish house of worship had been burned. The same year saw an arson attack against the so-called Jewish barracks of the former Nazi concentration camp Sachsenhausen. In 2003 neo-Nazis planted a bomb at the site of the new Jewish synagogue of Munich (it was removed before it could explode). There were also threats of kidnapping and assassinations against prominent Jewish figures. All and all, these attacks could no longer be written off as residues of the Nazi era. New right-wing groups openly voiced anti-Jewish slogans. Once again German Jews felt threatened in their own country. The sight of police guarding Jewish retirement homes, museums, memorials, and synagogues was a new chapter in the history of postwar German Jewry.

Prominent Jews now were accompanied by bodyguards. Outings by young people had to be protected by police. In the summer of 2000, a bombing at a Düsseldorf transit station injured six Jews. During the fall of that year, gasoline bombs were thrown at synagogues in Düsseldorf, and windows were smashed at the Kreuzberg synagogue in Berlin.[37] On October 9, 2019, on Yom Kippur, the holiest day of Judaism, a heavily armed twenty-seven-year-old man sought to enter a synagogue in Halle, a city in the former East Germany. His proclaimed intent was to kill as many Jews as possible, and only a locked door prevented a terrible massacre. Most of these attacks, including physical assaults on individual Jews carrying a *kippah* or Star of David, have been traced to members of extreme-right groups or lone individuals embracing a quasi-Nazi ideology.[38]

With the arrival of predominantly Muslim refugees from the Near East, the situation worsened. In August 2010 four youths of Middle Eastern appearance attacked rabbi Daniel Alter in Berlin as he was walking with his six-year-old daughter. He later underwent surgery for a fractured cheekbone. An increase in the badgering of Jewish pupils, primarily by Arab children, caused some Jewish students to transfer to Jewish and private schools. Hostility to Jews has been found to be more prevalent among Muslim youths than among young people generally.[39]

Following the influx of predominantly Muslim refugees in 2015 and 2016, increasing antiforeign sentiments sparked crimes against the newcomers. Houses sheltering the refugees were bombed or set on fire. The rate of violence against Jews correspondingly rose as well. Research has shown that those Germans who feel most threatened by foreigners are also the most anti-Semitic. As the number of foreigners seeking asylum in Germany has increased during the last fifteen years, antiforeign sentiments, not to say xenophobia, have grown as well. Many Germans, it appears, are not so much worried about unemployment or the lower wages that might be caused by an influx of foreigners, but rather by a perceived threat to German traditions and values and what it means to be a German. This awakened nationalism regards the Jews, too, as outsiders. In other words, contemporary anti-Semitism is largely a result of hostility toward foreign cultures. *Völkisch* anti-Semitism used to denounce the Jews as rootless, cosmopolitan, aggressive, and, above all, alien. The new anti-Semitism spread by the extreme right has revived these stereotypes. The lack of contact with Jews (given the small number of Jews living in Germany today) has contributed to German acceptance of these prejudices disseminated through persistent anti-Jewish propaganda.[40] In 2013 788 criminal cases had been linked to anti-Semitism; in 2018 these had grown to 1,514, and in 2019 they reached 1,799.[41] Members of extreme-right groups were found to be responsible for the majority of these incidents, though the accuracy of this determination has been questioned. Felix Klein, the commissioner for Jewish Life in Germany and the Fight against Anti-Semitism, has acknowledged that the number of anti-Semitic incidents caused by Muslims is undoubtedly higher.[42]

The 2015 Anti-Semitism Survey of the American Anti-Defamation League (ADL) has supported this finding. Overall, some 16 percent of Germans were found to be harboring anti-Semitic attitudes, whereas for Christians this figure was 14 percent, and for Muslims it was 56 percent. Once again younger people were found to be less anti-Semitic, with only 10 percent considered anti-Semitic.[43] Outright anti-Semitic views are voiced by Germany's extreme-right parties.

For a time, the neo-Nazi Nationaldemokratische Partei Deutschlands (NPD, National democratic party of Germany), founded in 1964, did well and even entered several state parliaments. The government considered banning the NPD on account of its ideology, but the Federal Constitutional Court rejected this measure in 2017. Banning the party, the court reasoned, would not change the mindset of its members, who would either simply form a new movement under a different name or flock to other right-wing groups. The most important of new extreme-right political entities has been the Alternative für Deutschland (AfD, Alternative for Germany). Founded in 2013, AfD quickly showed surprising strength in local elections. In the national elections of 2017, the AfD managed to get 12.6 percent of the vote, and with ninety-four seats in the Bundestag it became the largest opposition party. For the first time in postwar German history, a rightist party had entered the German parliament. The AfD describes itself as "Euro-sceptic" and denies being anti-Semitic, yet some of its leading members are openly anti-Jewish.[44]

Greatly concerned about anti-Jewish attitudes among Germany's Muslims, a few Jews have joined the AfD. "The AfD is the only party that focuses on Muslims' hatred of Jews without playing it down," declared Dimitri Schulz, who emigrated to Germany from the Soviet Union in 1989. Schulz has announced the formation of a Jewish group within the AfD on his Facebook page, which also contains descriptions of anti-Semitic remarks and actions, especially from recently arrived asylum-seeking Muslims. Several Jewish leaders have admonished German Jews not to make common cause with an extreme-right organization whose members have downplayed, and at times denied, the Holocaust.[45] At a

Kristallnacht commemoration held at the Rykestrasse synagogue in Berlin on November 8, 2018, with German chancellor Angela Merkel in attendance, Josef Schuster, head of the Zentralverein, called on Germans to fight xenophobia and anti-Muslim sentiments and to oppose in particular the "spiritual arsonists" who belittle the Holocaust and mock its victims and survivors.[46]

Seeking to prevent a further growth in anti-Semitism and anti-Jewish violence, in November 2015 the Central Council of Jews in Germany urged the imposition of an upward limit on the number of refugees accepted in Germany. This idea was widely popular, and in October 2017 Chancellor Merkel indeed agreed to limit the number of asylum seekers allowed to enter Germany each year to two hundred thousand.

The Jewish activist Shahak Shapira, who was born in Israel but came to Germany at the age of fourteen, has strongly denounced this view. Not so long ago, she pointed out, German Jews begged for admission at the borders of the Netherlands and Switzerland, but, instead of granting them protection against Nazi fury, these countries increased the number of their border guards. Had Anne Frank not been refused admission to the United States, today she would be a grandmother in Boston. German Jews, Shapira argues, should consider the stream of Muslim refugees as an opportunity to improve relations between Jews and Muslims.[47] Sounding a more alarmist note, in late May 2019 Commissioner Klein suggested that Jews should not wear their skullcaps everywhere in public. Soon thereafter activists in Berlin organized a "Berlin Wears Kippah" campaign. Interior minister Horst Seehofer termed it "unacceptable" for German Jews to have to hide their faith.[48]

Despite the continued manifestation of anti-Jewish sentiments and occasional violence against Jews throughout the postwar years, for Jews from eastern Europe Germany remained an attractive destination, and, following the disintegration of the Soviet Union in 1990 and the resulting economic hardships, tens of thousands found a new home in Germany. The new attitude toward Jews had helped persuade the German government to open its doors to Jews from the former Soviet Union. Before the Berlin Wall came down in 1989, about 25,000 Jews lived in the Federal Republic of Germany (GFR) and another 500 or so in Communist East Germany. Most of the latter were elderly, and their numbers were diminishing. The opening of the borders, and the flood of immigration from the east, reversed all that and fundamentally changed the character of Jewish life in Germany. By 2001 about 80,000 Russian Jews had been admitted by the GFR as refugees. Not touched by the Holocaust, they have not felt guilty for living in Germany and do not regard Germans as the "children of perpetrators." Many have no interest in the Jewish religion, live in religiously mixed marriages, and have not joined official congregations. In 2010 there were 108 Jewish communities with about 105,000 members, about 80 percent of them from the former Soviet Union. Today the total number of Jews living in Germany is estimated at double that number, and possibly as large as 300,000. Still, the Jews of Germany constitute fewer than 0.3 percent of the total population.[49]

Living in the Land of the Murderers

The overall picture of postwar Jewish life in Germany would not be complete without allowing individual Jews to tell their own stories. What is it like for them to live in the land of the murderers? How serious are the problems created by anti-Semitism? Is it possible to have normal relations with the new generations of Germans?

The Jews who have written about their experiences in postwar Germany are not average individuals. For the most part they are writers, intellectuals, or public officials. And yet this select group is characterized by a healthy diversity. Some are happy. Others have reservations. Still others have left the country, citing a variety of reasons, the most common being a dearth of civic courage, the exaggerated importance of authority, and the lack of emotional warmth in the new Germany.[50]

Julius H. Schoeps is the son of Hans Joachim Schoeps, the German Jewish patriot who despite his Jewishness wanted to be accepted by the Nazis and, eventually, deeply disillusioned, went into exile in Sweden. After the war Schoeps took his family back to Germany. Young Julius attended German schools, acquired a PhD in history—specializing in German-Jewish history—and now serves as a professor at the University of Potsdam. As Julius Schoeps sees it, there have been more than enough reasons for him *not* to stay in Germany. Jewish cemeteries have been vandalized, respectable persons complain about political correctness which in Germany requires feeling guilty about Nazi crimes, and anti-Semitic incidents happen here and there. He decided, however, not to focus on such matters and instead build a satisfactory life as a Jew in Germany. He is happily married, has close German friends, and finds his career fulfilling. Schoeps describes himself as "a citizen of the German Federal Republic, who is Jewish [though not religiously] but is strongly influenced by a Protestant milieu, and who feels and thinks German."[51]

Schoeps acknowledges two difficulties with this position. First, much of the outside Jewish world finds it difficult to accept that Jews have chosen to live in post-Holocaust Germany, and those who do are made to feel defensive about their decision. Second, he experiences a "diffuse feeling of guilt" in dwelling among the people (or the children of people) who tried to destroy European Jewry. As a historian he has developed distance between himself and these horrendous events, but, he acknowledges, a strong sense of unease remains. Despite these difficulties, Schoeps says he leads a satisfying life. As a result of his origins and education, he is at home in the German language and German culture. Germany is where he belongs.[52]

The Holocaust literary critic Marcel Reich-Ranicki was a Polish-born Jew educated in Germany and was deported to Poland in 1938. His parents were killed at the Treblinka extermination camp; he survived, being hidden by a sympathetic family outside of Warsaw. After a stay in England, Reich-Ranicki returned to Germany in 1956. He wrote for the weekly *Die Zeit* (Time) and became literary editor of the daily *Frankfurter Allgemeine Zeitung* (General newspaper of Frankfurt), generally regarded as the best newspaper in Germany. In 1988 he launched the television program *Das literarische Quartet* (The literary quartet), which featured lively debates between the host and his literary guests, and Reich-Ranicki soon became known as the "literary pope of Germany." He received numerous medals, including the Goethe Prize for Literary Achievement in 2002. In his autobiography he writes that he is neither a Pole nor a German; his fatherland, he states, is "German literature."[53] Reich-Ranicki died in 2013 at age ninety-three.[54]

Ralph Giordano was a Holocaust survivor whose family was hidden in a German friend's cellar in Hamburg. After the war Giordano became a highly respected journalist and public intellectual. He died in 2014. When asked in 1979 why he continued to live in Germany, he answered: "Here I was born and have grown up, and here I live now for more than half a century. . . . I stay because the German language is part of my Heimat [home]; it is my tool, my anguish, and my delight. It is impossible for me to write or even think in another language." Giordano acknowledged that German democracy was afflicted by many problems, but noted that the "ugly German" (the pejorative term applied to Germans who are loud and boisterous while submissive to authority) was not the only German. He was comforted to know that many Germans of all ages detested the "ugly German" as vehemently as he did.[55]

Ignatz Bubis, born in 1927 in Breslau (today Wroclaw), survived a Nazi labor camp and returned to Germany after his liberation. He served as chairman of the Jewish community of Frankfurt and, later, of the Central Council of Jews (CCJ), the governing body of German Jews, from 1992 until his death in 1999. Bubis called himself a German citizen of the Jewish faith. Stressing the continuity with prewar Jewry, he said he was both Jewish and German. Until the end of the Weimar Republic, German culture had been Jewish and Jewish culture had been German. His rootedness in this culture, Bubis maintained, made life in Germany important for him. The Holocaust had destroyed normality in the relations between Jews and Germans, but Bubis harbored the hope that the passage of time would restore it. Toward the end of his life, Bubis grew increasingly concerned about the resurgence of extreme-right parties, worrying that the desired normal existence of Jews in Germany appeared more distant than ever. Possibly this sense of disappointment, as well as the vandalizing of the grave of his CCJ predecessor Heinz Galinski, induced Bubis's request to be buried in Israel.[56]

Henryk M. Broder was born in Poland in 1946. His parents were Holocaust survivors who moved the family to Cologne in 1958 on account of unabated Polish anti-Semitism. Today he is a journalist, author, and TV personality with a sardonic, not to say cynical, temperament. In his 2004 book *A Jew in the New Germany*, Broder expressed skepticism about the genuineness of Germany's concern with the Holocaust: "The further the Third Reich [and its crimes] recedes into history, the more jobs it creates. Hordes of historians, scholars, and researchers dissect and analyze the interstices of every last detail, however marginal it may seem. Scores of educators, journalists, and artists pick up the fragments, put them in place, and market them as curricula, articles, and works of art. You could say that, fifty years after its demise, the Third Reich has become a mammoth welfare-to-work program that translates into profit for countless small-business contractors."[57]

In the early 1990s the German government agreed to construct a memorial for the murdered Jews of Europe in the center of Berlin, and a competition was announced for a suitable design. Broder considers what happened next an example of the damage the Holocaust has done to the collective German psyche. Some 2000 sculptors and architects submitted 528 models. In Broder's view, Germany had not seen "a more impressive collection of kitsch, banality, and nonsense escalated to the point of absurdity since the 1936 Olympics." The competition, he argued, had demonstrated the impossibility of responding to the Holocaust with a memorial.[58] While Broder's ideas often are criticized as exaggerated and shrill, his conclusion that the Berlin memorial has failed to achieve its purpose is shared by others, both inside and outside of Germany. The memorial, designed by the American architect Peter Eisenman, consists of 2,711 slabs of stone, and no one has been able to put forth a convincing explanation for how these stelae memorialize the murdered Jews.

Although Broder is a member of the Jewish community of Berlin, he considers himself neither a genuine German nor a real Jew: "There are Jews, 'passport Germans' like myself, who can pass for Germans and who resolve their identity crises by boasting of their Jewishness at every opportunity it may be. To me, that is senseless babble from people who have nothing else to take pride in. You can only take pride in the things you can control. I have as much control over my Jewishness as I have over my eye color or shoe size. And when I think about it, I would really rather not be a Jew."[59] Broder is critical of his fellow intellectuals for "their free-floating sympathy toward the People of the Third World," which makes them side with the Palestinians over Israel to the point of believing that without Israel there would be no conflict in the Middle East. Broder does not want Israel to be beyond criticism, but he points out that the same people who find fault with Israel's settlement policy have no problem with China's occupation of Tibet or Turkey's suppression of the Kurds. They will honor any despot "as long as he decorates himself with the 'anti-imperialist' label." They are willing to overlook any atrocities as long as they are committed by their ideological allies.[60]

Richard Chaim Schneider was born in 1957 in Munich to parents who survived the Holocaust; now he works as a journalist. He is unhappy about the residues of anti-Semitism in Germany. He receives letters telling him to go to where he belongs, a common remark of German xenophobes. His parents, he says, invented elaborate justifications for living in Germany—they did not want Hitler's prophecy of making Germany *judenrein* (clear of Jews) to come true; they sought by their presence to create an eternal remembrance of Nazi crimes. The young Schneider has no use for such subterfuges. He lives in Germany today because of his family, his friends, his work, and, last but not least, the German language.

He was born in Germany and, on the whole, feels quite happy there. "Let us face it," he writes. "We live in Germany because we are doing well here. We are as materialistic and selfish as other Germans. They do not want to endanger their precious skin and therefore oppose a German military role abroad. We Jews feel the same way when we do not want to risk our lives in Israel."[61]

Some Jews have decided to leave the country in which they grew up. Lea Fleischmann, born in a DP camp, became a teacher in Germany, but she eventually gave up on trying to change the political attitudes of Germans, especially what she regarded as their servility to authority. In 1979 she emigrated to Israel. Discussing her decision to leave Germany in a widely read book *Dies ist nicht mein Land* (This is not my country), Fleischmann now calls herself a Jewess with a German passport, rather than a German of the Jewish faith.[62]

Yasha Mounk was born in 1982. His Jewish mother had left Poland for Germany in 1969, and Yasha lived his youth in what he calls "reasonably idyllic places" like Munich and Freiburg. He attended college in England, but German, he notes, is the only language he speaks without an accent. Growing up in Germany, the threat of anti-Semitic violence was distant and abstract: it no more defined his childhood than would the fear of being mugged for a kid growing up in an affluent American suburb. What made Mounk conclude he would never be a German was not violence or hatred but benevolence:

> Far from being openly anti-Semitic, most Germans I met were so keen to prove that they weren't anti-Semitic that they treated me with the kind of nervous niceness usually reserved for the mentally handicapped or the terminally ill. Driven by misplaced guilt and embarrassment about the unspeakable things their ancestors had done to mine, they ended up feeling limitlessly sorry for me. The effect of their pity and their virtue was to leave . . . [me] with the sense that I couldn't possibly have anything in common with them.[63]

Mounk felt distinctly unhappy when confronted with this philo-Semitism, and when he was offered an academic post in the United States he left Germany. He is now a lecturer at Harvard University and the host of the podcast *The Good Fight*.

As Mounk correctly observes, all things Jewish are currently fashionable in Germany. Germans attend Hebrew classes. Literary events include the recitation of a few choice poems in Yiddish. Blue-eyed Germans perform klezmer music before awed audiences. Jewish contributors to German culture such as the painters Marc Chagall and Otto Dix, as well as the writers Heinrich Heine and Stefan Zweig, have also attained a new popularity. There is a widespread interest in Jewish studies. Some fifty scholars occupy chairs in Jewish history at German universities.[64] Every year hundreds of new books are published on various Jewish subjects. Thousands of young Israelis spend several years in Berlin, enjoying the cosmopolitan atmosphere of the city. At times the good intentions Germans display toward Jews have a humorous aspect. For Brotherhood Week, the mayor of a small town in Bavaria held a buffet for which he ordered kosher meat served on sandwiches with cheese.[65]

Meanwhile, what has not been on the rise in Germany in recent years are Jewish traditions themselves. Between 1951 and 1994, 73 percent of all Jewish marriages involved a non-Jewish partner, the highest such ratio in the world.[66] No figures are available for more recent years, but the situation is unlikely to be fundamentally different. The majority of the children in mixed marriages are not raised as Jews; thus, there is the distinct possibility of the eventual disappearance of the Jewish population of Germany.[67]

Feeling at Home?

After Auschwitz, one might say, it would be rash to expect normality in the relations between Jews and Germans. The historian Dan Diner, who teaches in Israel and Germany, speaks of a negative symbiosis, by which he means that the life of Germany's Jews is determined in a negative fashion by their relationship with non-Jewish Germans and the Holocaust.[68] Encounters between German Jews and non-Jews are characterized by a self-consciousness and distrust that is considerably less prevalent in other countries. When an American Jew meets a non-Jew, it has been said, he generally will feel at ease unless that person manifests anti-Semitic attitudes. In Germany it is the other way around: the German Jew will be cautious about the meeting until the German has demonstrated that he is *not* an anti-Semite.[69]

The German politician and one-time foreign minister Joshka Fischer has called the question whether German Jews will once again feel "at home" in Germany a test of German democracy and its ability to create an open and tolerant society.[70] On the other hand, the German-Jewish author Rafael Seligmann has put part of the blame for the absence of a natural German-Jewish relationship on the Jews themselves, because, he argues, they live in a self-imposed new "ghetto": they have chosen to live in Germany without being part of German cultural life. Seligmann wants the Jews in post-Holocaust Germany to understand themselves as German Jews and end their isolation: "Jews have been part of German society for a thousand years, [and] it's about time Jews as well as non-Jews finally accept this."[71]

The opposite point of view has been argued by the German-Jewish writer and poet Max Czollek in his 2018 book *Desintegriert Euch* (Disintegrate yourselves), which attracted considerable attention from Jews and non-Jews alike. Czollek called on Germany's Jews as well as on other minority groups to stop trying to fit in and embrace their "otherness" so that Germany could become a truly multicultural, pluralistic society. In a conversation with the *New York Times* correspondent Valeriya Safronova in the fall of 2019, Czollek conceded that his link to the Jewish people was "extremely thin," but added that he was anxious to renew the thread with his ancestors. It remains unclear whether many Jews in today's Germany will share Czollek's outlier position.[72]

The historian Michael Wolffsohn appears to be the only German-Jewish intellectual who considers his living in Germany unproblematic. Wolffsohn was born in Palestine in 1947 to German-Jewish parents; in 1954, when he was seven, the family returned to Germany. Now a professor of contemporary history at the Universität der Bundeswehr (University of the armed forces) in Munich, Wolffsohn argues that the crimes of the former Nazi regime are no reason why modern Germans—Jews included—cannot be proud of their country. Hence Wolffsohn calls himself a "German-Jewish patriot."[73]

For most other Jews living in Germany, life is not so simple. Reminders of an uncertain rapport are all around them. The fact that well-meaning Germans continue to refer to the Jews in their midst as "fellow citizens" (*Mitbürger*) rather than simply as "citizens" is one of many reasons they consider the current German-Jewish relationship far from normal. To this day Germans hesitate to call someone a *Jude* (Jew) because of the negative connotation this term acquired during the Nazi era. Salomon Korn, head of the Jewish community of Frankfurt and a vice president of the Zentralrat, has suggested that an ordinary state of affairs could be considered achieved if German-Jewish normalcy is no longer a topic of discussion and German Jews are no longer seen as responsible for the politics of the State of Israel or the World Jewish Congress.[74] It remains an open question whether and when post-Holocaust Germany will ever reach this happy state of affairs.[75]

7

Being Jewish in Communist East Germany

According to the census of October 29, 1946, more than a year after the end of the war, some 4,500 Jews lived in the Sowjetische Besatzungszone, or SBZ (Soviet zone of occupation). This figure was incomplete. It did not include most of the Jewish Communists who had returned to Germany from exile abroad and who considered themselves German Communists rather than Jews and whose number would eventually reach about 3,500.[1] These "non-Jewish Jews," as the Marxist writer Isaac Deutscher referred to them,[2] denied their Jewishness, opposed Zionism, and embraced an assimilation far more self-effacing than that practiced by German Jews before 1933.[3] During the Weimar era, these individuals had fought for the Communist society that they believed would do away with all ethnic, social, and religious discrimination. Now, the part of Germany liberated by the Red Army promised to be the place where this Marxist utopia could be realized. Thus, in the Soviet zone these returnees began to recover the sense of community that the Communist party of Germany had provided for them. Once again, belonging to the party was an auspicious substitute for the biological family most of them had lost.[4]

Emergence of an "Anti-Zionist" Communist Regime

In October 1949 the SBZ became the German Democratic Republic (GDR). It functioned as an eastern bloc state, governed by the Sozialistische Einheitspartei, or SED (Socialist Unity party), that had been created in April 1946 out of the forced unification of the Social Democrats and the Communist party. From its beginning the SED was a Stalinist party following the Soviet model of a totalitarian regime that sought to dominate all aspects of life. Other parties were granted a nominal existence, but the SED's controlling role in the GDR was beyond dispute. The "shield and sword" of the party was the Ministerium für Staatssicherheit (Ministry for state security), known as Stasi, the regime's secret police. In addition to its 102,000 full-time personnel, the Stasi had as many as a half-million informers, known as Inoffizielle Mitarbeiter, or IMs (inofficial associates). The sway of the Stasi was worse than that of the Gestapo. The Nazi secret police had 40,000 officials watching a country of 80 million; the Stasi employed 102,000 to control 17 million.[5]

Officially, the East German state regarded the Jews' fate as proof of the barbaric character of "German fascism," but otherwise did not recognize the existence of a Jewish question. Anti-Semitism was a problem of capitalist societies, a tool of capitalist rulers to divert attention from the class struggle.[6] Since the German working class was anti-Fascist, by definition it did not bear guilt for the Holocaust. Indeed, anti-Semitism was attributed to only a small minority of Nazis who had lorded it over the German population. The twelve years of Nazi rule were seen as a kind of foreign tyranny. This view of the Nazi era corresponded to the wishes of the majority of Germans, both East and West, who saw themselves as victims and therefore not responsible for Auschwitz.[7]

This also meant that the GDR did not have pay restitution to the Jews. The victims of Fascism, the veteran Communist leader Walter Ulbricht declared in 1948, were now building their new state, and it would be ridiculous if they were to pay recompense to themselves: "And the Jews? Well, we have always been opposed to the Jewish capitalists in the same measure as to the non-Jewish ones. And if Hitler had not deprived them of their property, we would have done it."[8] In October 1945 the former Communist party member Jenny Matern objected to financial aid for Jews on the grounds that they were only interested in money. Negotiations with Israeli diplomats about a financial payment to the emerging Jewish state ended in failure.[9]

With the coming of the Cold War and the proclamation of the State of Israel, SED antipathy toward Jews only increased. The Cold War heightened the foment surrounding the purported links between Jews and West German imperialism. As for the State of Israel, the Soviet Union had in fact recognized the Jewish state on May 17, 1948, three days after it had come into being. Not only that: arms from Czechoslovakia, a Soviet bloc state, had played a crucial role in Israel's success in the Arab-Israeli War of 1948. Apparently, Stalin had believed that Israel's existence would help decrease British influence in the Middle East. But, by the end of 1948, as Israel emerged as a close ally of the Western powers, the Soviet Union switched sides and turned toward the Arab states. Soviet Jews were now denounced as "bourgeois nationalists," the term for Zionists, and for being "rootless cosmopolitans"—that is, internationalists. Ever since his struggle with Trotsky, a Jew, Stalin had had a residual fear of Jewish intellectuals, especially their internationalism.[10] After World War II, his disdain for Jews became even more pronounced, and during the last years of his life his anti-Semitism turned into an obsession.[11] Rootless "cosmopolitans" now became the code word for "Jews."[12] Both Zionists and cosmopolitans were held to promote the interests of American imperialism. This campaign was a replay of the drive by the Jewish sections of the Soviet Communist party in the 1920s, the so-called *Yevsektsiya* that had sought the destruction of Zionism and traditional Jewish life. Led by Simon Dimanstein, the Jewish cells staged show trials of offenders and confiscated the property of Jewish synagogues, hospitals, orphanages, and Hebrew schools. Simon Dimanstein himself was liquidated during the Stalinist show trials of the 1930s.

The anti-Jewish campaign after World War II also began with virulent attacks on Israel and Jewish culture. Publication of Yiddish books and newspapers was banned, and in April 1949 five of the most prominent Yiddish writers were imprisoned, with further arrests during subsequent months. The Soviet regime disbanded the Jewish Anti-Fascist Committee, under whose auspices the Yiddish actor Solomon Mikhoels and the Yiddish poet Itzik Feffer had visited the West in 1943 to build support for the Soviet war effort. The trial of the Jewish counterrevolutionaries ended with the execution of thirteen Yiddish writers on August 12, 1952. At the trial of Lászlo Rajk, the non-Jewish leader of the Hungarian Communist party in September 1949, three of Rajk's six codefendants were Jews. All of them were convicted of participating in a "worldwide Zionist plot" that had conspired with Yugoslavia's president, Josip Broz Tito, to overthrow the Hungarian Communist regime. One defendant "confessed" to having been a member of a "Trotskyite Zionist movement."[13]

Against this background, in November 1949 the SED began a purge of alleged Titoists, Trotskyists, and those adhering to "Social Democratism," all considered "agents of imperialism, no matter what flag they flew."[14] The Berlin Airlift, started in June 1948 to supply West Berlin, which was isolated by a Soviet-organized blockade, had come to an end in September 1949, four months after the blockade was lifted. Now that the international situation had become less tense, party head Walter Ulbricht used this drive for ideological purity to consolidate his centralized rule. Some 150,00 party members were expelled, most of them former Social Democrats. Those who had spent the war years in the West were particularly suspect. They were charged with having had ties to Noel Field, a U.S. State Department employee and Soviet spy, who, it was said, had served American imperialism and the subversive Marshal Tito. A Jewish origin was an additional handicap. In the files of those to be investigated by the Stasi, Jewish or Jewish-bourgeois descent was often noted. Jews were considered of doubtful loyalty because they had sympathy for Zionism.[15] Jewish Communists were also considered too independent in their thinking.[16]

Soviet bloc anti-Semitism reached its peak with the Prague show trials of fourteen Communist party leaders of Czechoslovakia in

November 1952. Eleven of the defendants were of Jewish origin, a fact noted in the indictment. The defendants were charged with participating in a "Jewish nationalist imperialist Zionist conspiracy" aimed at restoring capitalism. For defendants who had Czech-sounding names, the indictment gave in parentheses their original Jewish names—for Rudolf Slansky (Salzmann), for André Simone (Katz). Each name was followed by a designation, such as "son of a big merchant" or "son of a manufacturer." The defendants were forced to testify that their Jewish origin had caused them to become estranged from the working class. One confessed that his upbringing in a "Jewish bourgeois family" had led him into the camp of the enemies of Socialism. Another admitted working for the U.S. Overseas News Agency, "an organ of Jewish capitalists." In a Stalinist version of the *Protocols of the Elders of Zion*, prosecutors alleged the existence of a worldwide secret plot, led by a cabal of Western dignitaries meeting in a closed-door conference in Washington, DC, in 1947, where they had concocted the Morgenthau Plan. In 1944 U.S. secretary of the treasury Henry Morgenthau had proposed eliminating Germany's ability to wage war by destroying its arms industry and any other economic enterprise that could aid the production of weapons. In the Communist version of this plan, "Zionist organizations" in Czechoslovakia would carry out espionage and economic sabotage. Among the alleged conspirators was the Jewish charitable organization American Jewish Joint Distribution Committee, known as "the Joint," which had sent packages to needy Jews in Europe. The fact that the accused Jewish Communists had been self-hating Jews and sworn enemies of Israel was no hindrance to convicting them of "Jewish bourgeois nationalism."[17]

Among the Jewish defendants of the Slansky trial who were hanged on December 3, 1952, was Otto Katz, listed as André Simone. Known for his many pseudonyms (said to have numbered twenty-one) and his seductive character as a bon vivant, Katz had been a highly effective operative in the disinformation campaigns of the Communist International (Comintern) in the 1930s. He had also targeted Hollywood for its money and political support. Known there as Rudolph Breda, Katz served as the model for the anti-Fascist hero Victor Lazlo in the film *Casablanca* (1942) and for the central figure of Kurt Müller in Lillian Hellman's play *Watch on the Rhine* (1941).[18] As a German Communist party member, Katz had worked closely with Albert Norden, a rabbi's son who served in the SED's politburo from 1958 to 1967, eventually becoming of one the highest-ranking German Jewish Communists in the East Communist regime. The execution of his close friend Otto Katz as a traitor is said to have devastated him and to have challenged his loyalty to the Communist cause. But Norden, like most Communists, got over his crisis of belief with the help of the soothing conviction that, in the long run, the party is always right.[19]

On January 4, 1952, the GDR official newspaper *Neues Deutschland* (New Germany) published an official SED Central Committee statement summing up the lessons of the Slansky trial and denouncing the "Slansky bandits."[20] The evidence had proven that American imperialism had used the State of Israel and Zionist organizations in the people's republics to carry out espionage. Among those charged was the non-Jewish Paul Merker, a German Communist who had spent the Nazi years in exile in Mexico and had been expelled from the SED in 1950. According to the report, there was no doubt that Merker was a Zionist and an agent of the "American financial oligarchy." He had advocated for the creation of a Jewish state and compensation for Jewish capitalists in order to "enable U.S. finance capital to penetrate Germany." Merker had thus revealed himself as an enemy of the Soviet Union and his own people.[21]

During the winter of 1952/53, arrests, dismissals from jobs, and expulsions from the SED multiplied. Among the leading Jewish Communists to be expelled was Gerhart Eisler, a prominent member of the German Communist party during the Weimar period and head of the GDR news bureau.[22] In Dresden about 10 percent of Jewish Communists were arrested.[23] Members of

German Jewish communities were accused of being Zionists and working for the American CIA. Synagogue offices were searched and files confiscated. The magazine of the Jewish community of Berlin, *Der Weg* (The path), was banned. On January 6, 1953, Julius Meyer, the head of the Jewish community of Berlin and an SED delegate in the Volkskammer (East German parliament), was interrogated and pressured both to endorse the death sentences of the Slansky trial and to condemn Israel as a Fascist state. He refused (without repercussions). Soon thereafter the Communist regime divided the Jewish community of Berlin into "West" and "East."

On January 13, 1953, Stalin ordered the arrest of nine prominent doctors from Moscow who had been attending to major Soviet leaders. Six of them were Jews. In what would become known as the "Doctors' Plot," the nine were accused of being members of the Joint, "the international Jewish bourgeois nationalistic terrorist organization," and of having conspired to poison the Communist leadership. Panic spread among the Jewish population of East Germany. Meyer and the heads of the Jewish communities of Leipzig, Dresden, Halle, and Erfurt were among those who fled to the West. Among the four hundred Jews who decamped from the GDR in January was Leo Zuckermann, chief of staff for head of state Wilhelm Pieck.[24] His fellow Jewish Communist Alexander Abusch explained Zuckermann's defection as a result of his "long-standing Jewish-chauvinist outlook."[25] The large exodus further diminished the size of the numerically small Jewish communities in East Germany. In Leipzig the loss was half of the membership, leaving only 140 mostly aged Jews.[26]

The death of the Soviet dictator on March 5, 1953, may have prevented more severe anti-Jewish measures, but the anti-Zionist campaign continued. Among those arrested was Paul Merker, a non-Jew whose heretical support of the State of Israel and insistence that Jews were entitled to restitution rendered him politically unreliable. At one time a member of the SED politburo, he was now charged with being a cosmopolitan and in the pay of the Zionists in order to destroy Communism in Eastern Europe. Communist leaders probably chose a non-Jew as the key defendant in the alleged Zionist plot in order to not appear openly anti-Semitic. Convicted in a secret trial, Merker stayed in an East German jail until 1956, when he was released in the wake of Nikita Khrushchev's speech denouncing Stalin's crimes. His release was kept secret, however, and he was never again given an official position. Meanwhile, blurring the distinction between Jews and Zionists, the purge of most Jews from leading positions in the East German Communist regime remained in force. Thus, while the SED paid lip service to the new line coming out of Moscow, the party kept up its anti-Semitic policy by linking Jews to humanity's exploiters and imperialists.[27]

East German policy toward Israel and the Jewish question largely followed Soviet foreign policy. Hence, from 1953 on, the anti-Zionist position reigned supreme. The Zionists were regarded as a fifth column against which the regime counseled continuing vigilance. Much of this obsessive anti-Zionism was formulated by Jewish Communists such as Hermann Axen and Albert Norden.[28] At the outbreak of the 1967 Six-Day War, the GDR condemned Israel for its "aggression" and avowed its solidarity with the Arab states. In August 1973 the SED and the PLO signed an agreement committing the GDR to "material support" of the PLO in the joint struggle against "imperialism and Zionism." Between 1976 and 1982 the Stasi and the GDR defense ministry provided the PLO with thousands of modernized Kalashnikov assault rifles and grenades free of charge, as "solidarity" goods.[29] It was hoped, among other things, that this support would encourage the Arab states to recognize the GDR, an expectation that indeed proved correct.[30] A statement adopted by the SED Central Committee on April 6, 1973, charged that "international Zionism, supported by influential groups of American monopoly capitalism, constituted one of the most active elements of anti-Communism and anti-Sovietism," and in fact had taken on a "terroristic character."[31] On November 10, 1975, the GDR, together with all other Soviet bloc nations (except Rumania), voted for the U.N. resolution that Zionism is racism.[32]

Purge of the Jews from Communist Ranks

The purge of Communists who had spent the Hitler years in the West affected a large number of Jews. One of the high points of this campaign was the dissolution of the Communist front organization Vereinigung der Verfolgten des Naziregims, or VVN (Association of the persecuted by the Nazi regime) in February 1953. The official explanation was that the new GDR political order had destroyed all remnants of Fascism and therefore had made the VVN's existence superfluous. The real reason was probably the large number of Jews in the VVN, and their unwillingness to denounce Israel. On January 21 *Neues Deutschland* had reported the expulsion of several leading Jewish VVN members who were branded "Zionist agents."[33] Once the VVN was disbanded a month later, politically reliable VVN members were channeled into the newly formed Komitee der antifaschistischen Widerstandskämpfer (Committee of anti-Fascist resistance fighters), which included only one Jew in its leadership and was appropriately hostile to Israel.[34] Jews were also excluded from other Communist front organizations, though anti-Jewish measures in the GDR never reached the degree of intensity that would have threatened the lives of Jewish functionaries, as in the Soviet Union. The temporal proximity of the Holocaust and the openness to the West in Berlin limited the SED's freedom of action and therefore ruled out show trials of Jews.[35]

Anti-Semitism had never disappeared in East Germany, and the propaganda against the so-called Zionist and capitalist Jews could not but strengthen its continued manifestation. GDR leaders outwardly rejected the idea that their policies had anything to do with anti-Semitism, claiming that West—not East—Germany was swarming with Nazis and anti-Semites, but in fact the alleged link between Jews and capitalism reinforced long-standing anti-Semitic sentiments.[36] The fact that the SED's anti-Semitic actions were motivated by political rather than racial reasons was essentially irrelevant. While the regime officially opposed expressions of animosity toward minorities, the vilification of Israel and Jewish capitalists encouraged anti-Semitic violence. There were attacks against Jewish functionaries and institutions as well as desecrations of synagogues and cemeteries.[37] The GDR press did not report these incidents.[38]

A few Jewish Communists are said to have been unhappy about the harsh and crude attacks on the Jewish homeland. In public practically all of them went along with the anti-Zionist line, and at times excelled at extolling it. When affected directly by the purges, most of them affirmed their loyalty to the party, and many of them continued these declarations of fidelity to the Socialist cause even after their positions had become untenable and they had escaped to the West. A case in point is Markus Wolf, who was head of the Stasi's foreign intelligence section and for thirty-four years the Stasi's number-two man. After his flight to the West in 1990 he declared: "We fought for a combination of socialism and freedom, a noble objective that failed utterly but which I still believe is possible. . . . I am no defector."[39]

Alexander Abusch, born to Jewish parents in Cracow in 1902, had been a German Communist since the party's founding in 1918. In 1933 he emigrated to France and later spent most of the war years in exile in Mexico serving as editor in chief of the magazine *Freies Deutschland* (Free Germany). In 1946 he returned to Communist East Germany and rapidly rose in rank. He served as deputy minister of culture from 1954 to 1956 and deputy head of the council of ministers from 1961 to 1971. After the GDR's downfall in 1990, it became known that he had also been a longtime Stasi informant.

During the 1950 and 1952 purges of Communists who had lived in the capitalist West, Abusch successfully undertook self-criticism. In an essay entitled "My Errors in Mexico and their Lessons for the Present," he admitted that he and his comrades had not practiced enough "revolutionary vigilance."[40] Abusch had been a member of the German-Jewish organization Menorah, but he now declared himself liberated from the influence of his Jewish descent.[41] In a report on the activities of German Communists in Mexico, Abusch blamed himself for not having been more forthright in his opposition to Merker, who, in his articles for *Freies Deutschland*, had tried to promote "the interests of monopoly capitalism and Zionism."[42]

Seeking to minimize his own wrongdoing, Abusch denounced several of his Mexican fellow exiles to the Stasi. Impressed by Abusch's willingness to betray his erstwhile comrades, the Stasi enlisted him to "expose enemies of the party and the working class," assigning him to spy on his former companions in Mexico. To be on the safe side, the Stasi also established a file on Abusch that included damaging material, a routine practice, especially with Jewish agents. In this way Abusch weathered a major crisis and was able to continue his rising career as a Communist functionary. He became known as a rigid dogmatist who always toed the party line. His colleague Alfred Kantorowicz called him *"Parteigendarm"* (the policeman of the party)[43]—a reputation he maintained until his death in 1982.[44]

Most other Jewish Communists did not weather the purges as successfully. Rudolf Herrnstadt was born in 1903, the son of a wealthy Jewish family in Silesia. Forced by his father to work in the business, young Rudolf became a dedicated Communist. In 1939 he took refuge in the Soviet Union, where he was active in the National Committee for a Free Germany. Returning to Germany after the war, Herrnstadt was made editor in chief of the *Berliner Zeitung* and later of the official party newspaper *Neues Deutschland*. He also advanced to the SED politburo, thus becoming the highest-ranking Communist functionary of Jewish descent. But Herrnstadt's career came to an end in 1953, when he was denounced as a "Jewish agent" for having organized a "hostile party faction" aimed at gaining the party leadership. On July 26 he was expelled from the SED Central Committee and the politbureau. The SED started disciplinary proceedings against him, and the central control commission of the party pressured him into acknowledging his guilt. Complying with this demand, on August 31, 1953, he composed a lengthy memorandum that read in part: "I hereby declare that I fully accept the decision of the fifteenth plenary meeting of the central committee, especially those parts that concern me." As editor in chief of *Neues Deutschland*, he had accepted articles characterized by a Social-Democratic way of thinking that were "objectively false." In this way, Herrnstadt admitted, he had promoted a false and defeatist line, failed to support the interests of the working class, and adopted an "un-Marxist position." Furthermore, together with his comrade Wilhelm Zaisser, the head of the Stasi, he had falsely criticized the allegedly dictatorial leadership style of Walter Ulbricht, head of the party's Central Committee. This meant that he had failed to be guided by the "objective needs of the party as a whole."[45] On January 23, 1954, Herrnstadt was expelled from the SED and sidelined with a job as archivist in Merseburg.[46]

On December 1, after three months in exile in Merseburg, Herrnstadt retracted his confession. Even the possibility of expulsion from the party, he wrote in a thirty-seven-page statement of defense, would not make him admit to crimes he had not committed; it would mean lying to the party.[47] Three years later he endeavored to explain what had made him admit to the false accusations. At the time, Herrnstadt wrote, he had been convinced that he could not be more clever than the entire Central Committee. He had firmly believed that the party is always right, and he still adhered to this conviction. A Communist had to bow to party discipline at all times.[48]

After Khrushchev's speech in 1956 denouncing Stalin's crimes, Herrnstadt asked for rehabilitation, but the SED, under Ulbricht's firm control, turned him down. In a letter to Hermann Matern, a member of a commission appointed by Ulbricht to reexamine earlier disciplinary measures, Herrnstadt lamented the fact that the party, which he continued to believe in, was unwilling to grant him a hearing. The offenses of which he had been found guilty had caused his "moral and political annihilation" with ruinous consequences for him and his family.[49] In 1961, as the thaw coming out of Moscow made some headway, Herrnstadt was informed that he might be readmitted to the SED if he remained silent about the circumstances of his downfall, but he refused the offer. A year later, in what would turn out to be his last letter, he asked for help from Wladimir Semjonow, who as political advisor of the Soviet military administration in 1953 had participated in his purge, but this plea too remained unanswered. He remained a convinced Communist until his death in 1966. In a memoir published in 2008, his daughter Irina noted that her father had maintained his faith in the Soviet Union until the very end. His comrades had sought to destroy him, but he had kept faith with the party that to him was more important than anything else in the world. He had sought a more democratic SED, but he had never questioned the essential judgments of the party. A more radical reform would have been unrealistic for a dedicated Communist.[50] After the opening of the Berlin Wall and the downfall of the Communist regime in 1989, Herrnstadt was posthumously rehabilitated and restored to the SED.

The economist Jürgen Kuczynski, one of East Germany's most prominent academics, was another Jewish Communist for whom life outside the party was unimaginable. Born in 1904 as the son of a German-Jewish banker, Kuczynski joined the Communist party in 1930. After Hitler's accession, he served in the Communist underground and in 1939 took refuge in England. There he got to know the physicist Klaus Fuchs, another Communist exile, and persuaded him to work for Soviet intelligence. Kuczynski's daughter Ursula, working under the code name "Sonya," was the intermediary through whom Fuchs conveyed information about work on the atomic bomb. Returning to East Berlin in 1945, Kuczynski became president of the Society for the Study of the Culture of the Soviet Union, a post from which he was removed in 1950 by Soviet request because he was a Jew. Kuczynski attributed his dismissal solely to anti-Semitic attitudes on the part of the

Soviets. The German party, he argued as a loyal German Communist, was never anti-Semitic.[51]

On account of his outstanding professional reputation, Kuczynski was allowed a somewhat greater latitude for criticism of Communism under Stalin than that permitted to other Jewish East German Communists. His fault-finding was moderate, and yet it took six years until the publisher Aufbau-Verlag in East Berlin issued his book in 1983 containing some critical comments on Stalin. Written in the form of letters to his grandson, the work described Stalin as someone who had harmed some good and loyal comrades but had also achieved great things. He had created the Soviet Union as a strong industrial power and led his people to victory over Fascism. He had also been an outstanding propagandist for Marxism-Leninism. The building of a Socialist society was difficult, Kuczynski insisted, and it required a state under centralized leadership. Most individuals are politically naïve and given to acting against their own best interests. Hence East Germany needed the dictatorship of the proletariat to guide the country toward Socialism.[52]

In a memoir, also published in 1983, Kuczynski described himself as an "able Marxist social scientist and a reliable, useful comrade *[ein zuverlässiger, brauchbarer Genosse]*."[53] This was an accurate appraisal. Although he had occasional brushes with the SED leadership, he did well under both Walter Ulbricht and his successor Erich Honecker. When change came to the GDR in 1989, Kuczynski adjusted to that as well. While some of his erstwhile comrades now described the dark side of the SED dictatorship, Kuczynski continued to praise the GDR. He never abandoned his Communist faith, affirming: "I have not given up my childhood dream of a socialist Germany."[54]

Another convinced—not to say overzealous—Communist was Hilde Benjamin. Born Hilde Lange in 1902, she grew up in a Protestant family of converted Jews and, according to GDR nomenclature, was thus one generation away from being of Jewish descent. Lange studied law, and during the Weimar years was a practicing attorney of the Rote Hilfe (Red help), a Communist legal aid society. The Nazis, of course, considered her a Jew, and when they assumed power she lost her right to practice law. She managed to survive the war; her husband, Georg Benjamin, the brother of the writer Walter Benjamin, perished in the concentration camp Mauthausen. In 1946 she joined the SED, and from 1949 to 1953 she served as vice president of the GDR's Supreme Court. In this capacity she presided over a number of political trials. Her frequent death sentences earned her the byname "Bloody Hilde," and she was often compared to the ferocious Nazi judge Ronald Freisler, who as president of the "People's Court" was notorious for issuing verdicts of death. In 1953 Benjamin became minister of justice, a post she held until 1967, when she had to resign, ostensibly for health reasons; in fact, the politburo had concluded that her harsh verdicts and political fanaticism were impeding international recognition of the GDR. She died in 1967, an unrepentant Communist.[55]

The journalist and professor of literature Alfred Kantorowicz considered himself a "socialist humanist," an ideological outlook not easy to uphold in a state governed according to Marxist-Leninist principles. Born in 1899 as the son of a Jewish businessman, the young Kantorowicz volunteered for military service in World War I, and later studied German literature and law. For several years he worked as a journalist, and in 1931 he joined the Communist party. After Nazi storm troopers ransacked and looted his home in February 1933, Kantorowicz fled to France, where he became head of the Library of Burned Books, a collection organized by German exiles containing all books banned or burned in Nazi Germany. From 1936 to 1938 he fought in the Spanish Civil War and eventually reached safe haven in the United States. In 1946 he returned to East Berlin and founded the monthly magazine *Ost und West* (East and West), aimed at building bridges between the hostile ideologies of the Cold War. He also joined the SED and was made professor of German literature at Humboldt University, the oldest of Berlin's universities, founded in 1809 at the initiative of the famous philosopher and linguist Wilhelm von Humboldt.[56]

Kantorowicz kept a diary that mirrors his gradual disillusionment with what purported to be a new Socialist society. The realization that the so-called German Democratic Republic was ruled by a clique of men who suppressed intellectual and social freedom took time. For many years Kantorowicz believed that the rigidities and stupidities of the party bureaucracy were transitory phenomena that the party would gradually outgrow. Convinced of the "collective wisdom" of the party leadership, he supposed that any public criticism amounted to "soiling your own nest" and was therefore unacceptable. He would eventually acknowledge that the adamant beliefs that the end justified the means and that the Socialist ideal had to be implemented by force when necessary were grievous misconceptions.[57]

Kantorowicz's first public collision with the party bureaucracy took place in March 1949. The occasion was a "conversation" between the party leadership and the so-called *Kulturschaffende*, the creators of culture. GDR prime minister Otto Grotewohl delivered a lengthy discourse in which he outlined a "plan for culture"—in actuality, a rigid scheme to which all intellectuals were expected to conform. When it was Kantorowicz's turn to speak, he exclaimed that the plan for culture had nothing to do with culture, but simply amounted to a set of instructions on how to increase productivity. It deprived artists, poets, and musicians of their creative liberty, forced them into a "corset of standees at attention and yes-sayers," and amounted to agitprop.[58] Perhaps because of his renown, his comments passed without incident.

For the first time, Kantorowicz now began to think of leaving the GDR, but his friends Arnold Zweig and Ernst Bloch persuaded him to abandon this idea, arguing that the desertion of such a famous man like himself from the DDR would encourage reactionaries in the West. Meanwhile, his appointment at Humboldt University, he believed, created the possibility "to build walls around myself, to persevere in a decent manner in the ivory tower of scholarship."[59] The students had been indoctrinated by the party, but he was confident that he could *"die Mucken austreiben"* (drive out the bugs). The price to be paid for this endeavor was high; instead of building a new world of social justice, the SED under Ulbricht's leadership had done away with all freedom of discussion. On occasions like the GDR's birthday he had to compose a panegyric. To accomplish this, he wrote on October 7, 1952, "I needed an almost full bottle of Vodka."[60]

On November 27, 1952, *Neues Deutschland* reported, Slansky had been sentenced to death as a "Trotskyite-Titoist, Zionist, bourgeois-nationalist traitor, and enemy of the people of Czechoslovakia." Kantorowicz denounced the verdict of the Prague trial in his diary: "This is the language of Streicher, the mentality of Himmler, the atmosphere of interrogations by the Gestapo and of the proceedings of the people's court under Freisler. . . . Hitler, you have become popular not only in the West but also in the East."[61]

The East German uprising of June 17, 1953, affected Kantorowicz deeply. The insurgency had begun with demonstrations against unreasonable production quotas in East Berlin, but quickly spread to more than four hundred cities, towns, and villages throughout East Germany. As the outbreak expanded, it took on a more political character and revealed the breadth of discontent. Demonstrators demanded free elections and were heard to chant "Death to Communism." Russian tanks violently suppressed the rebellion, and several hundred people were killed. Kantorowicz decided to go public again. On July 3, 1953, at a meeting of the SED faction of the Humboldt University faculty, he rejected as self-serving the official explanation that the uprising was the work of Western provocateurs.[62] About three months later, he noted in his diary entry for September 30 that he would stop all work as an author and concentrate on teaching. To his friend Lion Feuchtwanger he explained that in past years he had published little and had anyway written mostly "for the drawer."

The year 1956 brought new tensions. In late October a spontaneous national uprising in Hungary demanded a more democratic political system and an end to Soviet hegemony. Twelve days later Soviet tanks rolled into Budapest and crushed the revolt; some 2,500 Hungarians died and about 200,000 fled to the West. The Hungarian revolution led Ulbricht to tighten censorship and repression. On December 30 the Communist leader wrote in *Neues Deutschland*: "The events in Hungary have taught us that when a party of the working class lets intellectuals carry out their subversion, the results are catastrophic." Kantorowicz, however, refused to sign a resolution condemning the anti-Communist uprising.

Soon thereafter Humboldt University students demonstrated for an increase in GDR financial support to avoid class overcrowding; the SED Central Committee mobilized special police units that quashed the rally. The desperate Kantorowicz doubled his efforts to encourage his students to continue to think critically. The all-important task was to build resistance to the "ideological straightjacket" that the regime sought to impose.[63] On December 2, 1956, Kantorowicz wrote in his diary: "The pressure is increasing, the air is getting more suffocating. The terror against the mind takes on increasingly unbearable forms." His Humboldt University colleague, professor of philosophy Wolfgang Harich, had been arrested and charged with "maintaining relations with the reactionary Petöfi-Circle in Hungary," an association accused of laying the intellectual foundations for the Hungarian uprising. Harich was given a prison sentence of ten years for having established a "conspiratorial counter-revolutionary group," and Kantorowicz concluded that the regime thus sought to set a warning example and intimidate any prospective dissenters.[64]

Fearing arrest, Kantorowicz once again contemplated escaping to the West, this time more seriously. He hesitated for several months, concerned that his flight would be regarded as desertion from the good fight he had waged. He also saw West Germany as a place where Nazis and their supporters held all too much sway. On the other hand, he admitted to himself, there one could at least remain silent. Hence in August 1957 Kantorowicz fled to safe haven in Hamburg. He did not feel good about this step. In the prestigious weekly *Die Zeit* he wrote on September 5: "I come not too late but too early. I should not have fled but continue to share the fate of those who over there maintain the opposition to the reign of terror of the Ulbricht-clique." Many, he conceded, would see his move as a naked attempt to save his own skin.[65]

By 1961 Kantorowicz had published his memoirs. He announced that at some future time he would describe what life is like "for a Jewish intellectual of the Left who comes as a German to the German Federal Republic."[66] This work never appeared, and we are thus left with this enigmatic reference to Kantorowicz's Jewish identity. It appears to be the only time Kantorowicz took up this issue. Like other Jewish Communists, he did not consider his Jewish origins to be of any significance. Kantorowicz died in Hamburg in 1979.

Staying in the Good Graces of the Communist Regime

It appears that only one Jewish Communist, Helmut Eschwege, insisted on affirming his Jewishness, and he would pay for this persistence. Born to Jewish parents in Hanover in 1913, Eschwege was a member of the Social Democratic party (SPD) between 1929 and 1933. In 1937 he arrived in Palestine, where he joined the local Communist party. For several years he was a civilian worker for the British Army; in 1946 he returned to East Germany as a convinced Communist and became an SED functionary. But unlike other Jewish Communists, Eschwege wanted to be regarded as of Jewish nationality—an insistence that would lead to his expulsion from the SED. Overcoming political and bureaucratic obstacles, he nonetheless succeeded in publishing several significant works on the history and persecution of German Jewry. These books, it has been said, were an indispensable source for the about-face in 1990 when the GDR finally issued an apology for its role in the crimes of the Nazis against the Jewish people.[67] Yet Eschwege also became an IM of the Stasi, and, with some interruptions, he continued to report on his Jewish acquaintances until the East Communist regime collapsed in 1989.

Eschwege's difficulties had begun in 1951, when the SED undertook enhanced scrutiny of Communist exiles who had spent the Hitler era in the West. In a questionnaire he was asked to write that his nationality was German. He objected, pleading to be listed as a Jew, on the grounds that he was unwilling to deny the Jewishness of his parents. Besides, after all he had experienced as a Jew, he felt like a Jew. He finally had to give in, but protested to the special party commission supervising the vetting. Even Stalin, he noted, had defined the Jews as a nationality. This affair, he would note in his memoirs, was the beginning of his difficulties with the SED, caused by the fact that he was a Jew who wanted to affirm this identity.[68]

Two years later, in March 1953, Eschwege was expelled from the SED. Among the reasons given were his "ideological confusion," which had made him insist on being of Jewish nationality, his visits to West Berlin which constituted a violation of party discipline, and his membership in the Jewish community of Dresden; he should have known that these petty bourgeois people constituted "class enemies." For the same reasons he also lost his job as department head at the Museum for German History. In response Eschwege told his former colleagues, "Now all Jews will be kicked out," a remark that led to the charge that he had endangered party unity, "the worst mistake a member of the party can make." Appealing to the control commission of the party, Eschwege won a victory. His position on the nationality question was found to be correct, and he was reinstated into the SED. Still, he was declared guilty of having infringed party discipline and given a reprimand.[69]

This was not the end of Eschwege's troubles. Together with some other Jewish community members, he protested against the SED's anti-Zionist campaign and its vilification of the State of Israel. In early 1965 the city of Dresden sponsored an exhibition of Arab artists that included caricatured depictions of Jews in the mode of Julius Streicher's infamous Nazi rag *Der Stürmer*. Eschwege asked the public prosecutor to bring charges of anti-Semitic agitation, which was illegal in East Germany, but the authorities declined to proceed.[70] As a result of these activities on behalf of Jews, Eschwege was accused of being a Zionist, and in January 1958 he was expelled from the SED for good. He was given a position as librarian at the Technical University of Dresden, but the GDR encumbered his scholarly work on German-Jewish history by prohibiting him from consulting relevant archives in the GDR and refusing his requests to visit libraries and archives in the West. He twice appealed his expulsion, to no avail. His attitude toward Israel, he was told, proved that he did not belong in the SED.[71] In 1982 he was asked to issue a statement condemning Israel's war in Lebanon. When he refused a prize his university had planned to bestow on him for his work on Jewish history was revoked.[72]

Eschwege was also denied permission to visit his aging mother in Israel, but eventually the GDR agreed, on the condition that he become a Stasi informant. Eschwege did not mention this quid pro quo in his memoirs, but the Stasi archives that became available after the Communist regime's downfall in 1989 document his work as an IM in great detail. He worked under the code names "Bock" and "Ferdinand." In August 1956 he was sent to West Germany, where he took photographs of important buildings in Cologne, Düsseldorf, Hamburg, and Hanover. He also provided detailed reports on members of the Jewish community in the GDR. His Stasi superiors lauded his contributions and gave him presents—money as well as books, and flowers on his birthdays. With some interruptions Eschwege continued his work for the Stasi until the last days of the GDR. Among the reports he filed in 1989 are descriptions of protest meetings in the Kreuzkirche (Church of the Holy Cross) of Dresden on October 17 that eventually led to the fall of the Berlin Wall. Eschwege's last recorded activity was a meeting with his Stasi contact on November 14, after the wall had fallen. He told the officer he had received an invitation to join the SPD and gave him a copy of the statutes of the new party.[73]

Like other Jewish Communists, Eschwege was strongly committed to the cause of Marxist Socialism. He was critical of some

GDR policies, but believed these to be aberrations that would be overcome in time. He considered leaving for the West, but friends dissuaded him by appealing to his Socialist honor: it was simply unacceptable to live in the country of the enemy of the working class. On account of the presence of so many former Nazis, there was said to be a direct continuation between the postwar Adenauer government and the Hitler regime. The fact that Eschwege shared many of the GDR's ideological positions may explain his long time working for the Stasi. He apparently hoped he could challenge the SED's rigidly negative posture toward Israel and Zionism. His Stasi connections, it has been surmised, may have also helped him gain access to materials essential for his research.[74] In retrospect it would seem that the Stasi got the better of the deal. Eschwege was one its most productive agents.

One of the ways in which Jewish Communists could try to protect their standing in the party was to confess their failings. Such was the approach taken by Leo Zuckermann. Born in 1908 in Elberfeld, Zuckermann became a Communist party member at the age of nineteen. He left Germany in 1933 and spent the Hitler years in Mexico. Among the ideological mistakes that were to follow him was his criticism of the 1939 Hitler-Stalin pact allying Europe's Fascist and Communist dictators and his advocacy supporting restitution for German Jews. Returning to East Germany, Zuckermann rapidly rose in rank, becoming chief of staff to GDR president Wilhelm Pieck. In 1950, as the purge of Communists who had returned from the West got underway, Zuckermann offered his resignation to Ulbricht on the grounds that during his years of exile as well as later he had committed serious mistakes:

> After my return I joined the Jewish community of Berlin, at that time known as Department of Racially Persecuted [sic]. Of course, I was not religious nor anything similar, However the massacres of the Jews by the Nazis and other atrocities, including the extermination of many relatives

> and acquaintances, had agitated me deeply. In the face of a lack of interest in this mass destruction on the part of the population at large and even open manifestations of anti-Semitism. . . . I took this step because I did not want to deny my Jewish origins. Joining [the Jewish community] was not dependent upon a declaration of religious belief, and at the time I considered it an act of solidarity with the persecuted Jews. In retrospect I have to acknowledge that this action represented a false and sentimental reaction. I do not want to excuse it but simply wish to explain it as a result of my growing up in an East-Jewish family that spoke Yiddish and Russian. Certain Jewish traditions and national feelings there were stronger as among German Jews. Meanwhile this problem has been solved in the GDR.[75]

This act of self-abnegation was successful, and Zuckermann retained his post with Pieck. Nonetheless, his Stasi file described him as of "German citizenship (Jew)"; non-Jews were not listed in this manner. When the anti-Semitic campaign of the eastern bloc reached its peak with the alleged discovery of the "Doctors' Plot" in January 1953, Zuckermann was one of several hundred Jews who fled to West Germany.

Gradually Zuckermann gained company, as other well-known Jews also decamped for the West. The philosopher Ernst Bloch abandoned the GDR in 1961, as did the composer Wolf Biermann in 1976 and the writer Jurek Becker in 1977. Those who stayed made their peace with the Communist regime in one way or another. To retain a significant position in the political or cultural life of the GDR necessitated not only proving that one was not a Zionist, but also remaining silent about one's Jewish background.

The East Communist regime also benefited from the support of a number of German-Jewish writers who did not formally become members of the ruling party. A good example of these fellow travelers was Stefan Heym, who had been born in 1913 as Helmut Flieg to an assimilated Jewish business family in Chemnitz. Flieg studied philosophy and journalism and wrote for Carl von Ossietzky's *Weltbühne*, a popular weekly magazine and the chief outlet for leftist intellectuals during the Weimar era. In 1933 he emigrated to Prague; in 1935 he moved to the United States and served in the U.S. Army during the war. Eventually discharged on account of pro-Communist activities, Heym returned to East Germany in 1953 and became a loyal supporter of the GDR, serving as a director of its Association of Authors (DSV). But Heym's relations with the authorities eventually deteriorated, and in 1989 he became one of the leading figures in the movement for a democratic renewal. In 1994 he was elected to the Bundestag as a Democratic Socialism (PDS) party delegate. He died in 2001 during a lecture tour in Israel.

As a returned pro-Communist intellectual, Heym received privileged treatment, such as a villa in Berlin-Grünau. He also wrote for the *Berliner Zeitung* and published several novels. On the first birthday after Stalin's death, in December 1953, Heym composed a panegyric published in the Soviet-controlled *Tägliche Rundschau* in which he called the Soviet dictator "a modest and simple human being" and "one of the most beloved men of our time."[76] After the outbreak of the Korean War, Heym wrote to president Dwight D. Eisenhower, his former commander-in-chief, returning to him the bronze star medal he had received in World War II. He could no longer wear this medal that "had been dishonored by the brutal and unjust war against the Korean people."[77] By contrast Heym regarded the Soviets' suppression of the East German workers' uprising on June 17, 1953, as necessary "to prevent war," and he voiced the same assessment after Soviet armored columns had quashed the Hungarian revolt against Communist rule in 1956. For this and other expressions of loyalty, Heym was awarded several prizes. After his death in 2001, David Binder of the *New York Times* called him "a star propagandist for the Communist regime."[78]

Gradually, it appears, Heym began to feel uneasy about his role as an officially favored author. As he recalled after the downfall of the Communist regime: "Year after year the perpetual Yes and the perpetual obedience, and as reward for this a benefit here and there."[79] In November 1976 Heym was one of twelve leading East German writers who protested against stripping the dissenting composer Wolf Biermann of his citizenship while he was on an officially authorized tour in West Germany. Relations between Heym and the East German authorities deteriorated further after he began to publish novels in the West for which he had failed to secure advance permission by the regime's censorship authorities. In 1966 he was summoned by minister of culture Robert Havemann and accused of speaking out against "the state of workers and peasants in West Germany and elsewhere." After the Munich-based publisher Bertelsmann released his anti-Stalinist novel *Collin* in 1979, he was convicted of violating currency laws and ordered to pay a penalty of 9,000 deutsche mark. He was also expelled from the German Association of Authors.[80]

During the late 1980s Heym supported the growing civil rights movement in East Berlin. In September 1989 he was one of the thirty-one initial signers of the illegally distributed resolution "Für unser Land" (For our country) expressing concern about the mass exodus from the GDR and the "unbearable ignorance of the leadership of the Party and the state" that prevented much-needed reforms: "We welcome the fact that citizens organize in groups representing direct democracy in order to take in hand the problems facing us. . . . We demand an opening of the media [to publicize] these problems." Within two weeks the resolution was signed by an additional 200,000 GDR citizens. At the big demonstration of November 4, 1989, on Berlin's Alexanderplatz (Place Alexander) five days before the fall of the Berlin Wall, Heym demanded a "democratic socialism" that would enable all to participate in governing the country.[81]

In line with his Marxist ideology, Heym believed that the new Socialist society would solve the Jewish question. But in the back of his mind he appears to have retained an emotional link to his Jewish origins. In his memoir, *Nachruf*, which tells the story of his life in the third person, Heym described his first visit to Israel and the ambivalence he felt on that occasion: "Is this land his land, are these Jews his people, does he feel warm all over, does he believe to be among brothers?" Answers to these questions, he went on to say, were difficult to find, and it may have taken a visit to Israel to raise these questions in the first place.[82] Toward the end of his life, Heym increasingly took up Jewish themes in his writings. In 1993 mayor Teddy Kollek bestowed upon him the Jerusalem Prize for contributing to the liberty of man in society.[83] Previous recipients had included Max Frisch, Graham Greene, Isaiah Berlin, Simone de Beauvoir, V. S. Naipaul, and Ignazio Silone. The Jewish world thus recognized Stefan Heym's life work as of significance, despite the ambivalence that characterized it.

Pressure to Condemn Israel

The Jewish congregations in East Germany were subjected to pressure as well. After the Berlin congregations had been divided into West and East in 1953, nine synagogues remained in the East. Officially they existed to practice the Jewish religion, and indeed the regime tolerated Jewish religious practice, but from early on it was understood that they also had a social function. As an editorial in the congregations' newspaper *Nachrichtenblatt* (News bulletin) put it: "The socialist social order guarantees all citizens a life of peace and equal rights. To be able to participate in this great task . . . is the desire of the small Jewish population of the GDR."[84] This meant, above all, issuing propagandistic statements in defense of the GDR and attacking the West German state, as suggested by the Communist leadership. Thus, in 1963, Heinz Schenk and Martin Riesenburger, functionaries in the Jewish community of Berlin, sent a letter to the UN Commission for Human Rights accusing the Federal Republic of Germany of "being polluted by the poison of anti-Semitism and racial hatred" while in the GDR human rights were fully safeguarded.[85] (After the opening of the Stasi files, it became known that the Stasi had sent out anti-Semitic chain letters ostensibly composed by West German senders such as "Comrades of the Waffen-ss" to Jewish leaders and to Jewish congregations in West Germany.)[86]

On June 11, 1967, *Neues Deutschland* published a statement signed by ten leading Jewish officials denouncing Israel's role in the Six-Day War: "As citizens of the German Democratic Republic of Jewish descent, we condemn most solemnly the aggression which the ruling circles of Israel have unleashed against their Arab neighbors. . . . It is the tragedy of the Jewish population of Israel that the rulers of their state follow a policy that is in the service of the strategic interests of the imperialist powers with regard to the Suez Canal and the Arab oil wells." This aggression, the statement went on to say, was a continuation of conduct that had begun when "reactionary circles" had created the State of Israel; now the rulers of Israel were working hand in glove with the "West-German imperialists," the Nazi murderers of the Jewish people. Together with their government, the GDR citizens of Jewish descent demanded an end to the aggression that the State of Israel had falsely described as a war of defense.[87]

Some Jewish leaders, a few of them SED members, refused to sign this statement. Helmut Aris, the head of the Association of Jewish Communities, declared: "Not so long ago, our brothers and sisters were murdered in Germany, and today they again lose their lives in the Near East." The well-known Jewish singer Lin Jaldati explained her refusal by noting that the PLO had advocated the destruction of the Jewish state. Albert Norden, a member of the SED politburo who had drawn up the statement, similarly did not affix his signature. As a Jewish Communist who had achieved high rank in the SED hierarchy, Norden was not interested in drawing attention to his Jewish origins.[88]

The authorities reacted in short order to this dissent by a few Jewish leaders. On June 28 state secretary for church affairs Hans Seigewasser reprimanded Aris and his deputy, who promised to reexamine their position. On July 27 the Stasi asked the head of the Jewish community of East Berlin to compile a list of all synagogue members. Such lists were usually created as preparatory to mass arrests. There were no such arrests in 1967, but the fact that the Stasi ordered this list is evidence that SED authorities regarded all Jews—even members of the Jewish community of East Berlin, known for their fidelity to the Communist state—as politically unreliable. In daily Communist discourse, being Jewish was generally equated with being a Zionist, an enemy of the state.[89] In this respect, the minutes of a meeting on January 30, 1973, again between Jewish leaders and the secretariat for church affairs (known in church circles as the "secretariat *against* church affairs"), noted the "provocative" attitude of some Jewish officials: "The overwhelming majority see themselves primarily as Jews and only then as citizens of the socialist GDR. They regard the imperialist aggressor Israel primarily as a Jewish state which has provided refuge to their brethren and also to their relatives."[90]

While the Communist state claimed to be the protector of Jews, its anti-Zionist propaganda helped to perpetuate anti-Semitic attitudes and anti-Jewish violence. Jewish cemeteries were desecrated, although authorities often dismissed these occurrences as the nonpolitical acts of playing children. In October 1976 two explosions damaged the offices of the Jewish community of Halle. There were several other incidents.

Discovering Jewishness in the Second Generation

The official position of the governing party was that membership in the SED was irreconcilable with joining the Jewish community. However, growing numbers of Jews did precisely that. Salomea Genin's family had emigrated to Australia in 1939. There she became a member of the Communist party, and in 1954 she returned to East Germany to participate in building a new Socialist society. After a long tour of duty working for the Stasi in West Berlin, she was allowed to move to the Communist sector and become an SED member in 1963. In an article published years later with the subtitle "How in the GDR I Was Transformed from a Communist into a Jewess," Genin described what made her join the Jewish community in May 1972. She had come back to East Germany in order to find a sense of roots, but had been disappointed. She had seen herself as part of the world Communist movement, but something was missing. Reading Jewish history, almost "unwillingly and shaken up," Genin began to feel like a Jew who had barely escaped death. She reacted vehemently whenever a German comrade revealed ignorance of the Holocaust. In 1989 she declared her exit from the SED, which she had come to realize did not want Jews as members. She joined the Neues Forum (New forum), a broad-based political movement in opposition to the Communist state.[91]

Salomea Genin's experience was not unique. Many young people, the sons and daughters of convinced Jewish Communists, had been brought up in ignorance of their ancestry. Seeking a more meaningful identity than that provided by the worn-out Communist ideology, these second-generation Jews took up the study of Jewish history and became intrigued by their newly discovered roots. In some cities they formed small groups interested in Jewish culture, such as Wir für uns (We for us), which came into being in East Berlin in 1986.[92] Group members found in this new setting a substitute for their former political engagement—an emphasis on the personal, on one's family, on the history of the Jewish people.[93]

The journalist and social activist Anetta Kahane, born in 1954, grew up as the daughter of German Communists who had returned to East Germany after the collapse of the Nazi regime. At the age of fourteen she began to listen to Jewish music, study Hebrew, and carry a pendant with a Star of David; as an adult she would see to it that her daughter became a bat mitzvah. Kahane undertook Latin American studies at the University of Rostock and later at Humboldt University in Berlin. In 1974, seeking to improve her situation, she began service as an IM for the Stasi under the code name "Victoria"; her reports on students and artists would amount to more than eight hundred pages. After ending her Stasi service in 1982, she was no longer able to travel abroad. She became active in the budding GDR civil rights movement, and after the downfall of the Communist regime she labored on behalf of foreigners and other minority groups. In 1998 she founded the Amadeu Antonio Foundation, which works against xenophobia and anti-Semitism in the united Germany.[94]

The writer Barbara Honigmann was born in 1949 to an ardent Communist mother who, while in England, had convinced Kim Philby to become a spy for the Soviet Union. Disappointed by a Socialism that had failed to live up to expectations, the younger Honigmann joined the Jewish community of East Berlin, which her parents had left in the 1950s. There she met other like-minded young people, and together they took up the study of Hebrew. "Our meetings," she recalled in a memoir, "had something conspiratorial. Reading the Bible in Hebrew was like reading a banned book. The task to which we dedicated ourselves was the recovery of our Jewishness." In this group Honigmann also met her future husband, Peter, who was to become a well-regarded Jewish historian. When their first son was born, they decided that he would not only be "of Jewish descent," but a person with whom they would lead a Jewish life. They called their Jewishness "kosher light." They wanted to be different from those who felt like Jews only when they went on pilgrimage to Jerusalem or Auschwitz.[95]

Barbara and Peter Honigmann made a second atypical decision. The Jewish communities in East Germany were too small for a meaningful Jewish life, they concluded; moreover, the strained way in which Germans related to their Jewish fellow citizens was a turnoff. The Nazi past was continuing to hover over their lives. "I sometimes think," Barbara Honigmann wrote, "as if only now the often-celebrated German-Jewish symbiosis . . . has been achieved because Germans and Jews have become a pair in Auschwitz." Hence the Honigmanns departed for Strasbourg. They were now outside of Germany, but, living in the former German Alsace, they remained close to the German culture with which they continued to identify. Existentially, Honigmann would later write, she considers herself more Jewish than German, but, culturally, she belongs to Germany and she is a German writer.[96]

The GDR Abandons "Anti-Zionist" Policy

By the 1980s East German Jews had begun to show a new willingness to protest manifestations of anti-Semitism. On December 11, 1985, Peter Kirchner, a Holocaust survivor and head of the Jewish community of East Berlin, addressed a letter to the editor in chief of the *Berliner Zeitung* strongly objecting to the illustration of an Israeli officer in the preceding day's paper. The artist, Kirchner pointed out, had given the officer a nose that replicated the vicious Jewish caricatures of Streicher's *Der Stürmer*. He should be held accountable for this drawing, for which there was no excuse.[97]

These developments within the Jewish community coincided with the Communist regime's new, more conciliatory attitude toward its Jewish citizens. The changed policy was dictated in part by the GDR's desire to receive international recognition and become a member of the United Nations. Moreover, the East German economy was in such bad shape that only a cooperative relationship with the capitalist West could prevent a complete collapse.

The turnaround began with concern about the disappearance of Jewish life in East Germany. Ever since the Jewish congregations of Berlin had been divided into West and East in 1953, the life of Jews in the East had entered a period of sharp decline. In 1956 there were about 2,300 Jews in East Germany, 1,279 of them in East Berlin. By 1965 the total number of Jews in East Germany had been reduced to 1,500, most of them elderly pensioners, and by 1986 it was down to 350.[98] Since 1969 none of the congregations had a rabbi. The impression this state of affairs left on the outside world was not good.[99] Against this background informal talks between the GDR and the World Jewish Congress got underway in the mid-1980s. This important American-led Jewish organization, it was hoped, would help the GDR gain most-favored-nation status in its economic relationship with the United States and, eventually, entry into the World Trade Organization. As a gesture of goodwill, in October 1988 SED general secretary Erich Honecker personally bestowed upon World Jewish Congress

President Edgar Bronfman the GDR's highest medal, the Stern der Völkerfreundschaft (Star of the friendship between nations). Bronfman's price for helping the GDR was $100 million dollars in restitution for the victims of the Holocaust, but the GDR was unwilling to make a definite commitment.[100]

At the same time, the GDR adopted a new policy toward Israel. The GDR's lavish commemoration of the fiftieth anniversary of Kristallnacht in November 1988 was attended by Jewish delegations from various parts of the world, including Israel. An official delegation under the leadership of GDR minister for church affairs Kurt Löffler visited Israel and was well received. Löffler's deputy, the Jewish Communist Klaus Gysi, had been working for some years toward an improved relationship with the country's Jews. He had appointed a new rabbi, returned confiscated Jewish archives, and restored the famous Neue Synagogue (New synagogue) of Berlin on Oranienburger Street.[101]

Reunification and Its Aftermath

The final act in this process of reconciliation came soon thereafter. In August 1961 the GDR government had built a wall between East and West Berlin that would eventually extend to encompass the entire border with West Germany. This barrier, it was said, had become necessary to prevent Western fascists from entering the GDR. Escapes from the GDR continued, though in seeking freedom in the West many lost their lives. Meanwhile, in May 1989, Hungary opened its border fence with Austria. The Hungarian Communist regime was in serious economic difficulties and showed signs of turning toward the West. With this end of the Iron Curtain, the trickle leaving East Germany turned into a flood. The wall between East and West Germany that had stood for more than two decades came down on November 8, 1989, when a misunderstood message from the SED leadership allowed an ecstatic crowd in Berlin to cross into the West. Others brought hammers and picks and started to destroy the hated barrier. At a special conference on December 16, the SED added the words *Partei des demokratischen Sozialismus*—PDS (Party of Democratic Socialism) to its name in order to dissociate itself from its repressive past. But this maneuver failed to produce its desired result.

On March 18,1990, in a truly free election, the GDR, still formally in existence, chose its first and last democratic parliament, the Volkskammer (People's chamber). With the East German economy near total collapse, the SED-PDS was badly defeated; a new government headed by the Christian Democrat Lothar de Mazière took its place. And then came a momentous event. On April 12, drawing on ideas the jurist Lothar Kreysig and the Jewish historian Helmut Eschwege had enunciated many years earlier, the Volkskammer took as its first act the adoption—by a vote of 379 to 0 (with 21 abstentions)—a resolution of apology for the crimes of the Nazis against the Jewish people:

> We, the first freely elected parliamentarians of the GDR, acknowledge the responsibility of the German people of the GDR for their history and their future and declare unanimously before the world's public:
>
> During the time of National Socialism, Germans inflicted immense suffering on the people of the world. Nationalism and racial delusions resulted in genocide, especially against the Jews of all European countries, the people of the Soviet Union, the Polish people and the Sinti and Roma. . . .
>
> We request the forgiveness of the Jews in the entire world. We request the people of Israel to forgive us for the hypocrisy and hostility of the official policy of the GDR toward the State of Israel and for the persecution and debasement of Jewish compatriots in our country after 1945.
>
> We declare our willingness to contribute as best we can to the healing of mental and physical sufferings of the survivors and to provide just compensation for material losses. . . .
>
> This guilt must never be forgotten. From it we want to derive our responsibility for the future.[102]

During its short life, the new GDR government acted on these promises. In negotiations with GDR foreign minister Markus Meckel, Israeli diplomats put forth the conditions for establishing diplomatic ties, among them entering negotiations over restitution, changing school curricula, ending the GDR's pro-Arab foreign policy, and ceasing the training of terrorists for warfare against Israel.[103] The GDR also invited persecuted Soviet Jews to live in East Germany.[104]

While West Germany's chancellor Helmut Kohl vigorously pursued the reunification of Germany, SED-PDS head Gregor Gysi, son of the former minister for church affairs Klaus Gysi, sought to save the GDR's sovereignty by mobilizing Jewish fears of a united Germany. A large and powerful Germany, he argued, was bad for the world, and especially bad for the Jews. In view of Germany's militaristic past, many Jews in Europe and America shared these sentiments.[105] Gysi also approached rabbis all over the world for financial help to safeguard the GDR's independence. Foreign minister Oskar Fischer declared that the partition of Germany was a precondition for a stable Europe. But these self-serving efforts failed. The Christian-Democratic government of East Germany urged Germany's quick unification, and, on August 31, 1990, the former GDR became part of the Federal Republic of Germany.[106]

With German unification the forty-five-year long tribulations of the Jews of East Germany at the hands of their Communist government had come to an end. But this did not mean the end of anti-Semitism. During the Communist era, xenophobic manifestations had been treated as taboo; officially, anti-Semitism did not exist in the land of Socialism. However, after unification and the coming of democracy, many of the East's young people in particular, leading insecure lives, now felt free to express anti-Semitic sentiments. With incomes lagging behind those in the western part of Germany, they blamed Jews, together with asylum seekers, Gypsies, and other foreigners, for their deprived situation. In 1997 anti-Semitism in the former East Germany was 15 percent higher than in the western part. Official figures on the geographical distribution of anti-Semitic acts in subsequent years do not exist, but reports by groups active in fighting xenophobia show that this disparity in the strength of anti-Semitism has continued. The former eastern states have the highest number of neo-Nazis and potentially violent individuals by one hundred thousand inhabitants.[107] Since 1990 about every ten days a Jewish cemetery in the former East Germany is desecrated. Swastikas and anti-Semitic graffiti have been sprayed on Jewish houses. At soccer games epithets such as "Gas the Jews" have been directed against Jewish teams. Most of these anti-Jewish outbursts have come from the extreme-right youth subculture that includes neo-Nazi skinheads and so-called *Freie Kameradschaften* (free comradeships), informal groups of five to twenty members that manage to escape supervision by the organs of state security.[108]

The Arduous Life of East German Jewish Communists

During the GDR era, most Jewish Communists had experienced a difficult life. They had done their very best to vilify Israel, but deep down even many of those who called themselves "Jews by descent" may not have felt very good about the barrage of hateful pronouncements against the Jewish homeland. Moreover, could they really believe that their Jewish Czech comrades, many known to them personally, were "Trotskyite-Titoist traitors" who as agents of "international finance capital" had formed a "Jewish nationalist imperialist Zionist conspiracy"? Kurt Goldstein, the artistic director of Stimme der DDR (Voice of the DDR [GDR]), like all GDR media an SED propaganda tool, reminisced in 1991 that in his lifetime he had carried three burdens: "To be a German, to be a Jew, and to be a Communist." Asked why he had not protested against the anti-Semitism of the Communist regime, he answered: "Since we did not want the Germany of Globke [a former Nazi official and for ten years chief of staff of chancellor Konrad Adenauer] . . . we swallowed the horrible toads which our party and government fed us. Today I know that this was a mistake."[109] Barbara Honigmann's parents were dedicated Communists; she surmises that they put up with the constant suspicions, control procedures, and purges of Communists of bourgeois and Jewish background because they saw them as "terrestrial trials demanded of them as the price for future salvation."[110]

Among other reasons for "swallowing the toads" was a careerist's desire to preserve the privileges that came with positions in the GDR bureaucracy. Initially, Beatrice Zweig, wife of the writer Arnold Zweig, found it extremely difficult to live in the land of the murderers, but she eventually adjusted in large measure because of the financial security and the house and garden provided to her celebrity husband. Visitors from the West were amazed by how Arnold Zweig bragged about his material success and the many honors the regime had bestowed on him.[111]

There was also the pernicious doctrine of the ultimate wisdom of the party. In 1924, when Trotzky was still in the good graces of the Soviet Communist party, he had given this idea its classic formulation: "In the last instance the party is always right, because it is the only historic instrument which the working class possesses for the solution of its fundamental tasks. . . . I know that one ought not to be right against the party. One can be right only with the party and through the party because history has not created any other way for the realization of one's rightness."[112] Years later "The Party, the Party Is Always Right" became the official SED anthem, composed by the Jewish composer Louis Fürnberg.[113]

The well-known writer Anna Seghers was typical of Jewish Communists who were privately critical of the party's repressive discipline but remained loyal to it, defending it—or at least not publicly opposing it—at such crucial junctures as the Workers' Uprising of 1953 and the Prague Spring of 1968. In 1952, at a time when numerous Jews were being arrested or dismissed from their jobs, Seghers accepted the International Stalin Peace Prize. The SED used her reputation as a highly regarded literary figure to promote the alleged exalted cultural achievements of the East German Communist regime, and Seghers did not object. Hermann Axen, who rose to become a member of the SED politburo, was one of a few Jewish Communists who would acknowledge in retrospect, after the GDR's downfall, the poor judgment that had made him and his comrades vest blind faith in the party.[114]

The Jewish Communists shored up the Communist regime and in this way prolonged their own travail. In order to prosper in the GDR, they had to deny their Jewish origins, and many of them did so with a vehemence that bordered on self-hatred. The forces that finally brought down the GDR were driven by humanistic values that the Jewish Communist had abandoned long ago as bourgeois ideology. And this was their final tragedy. The Jewish Communists had wanted to build a new society of social justice, but ended up perpetuating a regime of moral corruption and degradation.

Conclusion

For over half a century—between the last decades of the nineteenth century and Hitler's rise to power in 1933—relations between Germans and Jews took on a highly amicable and intimate form. The Jews "were as German as the Germans," the former Berlin rabbi Joachim Prinz noted in his autobiography, "and sometimes even more so."[1] The idea of a German-Jewish symbiosis, first formulated in the 1920s, therefore accurately reflected German Jews' conviction that they were Germans and belonged to a community of Jews and non-Jews in which one's religious or ethnic background was irrelevant. In 1933 this belief turned out to have been an illusion; Jews became pariahs in German society. The vanity of complete assimilation was exposed with utmost clarity and left no room for controversy.[2]

Yet even after the Holocaust, for most German Jews the German-Jewish symbiosis retained a powerful significance. Hitler had destroyed this special relationship, but it lived on in their memory as an intellectual and cultural tradition that continued to resonate and thrive.[3] Driven into exile, the poets Nelly Sachs and Else Lasker Schüler used the German language as a matter of course to express their grief over the end of German-Jewish dialogue. Late in 1947 the historian Gustav Meyer wrote in his autobiography that "memories of one's family, abodes of one's youth, and one's mother tongue" keep alive the idea of the lost homeland.[4]

According to Leo Baeck, three times in the history of the Jewish people, the encounter with another culture had led to highly creative results: during the Hellenistic period in antiquity; the

Spanish-Arab era of the Middle Ages; and, finally, the meeting with German culture.[5] "There has rarely been a confluence of two cultural, ethnic, or religious traditions," Amos Elon has written, "that proved so richly creative at its peak."[6] Weimar culture constituted true greatness, in an era of eminent Jewish writers and painters, of outstanding composers and scholars. Can one think of Weimar's artistic, literary, and scientific life without the contributions of Arnold Schönberg and Gustav Mahler, Max Reinhardt and Bruno Walter, Kurt Weill and Lion Feuchtwanger, Jakob Wassermann and Otto Klemperer, Albert Einstein and Arnold and Stefan Zweig?! Between 1918 and 1933, German Jewry comprised 1 percent of the German population, but no fewer than twelve German-Jewish personages of distinction received the Nobel Prize for their cultural achievements.

Anti-Semites charged that Jews dominated German culture and society in general; the colloquial form of this allegation was *Verjudung* (Jewification). But, as the philosopher Ernst Bloch would later recall, few Germans at the time were interested in whether Kurt Weill's music for *The Threepenny Opera* was Jewish and Bertolt Brecht's text for the same work German.[7] German Jews had integrated into the fabric of German cultural life and achieved a level of assimilation with few parallels in the rest of Europe. Martin Buber, a philosopher not given to excessive pro-German sentiments, called the bond between Jews and Germans at this time more fruitful than at any other time in the Jewish diaspora and insisted in November 1933 that it could not be ended by any action on the part of the Germans.[8] Writing in January 1939, Buber referred to the German-Jewish encounter as "genuine and natural."[9]

Of course this is not a complete picture. Side by side with success, Jews encountered resentment and hostility.[10] As Jews progressed in integrating into German society, so did resistance aimed at halting this advance—the ferociousness of the backlash correspondingly increasing with Jewish achievement. The Weimar years—the high point of Jewish emancipation and assimilation—

also witnessed an escalating anti-Semitism, including a multiplicity of organizations openly committed to violence against Jews. While some Jews easily mixed with artists, musicians, and leftist intellectuals, most experienced a growing social isolation. Hence Gershom Scholem was not entirely wrong when he called the love affair between Jews and Germans largely "one-sided and unreciprocated."[11] But "not entirely wrong" is not entirely right. "If there were those who continued to deny Germany's Jews the right to speak as Germans," the historian Peter Gay insists, "there were many others who were glad to grant it to them."[12]

Scholem dismissed Gay's position as "chutzpah," a Hebrew word meaning presumption and arrogance.[13] But surely a society that enabled a Jew (Walther Rathenau) to become a foreign minister could not be all bad. A sense of German identity made sense; even the Zionists affirmed their German roots. Shortly before the Great War, the sociologist Franz Oppenheimer had written in the *Jüdische Rundschau*, the magazine of the German Zionist Federation, "I am not an assimilationist, but I am assimilated. . . . My Deutschtum [being German] is sacred to me." Oppenheimer professed not only his *Deutschtum*, but also his *Heimatbewusstsein* (awareness of home) and *Stammesbewusstsein* (awareness of clan).[14] The German Zionists did not consider themselves strangers in their own land. During the Weimar years, fewer than two thousand actually emigrated to Palestine, and many of those, unprepared for the harsh conditions of life in the primitive Middle East, returned to their German homes shortly thereafter.

Being German had been a cultural phenomenon before it led to German unification as a state in 1871. This shared language and literary tradition had united Prussians and Bavarians as well as Protestants, Catholics, and Jews. Beginning with Moses Mendelssohn, this heritage attracted thousands of East European Jews who regarded German culture as the embodiment of enlightenment. The poet Heinrich Heine (who was born Jewish and later converted to Christianity) called Germany "the home of philosophy, the mother soil of prophecy and the citadel of pure spirituality."[15]

The phenomenon of a German-Jewish symbiosis was first mentioned in 1927 by the anti-Semitic German writer Wilhelm Stapel, who vigorously rejected such a merger of traditions. Gershom Scholem was probably the best-known Jewish scholar to similarly deny the existence of a convergence; he spoke instead of a "so-called German-Jewish symbiosis."[16] The alleged commonality of German and Jewish essence, he argued, "existed only on the part of Jews who sought it." It represented wishful thinking and constituted an "illusion."[17] Scholem's provocative position gave rise to a debate that continues to the present day.

Many well-known scholars agree with Scholem. Leo Baeck, the preeminent intellectual leader of German Jewry, called the idea of an intellectual and social symbiosis a "dream" that vanished in Auschwitz.[18] Rabbi Joachim Prinz stated that he always had "a sense of distance" between himself as a Jew and the German people: "I never sang the national anthem of Germany. Long before Hitler, I realized we were living in a fool's paradise."[19] The German historian Wolfgang Benz maintains that the "legend" of a symbiosis is false and based on a simplified view of history.[20] The Israeli historian Yehuda Bauer speaks of a "one-sided love affair."[21] The American historian George Mosse calls its failure "obvious."[22] The author Amos Elon regards the notion of a German-Jewish symbiosis "dubious" and "always suspect," though at the same time he speaks of a deeply felt "duality of German and Jew—two souls within a single body."[23]

Other scholars have given the idea of a German-Jewish symbiosis a more positive assessment. Peter Gay concludes that the "Jewish-German symbiosis was not a mirage . . . but a reality that had been wantonly destroyed."[24] Martin Buber calls the symbiosis "natural" and "genuinely fruitful," though he adds that he was aware that it might not last.[25] The historian Fritz Stern argues that if the hope for a German-Jewish symbiosis is to be judged an illusion, then it must also be acknowledged that for a brief moment in history it was an enticing illusion, an illusion productive of greatness.[26] The German historian

Manfred Voigts maintains that the close relationship of German and Jewish intellectual life was not an invention of the Jews, but a reality in the realm of literature, art, and culture generally.[27] The German critic Hans Mayer similarly speaks of a "Jewish-German literary symbiosis."[28] Most of these scholars have ignored the fact that even many German intellectuals who accepted German Jewry's important contributions to German culture did not regard the Jews as fully German. A typical representative of this outlook was Thomas Mann. In a letter to the émigré author Hermann Kesten dated January 30, 1938, the famous author acknowledges that "without you Jews there would be no real recognition of German literary works."[29] This complimentary view of course implies that German Jews were somehow separate from German literature.

While Scholem denied the existence of a German-Jewish symbiosis in the pre-Nazi period, he did not rule out a true dialogue after the Holocaust. "I am not among those who altogether refuse and oppose the resumption of such relations," he wrote in 1962. "In order to render such a resumption fruitful in a serious sense, one requires, however, not only knowledge of what is, but also of what was."[30] The publication of scholarship about Jewish history in the postwar Germany, Gershom believed, could create a productive discourse between Jews and Germans. Not surprisingly, given Scholem's sense of his own importance in Jewish scholarship, this view led to his endeavor to gain recognition and honor in the new Germany. He made frequent trips there, accepted numerous prizes, gave lectures, and arranged for the German publication of his books and articles. His biographer Noam Zadoff surmises that Scholem's renewed interest in all things German reflected Gershom's conviction that he had failed to realize the Zionist dream, together with the longing of an old man for the time of his youth, "when Berlin was the center; Jerusalem was a peripheral, rocky landscape; and the dream was still a dream."[31]

According to Scholem, German Jews showed "an astonishing lack of critical insight into their own situation."[32] In 1968 he told the German philosopher Karl Löwith that the German Jews with their passionate commitment to being German had lived a "lie" for which they eventually paid dearly.[33] Critics of this position have pointed out that Orthodox Jews and Zionists who opposed assimilation fared no better at the hands of the Nazis.[34] The deep attachment of most German Jews to their homeland may have contributed to misjudging the nature of Nazi rule, though most Germans similarly failed to anticipate the horrors that lay ahead.

The historian Peter Pulzer has argued that, for the most part, it was the Jews' very familiarity with prejudice and discrimination rather than their illusions about a German-Jewish symbiosis that made them underestimate the significance of Hitler's ascension in 1933, and I agree with this finding. The Jews had coped with mistreatment before and they expected to cope with it again. They had survived the onslaught of the crusaders, the Hep! Hep! riots, verbal abuse by the historian Treitschke and the court preacher Stoecker, as well as the violence of the Nazis and Schutz-und Trutzbund in the 1920s. Over the years they had gained considerable experience in fighting anti-Semitism, and they could count on some friends in high places. These defense mechanisms had worked before and were expected to handle the new situation as well. Finally, together with most Germans, the Jews failed to fathom the fanatical nature of Hitler's hatred and the lengths he and his entourage were prepared to go in pursuing their Jewish victims. The physical destruction of an entire people was simply beyond the mental horizon of just about everybody in 1933.[35]

And there was another tragic misjudgment. Attached as they were to their German homeland, the Jews expected better of their neighbors. "They imagined themselves to be surrounded by friends and discounted their enemies," Rabbi Prinz has written.[36] The prominent German cantor Joseph B. Levy adhered to this wishful thinking even after he had to emigrate in 1939. "It should not be forgotten," he wrote in 1940, "that the attitude of a large part of the Christian population, perhaps the majority, towards the Jews was basically friendly, often kind and sympathetic."[37]

This trust in the basic decency and humanity of the German people was to be bitterly disappointed. The onslaught on the Jews during the following years took place in full public view, but hardly any voices were raised against it. Only a tiny minority of Germans helped to hide Jews, and in the majority of cases these were acquaintances and friends. Tens of thousands of ordinary Germans were active participants in the Final Solution. The people who had produced Schiller and Goethe, Bach and Beethoven, now excelled in the organized murder of men, women, and children, by mass shootings in execution pits or asphyxiation in gas chambers, while practically all those not participating were demonstrably silent. The horrible fate of the Jews deported to the East became widely known, but it was met with indifference. Despite the short interlude of Weimar democracy, German society remained characterized by a sense of political servility, a weak conscience in public affairs. This deliberate turning away from personal responsibility left the Jews at the mercy of a state that had no mercy.[38]

The memory of the terrible events over the twelve years of the Hitler regime could not but affect Jewish life in postwar Germany. Some Jews, such as the Jewish official Ignatz Bubis, sought to pick up where matters had ended in 1933, calling themselves German citizens of the Jewish faith yet again. But for most Jews, whether survivors or returnees from exile, it was problematic to live in the land of the murderers. The historian Dan Diner speaks of a negative symbiosis: the experience of the Holocaust and the mindset of non-Jewish Germans set the benchmarks for that intersection. Hard-set anti-Semitic attitudes survived the downfall of the Nazis, and new anti-Jewish sentiments emerged in the 1980s in the wake of changed critical attitudes toward Israel. Large numbers of Germans wanted to draw a final line under the Nazi past. This changed political climate also brought increases in anti-Jewish violence, most of it by right-extremists but also by newly immigrated Muslims: police now had to guard Jewish synagogues, museums, retirement homes, and even outings of

Jewish youngsters. Concurrently, a prevailing philo-Semitism among well-meaning Germans contributed to artificial relations with their Jewish compatriots. The abnormality in the German-Jewish relationship became the new normality.[39]

In accordance with Marxist theory, in the part of postwar Germany under Communist rule the Jewish question was expected to be solved automatically. Religion was regarded as the opium of an oppressed people, and anti-Semitism as a tool of the capitalist ruling class. Once that class had been overthrown, and a new Socialist society established, both religion and anti-Semitism would disappear and Jews would enjoy a new freedom. Jewish Communists did their level best to conform to this prediction. They denied their Jewishness with a vehemence that bordered on self-hatred and embraced an assimilation far more self-effacing than that practiced by German Jews before 1933.

Yet the Marxist utopia failed to materialize. The SED—the Stalinist-style Communist party that ruled the country by use of an extensive machinery of control, the Stasi—created a society in which independently thinking persons were not welcome. Following Soviet direction, the GDR denounced Zionists and Israel as instruments of American imperialism, and the anti-Zionist propaganda helped perpetuate anti-Semitic attitudes and anti-Jewish violence. During repeated purges that blurred the line between Jews and Zionists, Jewish Communists lost their leading positions in state and party (even though most of them never abandoned their faith in the Communist cause). To this day, anti-Semitism is more widespread in the former East Germany than in the rest of united Germany.

For most Jews, the idea of a German-Jewish symbiosis died in Auschwitz. Yet the Holocaust has not decisively refuted the *possibility* of such a mutually beneficial relationship of Jews and non-Jews, provided one does not embrace a questionable theory of historical necessity.[40] The Nazis' anti-Semitic enterprise drew on sentiments and forces present in Germany for a very long time, but the Jewish catastrophe was not inevitable and foreseeable.

Historical events have causes, but they do not necessarily have only one possible outcome.[41] Without the badly mistaken policies of chancellor Heinrich Brüning and the political naïveté of the bankers and noblemen around president Paul von Hindenburg, Hitler's National Socialists would not have been able to ascend to power. Without Hitler's control of the machinery of state, there would have been no Shoah.

The fact that the Nazi takeover in 1933 was not inescapable does not mean that it constituted a kind of "industrial accident" that ran counter to the inherent logic of German history.[42] Nor does it absolve German society of its responsibility for Hitler's destructive policies. The vast majority of the populace exhibited unconcern, certainly passivity, regarding the terrible fate of the Jews. In view of all of this history, it is doubtful that German-Jewish relations can ever return to a form worthy to be called "symbiotic." Some 80 percent of Jews in today's Germany hail from the former Soviet Union, and to the extent that these Jews have an attachment to German culture, this bond has no special Jewish component. There is anecdotal evidence of some second-generation Jews showing an interest in all things Jewish, but there is no Baeck or Rosenzweig to lead a Jewish cultural renaissance of the kind experienced in the Weimar era. For those men Jewishness and being German were inseparable, and they inspired a confluence of two civilizations that was immensely fruitful for both Jews and Germans. That cultural greatness will remain an achievement to be remembered with pride, but it seems unlikely ever to be repeated.

Notes

1. Struggle for Emancipation

1. This account of medieval Jewish life is based largely on Kampmann, *Deutsche und Juden.*
2. Kampmann, *Deutsche und Juden*, 32–33.
3. Leschnitzer, *Magic Background of Modern Antisemitism*, 25.
4. Leschnitzer, *Magic Background of Modern Antisemitism*, 111–12.
5. Mosse, *German Jews beyond Judaism*, 15.
6. Grab, *Deutsche Weg der Judenemanzipation*, 12–13; Traverso, *Jews and Germany*, 9.
7. von Dohm, *Concerning the Amelioration of the Civic Status of the Jews.*
8. Sorkin, "Emancipation and Assimilation," 18.
9. Until this time, Jewish names generally changed with every generation. For example, Moses, the son of Mendel, would be called Moyshe ben Mendel.
10. Kampmann, *Deutsche und Juden*, 136; Grab, *Deutsche Weg der Judenemanzipation*, 18.
11. Quoted in Roemer, *Jewish Scholarship and Culture in Nineteenth-Century Germany*, 58.
12. Voigts, *Deutsch-jüdische Symbiose*, 240.
13. Schoeps, *Deutsch-jüdische Symbiose oder die Missglückte Emanzipation*, 54, 28–29.
14. Berding, *Moderner Antisemitismus in Deutschland*, 40–41.
15. Bering, *Name als Stigma*, 390–91.
16. Aschheim, *Brothers and Strangers*, 8–11.
17. Mendes-Flohr, *German Jews*, 27–28.
18. Elbogen, *Geschichte der Juden in Deutschland*, 242.
19. Stern, *Dreams and Delusions*, 103.

20. Mendes-Flohr, *German Jews*, 30–31.
21. See the balanced discussion in Voigts, *Zwischen Antisemitismus und deutsch-jüdischer Symbiose*, 77–81.
22. Grab, *Der deutsche Weg der Judenemanzipation*, 15.
23. Bauman, *Modernity and Ambivalence*, 126.
24. Voigts, *Zwischen Antisemitismus und deutsch-jüdischer Symbiose*, 218–19; Hertz, *How Jews Became German*, 52.
25. Reich-Ranicki, *Über Ruhestörer*, 40.
26. Katz, *Out of the Ghetto*, 201.
27. Rohrbacher, *Gewalt im Biedermeier*, 287–88.
28. Quoted in Elbogen, *Geschichte der Juden in Deutschland*, 192–93.
29. Berding, *Moderner Antisemitismus in Deutschland*, 74–75.
30. Volkov, "Reflections on German-Jewish Historiography," 316.
31. See Riesser, *Auswahl aus seinen Schriften und Briefen*.
32. Berding, *Moderner Antisemitismus in Deutschland*, 32.
33. Elbogen, *Geschichte der Juden in Deutschland*, 219, 238–39; Berding, *Moderner Antisemitismus in Deutschland*, 48.
34. Weltsch, *Deutsche Judenfrage*, 12.
35. Schoeps, *Deutsch-jüdische Symbiose*, 154.
36. An abbreviated version of Marr's work, *Sieg des Judentums über das Germanenthum*, can be found in Levy, *Antisemitism in the Modern World*, 76–93.
37. Niewyk, "Solving the 'Jewish Problem,'" 369; Scholem, "Juden und Deutsche," 177–201.
38. Angress, "Prussia's Army and the Jewish Reserve Officer Controversy before World War I," 25; Bieber, "Anti-Semitism as a Reflection of Social, Economic and Political Tensions in Germany," 42.
39. Treitschke's 1879 essay "Ein Wort über unser Judentum" is reprinted in Levy, *Antisemitism in the Modern World*, 69–73.
40. There has been some discussion about whether these words were meant literally and whether Dühring should therefore be regarded as an advocate of genocide. Regardless, there can be no doubt that Dühring sought to make Germany free of Jews (*judenrein*). Theodor Herzl, considered the father of the modern Zionist idea, pointed to Dühring's book as one of the anti-Semitic writings that awakened in him an interest in Judaism.
41. Berding, *Moderner Antisemitismus in Deutschland*, 149.
42. Quoted in Bein, "Jewish Parasite," 12.

43. Berding, *Moderner Antisemitismus in Deutschland*, 99–100; Niewyk, "Solving the 'Jewish Problem,'" 364.
44. Berding, *Moderner Antisemitismus in Deutschland*, 106–7; Levy, *Antisemitism in the Modern World*, 25.
45. Wistrich, *Socialism and the Jews*, 350.
46. Marx, *World without Jews*, 45.
47. Quoted in Johannsen, *Klärung*, 13.
48. Quoted by Traverso, *Jews and Germany*, 20. See also Schay, *Juden in der deutschen Politik*, 46–47.
49. See Angress, "Prussia's Army and the Jewish Reserve Officer Controversy before World War I," 19–42.
50. Traverso, *Jews and Germany*, 14.
51. Zipes, "Cultural Operations of Germans and Jews as Reflected in Recent German Fiction," 172.
52. Quoted in Mosse, "From 'Schutzjuden' to 'Deutsche Staatsbürger jüdischen Glaubens,'" 91.
53. Schoeps, *Das Gewaltsyndrom*, 42; Traverso, *Jews and Germany*, 11; Volkov, *Germans, Jews, and Antisemites*, 24.
54. Niewyk, "Solving the 'Jewish Problem,'" 339; Suchy, "Verein zur Abwehr des Antisemitismus," 205–39.
55. Scholem, *From Berlin to Jerusalem*, 27.
56. Traverso, *Jews and Germany*, 17.
57. Quoted in Stern, *Gold and Iron*, 477.
58. Honigmann, *Austritte aus der Jüdischen Gemeinde Berlin*, 8.
59. Klemperer, *Curriculum Vitae*, vol. 1, 350–52.
60. Quoted in Stern, *Gold and Iron*, 471.
61. Quoted in Volkov, *Germans, Jews, and Antisemites*, 40.
62. Goldstein, "German Jewry's Dilemma," 253.
63. Löwenfeld, *Schutzjuden oder Staatsbürger?*, 25.
64. Quoted in Aschheim, *Brothers and Strangers*, 50.
65. Volkov, *Germans, Jews, and Antisemites*, 264–65.
66. Aschheim, *Brothers and Strangers*, 37.
67. Barnouw, *Visible Spaces*, 87.
68. Quoted in Von Borries, *Selbstzeugnisse des deutschen Judentums*, 17. See also Katz, "Berthold Auerbach's Anticipation of the German-Jewish Tragedy," 215–70.
69. Quoted in Traverso, *Jews and Germany*, 25.
70. Quoted in Reinharz, *Fatherland or Promised Land*, 225.
71. Elon, *Pity of it All*, 225.

72. Grab, *Deutsche Weg der Judenemanzipation*, 34.
73. Aschheim, *In Times of Crisis*, 67.
74. Cohen, *Deutschtum und Judentum*, 37–38. See also Schwarzschild, "Germanism and Judaism," 154–55.
75. Scholem, *From Berlin to Jerusalem*, 26.
76. Mendes-Flohr, "*Kriegserlebnis* and Jewish Consciousness," 228.
77. Quoted in Angress, "German Army's 'Judenzählung' of 1916," 117.
78. Schoeps, *Gewaltsyndrom*, 45; Grab, *Deutsche Weg der Judenemanzipation*, 34. See also Vogel, *Stück von uns!*, 146–48.

2. Heyday of Assimilation

1. Grab, *Deutsche Weg der Judenemanzipation*, 35; Pulzer, "Between Hope and Fear," 274.
2. Brenner, *Renaissance of Jewish Culture in Weimar Germany*, 24.
3. Brenner, *Renaissance of Jewish Culture in Weimar Germany*, 5–7.
4. Leo Baeck Institute, https://www.lbi.org/about/leo-baeck (accessed January 21, 2020).
5. See also Bamberger, *Leo Baeck*; Neimark, *One Man's Valor*; Seligman, *Leo Baeck*.
6. Barkai and Mendes-Flohr. *Deutsch-Jüdische Geschichte der Neuzeit*, vol. 4, 135–40.
7. Barkai and Mendes-Flohr. *Deutsch-Jüdische Geschichte der Neuzeit*, vol. 4, 143–46.
8. Reichmann, *Grösse und Verhängnis deutsch-jüdischer Existenz*, 23; Barkai, "*Wehr dich!*," 120.
9. Barkai and Mendes-Flohr, *Deutsch-jüdische Geschichte der Neuzeit*, 86.
10. Fuchs, *Um Deutschtum und Judentum*, 365; see also Stern, *Warum hassen sie uns eigentlich?*, 89.
11. Fuchs, *Um Deutschtum und Judentum*, 240.
12. Marx, *Deutsche Judentum und seine jüdischen Gegner*, 9.
13. Stern, *Warum sind wir Deutsche?*, 26, 31, 89.
14. Quoted in Mendes-Flohr, *German Jews*, 59.
15. Quoted in Mendes-Flohr, "Between Germanism and Judaism, Christians and Jews,"161.
16. The best biography of Einstein is Isaacson, *Einstein*.
17. Sanders, *Days Grow Short*.
18. Toller, *I Was a German*, 285–86.
19. Liptzin, *Germany's Stepchildren*, 198.

20. A good appreciation of his work can be found in Spalek, *Lion Feuchtwanger.*
21. Zweig, *Welt von Gestern*, 415.
22. Partial estate, Vienna Library. See also Styan, *Max Reinhardt.*
23. See Salamon, *Arnold Zweig*; Wiznitzer, *Arnold Zweig.*
24. Wistrich, *Socialism and the Jews*, 74.
25. Letter to Mathilde Wurm, January 16, 1917, cited by Von Borries, *Selbstzeugnisse des deutschen Judentums*, 172.
26. Quoted in Hermand, "Juden in der Kultur der Weimarer Republik," 23. See Heller, *Untergang des Judentums.*
27. Cited by Traverso, *Marxists and the Jewish Question*, 193.
28. Niewyk, *Jew in Weimar Germany*, 69.
29. Lessing, *Jüdische Selbsthass*, 212.
30. Liptzin, *Germany's Stepchildren*, 186–87.
31. Poor, *Kurt Tucholsky and the Ordeal of Germany*, 218–19.
32. Quoted in Reich-Ranicki, *Über Ruhestörer*, 23.
33. Schulin, "Walther Rathenau und sein Integrationsversuch als 'Deutscher jüdischen Stammes,'" 13–38.
34. Loewenberg, *Walther Rathenau and Henry Kissinger*, 17; Pois, *Walther Rathenau's Jewish Quandary*, 120.
35. The translation is by Robertson, *"Jewish Question" in German Literature*, 298.
36. "Höre, Israel!" *Zukunft*, March 6, 1897, in Rathenau, *Schriften*, 89–93.
37. Loewenberg, *Walther Rathenau and Henry Kissinger*, 7.
38. Letter to Wilhelm Schwaner, January 23, 1916, in Rathenau, *Schriften*, 114.
39. Rathenau, "Staat und Judentum," *Gesammelte Schriften*, vol. 1, 206.
40. Stapel, "Antigermanismus," 421.
41. Meiring, *Christlich-jüdische Mischehe in Deutschland*, 92.
42. Quoted in Marx, *Deutsche Judentum und seine jüdischen Gegner*, 25.
43. Toury, "Gab es ein Krisenbewusstsein unter den Juden während der 'guten Jahre' der Weimarer Republik?," 146.
44. Wallach, *Passing Illusions*, 46–47.
45. Niewyk, *Jews in Weimar Germany*, 114.
46. Mayer, *Widerruf*, 373.
47. Hermand, *Judentum und deutsche Kultur*, 117.

48. See Luise, *Correspondence of Hannah Arendt and Gershom Scholem*, 201–5 and 212–14.
49. The most recent biography of Scholem is Biale, *Gershom Scholem*, published in 2018. See also Engel, *Gershom Scholem*.
50. Krojanker, *Zum Problem des neuen deutschen Nationalismus*, 35.
51. Reichmann, "Der Bewusstseinswandel der deutschen Juden," 568; Bolkosky, *Distorted Image*, 7.
52. Quoted in Barkai and Mendes-Flohr, *Deutsch-jüdische Geschichte der Neuzeit*, 100.
53. Heyworth, *Otto Klemperer*.
54. See also Ryding and Pechefsky, *Bruno Walter*.
55. See Frisch, *Schoenberg and His World*.
56. https://www.facinghistory.org/holocaust-and-human-behavior/chapter-4/antisemitism-and-jewish-identity (site discontinued).
57. Goran, *Story of Fritz Haber*.
58. Meiring, *Christlich-jüdische Mischehe in Deutschland*, 95.
59. Meyer, "Mixed Marriage,"54; Goran, *Story of Fritz Haber*.
60. Meiring, *Christlich-jüdische Mischehe in Deutschland*, 98.
61. Traverso, *Jews and Germany*, 30–31; Grab, *Deutsche Weg der Judenemanzipation*.
62. Niewyk, *Jews in Weimar Germany*, 28.
63. Pulzer, *Rise of Political Anti-Semitism*, 300.
64. Berding, *Moderner Antisemitismus in Deutschland*, 180–81, 186.
65. Quoted in Adler-Rudel, *Ostjuden in Deutschland*, 24.
66. Berding, *Moderner Antisemitismus in Deutschland*, 183; Barkai and Mendes-Flohr, *Deutsch-jüdische Geschichte der Neuzeit*, 52.
67. Adler-Rudel, *Ostjuden in Deutschland*, 209.
68. Quoted in Bein, "Jewish Parasite," 18.
69. Berding, *Moderner Antisemitismus in Deutschland*, 196.
70. Adler-Rudel, *Ostjuden in Deutschland*, 130.
71. Niewyk, *Jews in Weimar Germany*, 53.
72. Lewy, *Perpetrators*, 125.

3. Jewish Patriots

1. Quoted in Dunker, *Reichsbund jüdischer Frontsoldaten*, 186.
2. Dunker, *Reichsbund jüdischer Frontsoldaten*, 7–10.
3. Pierson, "Embattled Veterans," 150–52.
4. Niewyk, *Jews in Weimar Germany*, 92.
5. Gay, *Berlin-Jewish Spirit*, 13–14.

6. Niewyk, *Jews in Weimar Germany*, 92.
7. Pierson, "Embattled Veterans," 145.
8. Dunker, *Reichsbund jüdischer Frontsoldaten*, 92–95.
9. Pierson, "Embattled Veterans," 147.
10. Grady, "Fighting a Lost Battle," 128.
11. Quoted in Pierson, "Embattled Veterans," 150.
12. Pierson, "Embattled Veterans," 148n54.
13. Reichsbund jüdischer Frontsoldaten, *Jüdischen Gefallenen des deutschen Heeres*.
14. Pierson, "Embattled Veterans," 149.
15. Matthias Hambrock, *Etablierung der Aussenseiter*, 43–44, 100.
16. Naumann, *Von Zionisten und Jüdischnationalen*, 15, 44.
17. Peyser, *Nationaldeutsche Juden und ihre Lästerer*, 11.
18. Peyser, *Nationaldeutsche Juden und ihre Lästerer*, 30–31. See also Naumann, *Vom nationaldeutschen Juden*, 12.
19. Quoted in Aschheim, *Brothers and Strangers*, 221.
20. Naumann, *Vom nationaldeutschen Juden*, 35; Rheins, "Der Verband nationaldeutscher Juden," 245.
21. Marx, *Deutsche Judentum und seine jüdischen Gegner*, 58. See also Barkai, *"Wehr dich!,"* 140.
22. Rheins, "Verband nationaldeutscher Juden," 253–54.
23. Hambrock, *Etablierung der Aussenseiter*, 241; Foerder, *Stellung des Centralvereins zu den innerjüdischen Fragen*, 19.
24. Hambrock, *Etablierung der Aussenseiter*, 479.
25. Quoted in Hambrock, *Etablierung der Aussenseiter*, 374.
26. Hambrock, *Etablierung der Aussenseiter*, 405.

4. German-Jewish Youth Movement

1. Mosse, "Influence of *Völkisch* Ideas on German Jewry," 85–86.
2. Quoted in Laqueur, *Young Germany*, 7.
3. Stadura, *German Youth Movement*, 64.
4. Borinsky and Milch, *Jugendbewegung*, 25–26.
5. Laqueur, *Young Germany*, 32–36.
6. Gay, *Weimar Culture*, 78; Laqueur, *Young Germany*, 32–38.
7. Trefz, *Jugendbewegung und Juden in Deutschland*, 32; Laqueur, *Young Germany*, 76.
8. Trefz, *Jugendbewegung und Juden in Deutschland*, 34.
9. Trefz, *Jugendbewegung und Juden in Deutschland*, 37.
10. Quoted in Laqueur, *Young Germany*, 80.

11. Blüher, *Secessio Judaica*, 37.
12. Pulzer, *Rise of Political Anti-Semitism*, 309
13. Letter of April 14, 1913, quoted in Meier-Cronemeyer, "Jüdische Jugendbewegung," 18.
14. Adrianssen, *Rhythm of Eternity*, 68–69.
15. Trefz, *Jugendbewegung und Juden in Deutschland*, 77–81.
16. Trefz, *Jugendbewegung und Juden in Deutschland*, 39.
17. Meier-Cronemeyer, "Jüdische Jugendbewegung," 51–52; Trefz, *Jugendbewegung und Juden in Deutschland*, 13.
18. Hetkamp, *Jüdische Jugendbewegung in Deutschland*, 46; Brenner, *Renaissance of Jewish Culture in Weimar Germany*, 46.
19. Quoted in Paucker, "Zum Selbstverständnis jüdischer Jugend in der Weimarer Republik und unter der nationalsozialistischer Diktatur," 119.
20. Reichmann, "Bewusstseinswandel der deuschen Juden," 588.
21. Bergbauer and Schüler-Springorum, *"Wir sind jung, die Welt ist offen."*
22. Hans Litten, together with other leftists, was arrested after the Reichstag fire on February 27, 1933, and spent the next five years in various concentration camps. He committed suicide in 1938.
23. Kneip, *Jugend der Weimarer Zeit*, 166; Trefz, *Jugendbewegung und Juden in Deutschland*, 127.
24. Paucker, *Deutsche Juden im Kampf um Recht und Freiheit*, 188.
25. Trefz, *Jugendbewegung und Juden in Deutschland*, 151.
26. Maoz, "Werkleute," 181–82.
27. Gerson, *Werkleute*, 9.
28. Rinott, "Major Trends in Jewish Youth Movements in Germany," 19.
29. See Bergbauer, *Jüdische Jugendbewegung in Breslau.*
30. Paucker, *Deutsche Juden im Kampf um Recht und Freiheit*, 119.
31. Reinharz, "Hashomer Hatzair in Nazi Germany," 327.
32. Schatzker, "Jewish Youth Movement in Germany in the Holocaust Period," 320.
33. Paucker, *Deutsche Juden im Kampf umRecht und Freiheit*, 187.

5. Seeking a Place under Nazi Rule

1. Wild, "Violence against Jews in Germany," 181, 209.
2. Messerschmidt, *Wehrmacht im NS-Staat*, 41.
3. Quoted in Brenner, *Renaissance of Jewish Culture in Weimar Germany*, 213.
4. Quoted in Schoeps, *Gewaltsyndrom*, 113.

5. Barkai, *Deutsch-Jüdische Geschichte*, 189–90.
6. Benz, *Jüdisches Leben in der Weimarer Republik*, 79.
7. See also the insightful remarks of the prominent Zionist Robert Weltsch in his preface to S. Adler-Rudel, *Jüdische Selbsthilfe unter dem Naziregime*.
8. Adler-Rudel, *Jüdische Selbsthilfe unter dem Naziregime*, 184.
9. Baker, *Days of Sorrow and Pain*, 159.
10. Levine, "Jewish Leadership in Germany and the Nazi Threat in 1933," 188–89.
11. Munk, *Juden und Umwelt*, 34.
12. Trachtenberg, *Greuelpropaganda ist eine Lügenpropaganda sagen die deutschen Juden selbst*.
13. Quoted in Benz, *Juden in Deutschland*, 31.
14. In 1955 Baeck and other German-Jewish intellectuals who were meeting in Jerusalem founded there an institute for the study of German Jewish history and culture. Honoring Baeck's preeminent standing in this field, it was named the Leo Baeck Institute, and he became its first president. Baeck died a year later, on November 2, 1956.
15. Prinz, *Wir Juden*, 154–61. In 1937 Prinz came to the United States, where he became rabbi of Temple B'nai Abraham in Newark, New Jersey. He also was appointed president of the American Jewish Congress and took an active part in the struggle for civil rights. Together with Martin Luther King Jr., he was one of ten religious leaders who helped organize the 1963 March on Washington. Prinz died in 1988.
16. See Mendes-Flohr, *Martin Buber*.
17. Quoted in Barkai, "*Wehr dich!*," 17.
18. Barkai, "*Wehr dich!*," 275, 277.
19. Barkai, "*Wehr dich!*," 293.
20. Hirschberg, "Der Centralverein deutscher Staatsbürger jüdischen Glaubens," 29.
21. Barkai, "*Wehr dich!*," 285, 287, 319.
22. Cohn, *No Justice in Germany*, 21, 28, 176, 199.
23. Barkai, "*Wehr dich!*," 312–13.
24. Reichmann, *Grösse und Verhängnis deutsch-jüdischer Existenz*, 61.
25. Quoted in Barkai, "*Wehr dich!*," 375.
26. Hermann, *Dritte Reich und die deutsch-jüdischen Organisationen*, 66–67.

27. Blasius and Diner, *Zerbrochene Geschichte*, 129.
28. Levine, "Jewish Leadership in Germany and the Nazi Threat in 1933," 194.
29. Dunker, *Reichsbund jüdischer Frontsoldaten*, 134.
30. Freund, "Deutschtum und Judentum," 146–47.
31. Herzfeld, "Geist eines neuen Emanzipationskampfes," 96–98.
32. Herzfeld, "Geist eines neuen Emanzipationskampfes," 131.
33. Maybaum, "Absage an den RJF," 259–61.
34. Boas, "German-Jewish Internal Politics under Hitler 1933–1938," 11n38.
35. Hermann, *Dritte Reich und die deutsch-jüdischen Organisationen*, 68.
36. Dunker, *Reichsbund jüdischer Frontsoldaten*, 133; Grady, "Fighting a Lost Battle," 15.
37. Hermann, *Dritte Reich und die deutsch-jüdischen Organisationen*, 95.
38. Hermann, *Dritte Reich und die deutsch-jüdischen Organisationen*, 96.
39. Hermann, *Dritte Reich und die deutsch-jüdischen Organisationen*, 97–98.
40. Grady, "Fighting a Lost Battle," 8–11.
41. Grady, "Fighting a Lost Battle," 126.
42. Messerschmidt, *Wehrmacht im NS-Staat*, 45.
43. Hermann, *Dritte Reich und die deutsch-jüdischen Organisationen*, 139–40.
44. Dunker, *Reichsbund jüdischer Frontsoldaten*, 173.
45. Summary of meeting by R. von Stutterheim, June 2, in Hermann, *Dritte Reich und die deutsch-jüdischen Organisationen*, 135–36.
46. Hermann, *Dritte Reich und die deutsch-jüdischen Organisationen*, 50.
47. Dunker, *Reichsbund jüdischer Frontsoldaten*, 177.
48. Grady, *German-Jewish Soldiers of the First World War*, 181.
49. "Aachen: Die vormalige Gallwitz Kaserne hat einen neuen Namensgeber," *Aachener Zeitung*, January 1, 2014.
50. "Gesinnung," October 1933, quoted in Hermann, *Dritte Reich und die deutsch-jüdischen Organisationen*, 31.
51. Holzmann, *Und es beginnt ein neuer Tag: Autobiographie*, 35, 45.
52. Dunker, *Reichsbund jüdischer Frontsoldaten*, 197.
53. Rheins, "Schwarzes Fähnlein, Jungenschaft," 192.
54. Rheins, "Verband nationaldeutscher Juden," 253.
55. Hambrock, *Etablierung der Aussenseiter*, 569, 633.
56. Hermann, *Dritte Reich und die deutsch-jüdischen Organisationen*, 80.
57. Quoted in Hermann, *Dritte Reich und die deutsch-jüdischen Organisationen*, 24.

58. Hermann, *Dritte Reich und die deutsch-jüdischen Organisationen*, 25–26.
59. Hambrock, *Etablierung der Aussenseiter*, 679–80.
60. Hermann, *Dritte Reich und die deutsch-jüdischen Organisationen*, 26–27.
61. Hermann, *Dritte Reich und die deutsch-jüdischen Organisationen*, 12.
62. Barkai, "*Wehr dich!*," 290–91.
63. Schoeps, "Jahr später," 123.
64. Schoeps, "Wir deutschen Juden," 211; and Schoeps, "Deutscher Vortrupp," 164–65.
65. Schoeps, *Bereit für Deutschland*, 23, 75.
66. Rheins, "Deutscher Vortrupp," 217.
67. Trachtenberg, *Greuelpropaganda ist eine Lügenpropaganda*, 26.
68. Schoeps, "Wir deutschen Juden," 197.
69. Quoted in Faber, *Deutschbewusstes Judentum und jüdischbewusstses Deutschtum*, 23.
70. Schoeps, "Wir deutschen Juden," 204–6, 215.
71. Schoeps, *Ja, Nein, Trotzdem*, 131–32.
72. Schoeps, "*Bereit für Deutschland*," 19.
73. Quoted in Rheins, "Deutscher Vortrupp," 224.
74. Schoeps, "*Bereit für Deutschland*," 162.
75. Schoeps, "*Bereit für Deutschland*," 167.
76. Schoeps, "*Bereit für Deutschland*," 9.
77. Hermann, *Dritte Reich und die deutsch-jüdischen Organisationen*, 64.
78. Nicosia, "End of Emancipation and the Illusion of Preferential Treatment," 246.
79. Beckhardt, *Jude mit dem Hakenkreuz*, 181.
80. Nicosia, "Revisionist Zionism in Germany II," 251.
81. Buber, "Krise der deutsch-jüdischen Gemeinschaft," 46.
82. Dippel, *Bound Upon a Wheel of Fire*, 95.
83. Zimmermann, *Deutschen Juden*, 33.
84. Hermann, *Dritte Reich und die deutsch-jüdischen Organisationen*, 147.
85. Dunker, *Reichsbund jüdischer Frontsoldaten*, 137, 155.
86. Boas, "German-Jewish Internal Politics under Hitler," 11n40.
87. Klemperer, *I Will Bear Witness*, 68–69.
88. Dunker, *Reichsbund jüdischer Frontsoldaten*, 160.
89. Rosenstock, "Exodus," 373–74.
90. Quoted in Matthäus, *Jewish Responses to Persecution*, 369.

91. Karesky was accused of taking money from the Gestapo. See Nicosia, "Revisionist Zionism in Germany II."
92. Adler-Rudel, *Jüdische Selbsthilfe unter dem Naziregime*, 219.
93. Seligmann, "Illegal Way of Life in Nazi Germany," 353–55.
94. Strafstetter, "Submergence into Illegality," 109.
95. See Stoltzfus, *Resistance of the Heart*.
96. Kershaw, "Persecution of the Jews and German Popular Opinion in the Third Reich," 284. See also Bankier, *Probing the Depth of German Antisemitism*.

6. Land of the Murderers

1. Brenner, "Transformation of the German-Jewish Community," 50–51.
2. Stern, *Whitewashing of the Yellow Badge*, 107; Grossmann, "Where Did All 'Our' Jews Go,?" 136–37.
3. Brenner, *After the Holocaust*, 95.
4. Brenner, *After the Holocaust*, 53.
5. Brenner, *After the Holocaust*, 49.
6. Brenner, *Geschichte der Juden in Deutschland*, 164.
7. Ginsburg, "Politik danach," 115.
8. Brenner, *After the Holocaust*, 66.
9. Brenner, *Geschichte der Juden in Deutschland*, 218–19.
10. Benz, "Jewish Existence in Germany from the Perspective of the Non-Jewish Majority," 102.
11. Benz, "Jewish Existence in Germany from the Perspective of the Non-Jewish Majority," 109.
12. Mounk, *Stranger in My Own Country*, 110.
13. Grossmann, "Where Did All 'Our' Jews Go?," 148.
14. Brenner, *Geschichte der Juden in Deutschland*, 249.
15. Stern, *Whitewashing of the Yellow Badge*, 375.
16. Sinn, "Going Public," 27.
17. Cf. Wojak, *Fritz Bauer*.
18. Bergmann and Erb, "Wie antisemitisch sind die Deutschen?," 50–51.
19. Brenner, *Geschichte der Juden in Deutschland*, 55.
20. Simon Tomlinson, "19 Million Germans Have Anti-Semitic Views," *Daily Mail*, May 16, 2014.
21. Ahlheim and Heger, *Unbequeme Vergangenheit*, 52.
22. Quoted in Mounk, *Stranger in My Own Country*, 137.
23. Antifa and Halle, *Trotz und wegen Auschwitz*, 8.

24. Quoted in Mound, *Stranger in My Own Country*, 139.
25. "Gedenkfeier für Manfred Stolpe," Der Bundespräsident, https://www.bundespräsident.de (accessed January 21, 2020).
26. Bergmann and Erb, *Anti-Semitism in Germany*, 18.
27. Korn, *Fragile Grundlage*, 20.
28. Quoted in Wiegel and Klotz, *Geistige Brandstiftung?*, 9; Salzborn, "Anti-Jewish Guilt and National Self-Victimization," 40–45.
29. Quoted in Brenner, *Geschichte der Juden in Deutschland*, 425.
30. Quoted in Wiegel and Klotz, *Geistige Brandstiftung?*, 8.
31. Wiegel and Klotz, *Geistige Brandstiftung?*, 33.
32. Broder, "Ein moderner Antisemit," 93.
33. Mounk, *Stranger in My Own Country*, 146.
34. Goschler and Kauders, "Positionierungen," 325.
35. See Katrina Bennhold, "Germany Says Boycott of Israel is Anti-Semitic," *New York Times*, May 18, 2019.
36. Diamant, *Geschändete Friedhöfe in Deutschland 1945 bis 1999*.
37. Bundesministerium des Innern, *Antisemitismus in Deutschland*, 55.
38. Melissa Eddy, Rick Gladstone, and Tiffany Hsu, "Gunman Strikes German Temple on Yom Kippur," *New York Times*, October 10, 2019.
39. Isaac Stanley-Becker and Alexander Rojkov, "Muslim Asylum Seekers Reckon with Germany's Nazi Past," *Washington Post*, August 13, 2017.
40. Legge Jr., *Jews, Turks, and Other Strangers*, 130.
41. Christopher Schuetze, "Anti-Semitic Crimes Sharply Increase," *New York Times*, May 28, 2020.
42. James Angelos, "The New German Anti-Semitism," *New York Times Magazine*, May 26, 2019.
43. ADL/Global 100, https://global100.adl.org/ (accessed January 21, 2020).
44. "Lucke macht 'Kampfansage' an AfD," *Pro Christliches Medienmagazin*, April 15, 2019.
45. Melissa Eddy, "Some German Jews Embrace Far Right," *New York Times*, September 27, 2018.
46. "German Jews Denounce Far-right Party at Kristallnacht Memorial," *Jewish Telegraphic Agency*, November 9, 2018.
47. Shapira, *Wird man ja wohl noch schreiben dürfen*, 212–13.
48. Christopher F. Schuetze, "German Official Advises Jews against Wearing Skullcaps," *New York Times*, May 27, 2019.

49. Peck, *Being Jewish in the New Germany*, 40–41.
50. Peck, *Being Jewish in the New Germany*, 40–41.
51. Rappaport, *Jews in Germany*, 49–51.
52. Schoeps, *Mein Weg als Deutscher und Jude*, 314.
53. Schoeps, *Deutsch-jüdische Symbiose*, 399.
54. Ralph-Ranicki, *Mein Leben*, 373.
55. Zipes, "Critical Embracement of Germany," 183–201.
56. Giordano, "Problem—der 'hässliche Deutsche,'" 188.
57. Bubis, *Juden in Deutschland*, 14, 21, 34; Brenner, *Geschichte der Juden in Deutschland*, 427.
58. Broder, *Jew in the New Germany*, 105.
59. Broder, *Jew in the New Germany*, 105.
60. Broder, *Jew in the New Germany*, 3.
61. Broder, *Jew in the New Germany*, 31, 23.
62. Schneider, *Zwischenwelten*, 219.
63. Fleischmann, *Dies ist nicht mein Land*, 227.
64. Mounk, *Stranger in My Own Country*, 31.
65. Rahden, "History in the House of the Hangman," 171, 176.
66. Brenner, *Geschichte der Juden in Deutschland*, 155; Mounk, *Stranger in My Own Country*, 100, 103.
67. Wolffsohn, *Meine Juden—Eure Juden*, 231.
68. Goldschmidt, *Legacy of German Jewry*, 233.
69. Diner, "Negative Symbiosis," 251–61.
70. Kreisler, "Misstrauen," 243.
71. Fischer, "Deutschland, deine Juden," 42.
72. Valeriya Safronova, "Rethinking the Jewish Place in Germany," *New York Times*, January 20, 2020.
73. Quoted in Gilman, "Negative Symbiosis," 55.
74. Wolffsohn, *Verwirrtes Deutschland?*, 153. See also Wolffsohn, *Meine Juden—Eure Juden*.
75. Korn, *Fragile Grundlage*, 158.

7. Being Jewish in East Germany

1. Maser, "Juden und jüdische Gemeinden in der DDR bis in das Jahr 1988," 400; Hartewig, "Zurückgekehrt," 3.
2. Deutscher, *Non-Jewish Jew and Other Essays*.
3. Combe, "DDR," 141.
4. Herf, *Divided Memory*, 385.
5. For the role of the Stasi, see Koehler, *Stasi*.

6. Kahane, “Wirkung eines Tabus,” 39.
7. Gerber, “Sieger der Geschichte,” 38, 41.
8. Quoted in Käppner, *Erstarrte Geschichte*, 59.
9. Dennis and La Porte, *State and Minorities in Communist East Germany*, 35.
10. O’Doherty, “GDR in the Context of Stalinist Show Trials and Anti-Semitism in Eastern Europe,” 304.
11. Ascher, *Stalin*, 185.
12. Azadovskii and Egorov, “From Anti-Westernism to Anti-Semitism,” 76.
13. Norwood, *Antisemitism and the American Far Left*, 146, 151.
14. Quoted in Herf, *Divided Memory*, 108.
15. Illichmann, *DDR und die Juden*, 85.
16. Honigmann, “Gibt es in der DDR Antisemitismus?,” 6.
17. Honigmann, “Gibt es in der DDR Antisemitismus?,” 155; Wistrich, *From Ambivalence to Betrayal*, 450.
18. Miles, *Nine Lives of Otto Katz*, 204.
19. Podewin, *Albert Norden*, 256.
20. “Lehren aus dem Prozess gegen das Verschwörerzentrum Slansky,” *Neues Deutschland*, January 4, 1953.
21. Kessler, *SED und die Juden*, 153–54.
22. Burgauer, *Zwischen Erinnerung und Verdrängung*, 182.
23. Eschwege, *Fremd unter meinesgleichen*, 184.
24. Kessler, “Verdrängung der Geschichte,” 44–45.
25. Meining, *Kommunistische Judenpolitik*, 165.
26. Niether, *Leipziger Juden und die DDR*, 136; Maser, “Juden und die jüdischen Gemeinden in der DDR,” 400.
27. Herf, “East German Communists and the Jewish Question,” 640, 646; Hartewig, *Zurückgekehrt*, 369.
28. Hartewig, *Zurückgekehrt*, 59.
29. Herf, *Undeclared War with Israel*, 356–58. See also Herf, “Im Krieg mit Israel,” 129–30.
30. The full text of the agreement of August 2, 1973, is given in Timm, *Jewish Claims against East Germany*, 545.
31. Timm, *Jewish Claims against East Germany*, 537.
32. Meining, *Kommunistische Judenpolitik*, 351.
33. Otto, *SED im Juni 1953*, 106. See also Illichmann, *DDR und die Juden*, 112–13.
34. Meining, *Kommunistische Judenpolitik*, 201.
35. Hartewig, *Zurückgekehrt*, 382.

36. Herf, *Undeclared War with Israel*, 451.
37. Niether, *Leipziger Juden und die DDR*, 260–61. See also Meining, *Kommunistische Judenpolitik*, and Klein et al., eds., *Visionen*, 220.
38. Groehler, "Holocaust in der Geschichtsschreibung der DDR," 52.
39. Wolf, *Man without a Face*, xii.
40. Herf, *Divided Memory*, 135.
41. Kessler, "Verdrängung der Geschichte," 40.
42. Wolffsohn, *Deutschland-Akte*, 146.
43. Kantorowicz, *Deutsches Tagebuch*, vol. 2, 279.
44. Meining, *Kommunistische Judenpolitik*, 156; Hartewig, *Zurückgekehrt*, 167–68.
45. The full text of this memo is reprinted in Stulz-Herrnstadt, *Das Herrnstadt Dokument*, 2–7.
46. Huhn, *Fall Rudolf Herrnstadt*, 8, 85. See also Grieder, *East-German Leadership*.
47. Stulz-Herrnstadt, *Herrnstadt Dokument*, 31.
48. Stulz-Herrnstadt, *Herrnstadt Dokument*, 1.
49. Letter of July 5, 1956, quoted in Müller-Enbergs, *Fall Rudolf Herrnstadt*, 336.
50. Liebmann, *Wäre es schön?*, 374, 386.
51. Kuczinski, "Wo wäre es anders gewesen?," 45.
52. Kuczinski, *Dialog mit meinem Urenkel*, 28.
53. Kuczinski, *Memoiren*, 417.
54. Bornemann and. Peck, *Sojourners*, 129.
55. Wagner, *Hilde Benjamin und die Stalinisierung der DDR Justiz*.
56. Kantorowicz, *Deutsche Schicksale*, 256.
57. Kantorowicz, *Deutsche Schicksale*, 35, 41. See also Krüger, *Ende einer Utopie*, 162–63.
58. Kantorowicz, *Deutsches Tagebuch*, vol. 1, 585–86.
59. Kantorowicz, *Deutsches Tagebuch*, vol. 1, 668.
60. Kantorowicz, *Deutsches Tagebuch*, vol. 2, 225.
61. Kantorowicz, *Deutsches Tagebuch*, vol. 2, 334–35.
62. Kantorowicz, *Deutsches Tagebuch*, vol. 2, 391.
63. Kantorowicz, *Deutsches Tagebuch*, vol. 2, 31.
64. Kantorowicz, *Deutsches Tagebuch*, vol. 2, 691.
65. Kantorowicz, *Deutsches Tagebuch*, vol. 2, 34.
66. Kantorowicz, *Deutsches Tagebuch*, vol. 2, 715.
67. Jander, "Antifaschismus ohne Juden," 219.
68. Eschwege, *Fremd unter meinesgleichen*, 66–67.

69. Eschwege, *Fremd unter meinesgleichen*, 73–79.
70. Eschwege, *Fremd unter meinesgleichen*, 106–7.
71. Eschwege, *Fremd unter meinesgleichen*, 88.
72. Eschwege, *Fremd unter meinesgleichen*, 278–79; Timm, *Jewish Claims against East Germany*, 550–51.
73. Meining, *Kommunistische Judenpolitik*, 235–37.
74. Hartewig, *Zurückgekehrt*, 193–94.
75. Letter of November 27, 1950, quoted in Hartewig, *Zurückgekehrt*, 361.
76. Heym, *Nachruf*, 560.
77. Heym, *Nachruf*, 558.
78. David Binder, "Stefan Heym, Marxist-Leninist Novelist, Dies at 88 on Lecture Tour in Israel," *New York Times*, December 18, 2001.
79. Heym, *Auf Sand gebaut*, 43.
80. Heym, *Nachruf*, 771–12, 833–36.
81. Temme, "Heym's Kritik am falschen Sozialismus," 141.
82. Fox, "Stefan Heym and the Negotiation of Socialist-Jewish Identity." In Temme, "Heym's Kritik am falschen Sozialismus," 3.
83. Wolffsohn, *Deutschland Akte*, 165.
84. Quoted (without date) in Joseph, *DDR und die Juden*, 69.
85. Meining, *Kommunistische Judenpolitik*, 275.
86. Meining, *Kommunistische Judenpolitik*, 272.
87. Full text in Kessler, *SED und die Juden*, 174–75.
88. Timm, "Eine ambivalentes Verhältnis," 28–29.
89. Meining, *Kommunistische Judenpolitik*, 216. See also Eschwege, *Geschichte der Juden im Territorium der ehemaligen DDR*, 156.
90. The full text of the minutes can be found in Timm, *Jewish Claims against East Germany*, 541–44.
91. Genin, "Rückkehr?," 309–26. See also Genin, *Ich folgte den falschen Göttern*.
92. Gay, *Safe among the Germans*, 252; Niether, *Leipziger Juden und die DDR*, 294–95.
93. Wroblewsky, *Unheimlich Liebe*, 156–57.
94. See also Kahane, *Ich sehe was, was du nicht siehst*.
95. Honigmann, *Damals, Dann, und Danach*, 29, 68.
96. Honigmann, *Damals, Dann, und Danach*, 15–17.
97. Timm, *Jewish Claims against East Germany*, 554.
98. Richarz, "Juden in der Bundesrepublik Deutschland und in der Demokratischen Republik seit 1945," 21.
99. Hartewig, *Zurückgekehrt*, 575.

100. Seligmann, *Mit beschränkter Hoffnung*, 275–76.
101. Hartewig, *Zurückgekehrt*, 575.
102. Timm, *Jewish Claims against East Germany*, 588; Hartewig, *Zurückgekehrt*, 617.
103. Herf, *Divided Memory*, 365.
104. Seligmann, *Mit beschränkter Hoffnung*, 295.
105. Gilman, "German Reunification and the Jews," 174.
106. Mertens, *Davidstern und Hammer und Sichel*, 343; Schubarth, "Xenophobia among East German Youth," 145–49.
107. Schubarth, "Xenophobia among East German Youth," 145–49.
108. Thomas Haury, "Communist Anti-Semitism in East Germany," *Jewish Center for Public Affairs*, August 1, 2007; "Geographical Distribution of the Extreme Right in Germany," *Myplace*, September 25, 2012. In the former East German states of Brandenburg and Saxony, the right-extremist AfD emerged as the strongest party in the May 2019 elections to the European parliament.
109. Meining, *Kommunistische Judenpolitik*, 524.
110. Honigmann, *Kapitel aus meinem Leben*, 124.
111. Sternberg, *Arnold Zweig*, 212, 218.
112. Stenographic report of the Thirteenth Party Congress, quoted in Ascher, *Stalin*, 60.
113. Volker Müller, "Dichterwitwe Lotte Fürnberg erinnert sich ihrer Lebensjahre mit Louis Fürnberg," *Berliner Zeitung*, January 26, 2001.
114. Axen, *Ich war Diener der Partei*, 119.

Conclusion

1. Prinz, *Rebellious Rabbi*, 146.
2. Bauman, *Modernity and Ambivalence*, 94
3. Rabinach and Zipes, *Germans and Jews since the Holocaust*, 4.
4. Quoted in Gay, *Freud, Jews, and other Germans*, 165.
5. Weltsch, *Deutsches Judentum*, 7.
6. Elon, *Pity of it All*, 6.
7. Bloch, "Sogenannte Judenfrage," 280.
8. Buber, "Krise der deutsch-jüdischen Gemeinschaft," 46.
9. Buber, "Ende der Deutsch-jüdischen Symbiose," 630.
10. Aschheim, *In Times of Crisis*, 149.
11. Scholem, "Jews and Germans," 36. The fullest exposition of Scholem's views on the German-Jewish relationship can be found in his *On Jews and Judaism*.

12. Gay, *Jews of Germany*, xii.
13. Aschheim, *Scholem, Arendt, Klemperer*, 39.
14. Pulzer, *Jews and the German State*, 343.
15. Quoted in Grunfeld, *Prophets without Honor*, 1.
16. Scholem, "Jews and Germans," 35.
17. Scholem, "Wieder den Mythos vom deutsch-jüdischen Gespräch," 7–8.
18. Quoted in Benz, "Jewish Existence in Germany," 110.
19. Prinz, *Rebellious Rabbi*, 146.
20. Benz, "Legend of German-Jewish Symbiosis," 101.
21. Yehuda Bauer, "'German-Jewish Symbiosis' against the Background of the '30s," Shoah Resource Center, www.yadvashem.org (accessed December 19, 2019).
22. Mosse, *German Jews Beyond Judaism*, 72–73.
23. Elon, *Pity of It All*, 11, 5.
24. Gay, *Freud, Jews and Other Germans*, 165.
25. Quoted in Schulte, *Deutschtum un Judentum*, 151.
26. Stern, *Dreams and Delusions*, 114.
27. Voigts, *Deutsch-jüdische Symbiose*, 11.
28. Mayer, "Gedächtnis und die Geschichte," 13.
29. Cited by Hayman, *Thomas Mann*, 437–38.
30. Scholem, *On Jews and Judaism in Crisis*, 67, quoted in Zadoff, *Gershom Scholem*, 209.
31. Zadoff, *Gershom Scholem*, 250.
32. Scholem, "Jews and Germans," 37.
33. Aschheim, *Scholem, Arendt, Klemperer*, 19.
34. Voigts, *Zwischen Antisemitismus und deutsch-jüdischer Symbiose*, 267.
35. Pulzer, *Jews and the German State*, 345–46.
36. Prinz, *Rebellious Rabbi*, 86.
37. Joseph Levy's essay "Good Germans, Bad Germans" was part of a collection of memoirs by German Jewish refugees collected by Harvard University in 1940. It is reproduced in Limberg and Rübstatt, eds., *Germans No More*, 80–83.
38. See Lewy, *Perpetrators*.
39. Schoeps, *Gewaltsyndrom*, 11.
40. Bieber, "Anti-Semitism as a Reflection of Social, Economic and Political Tension," 62.
41. Pulzer, *Jews and the German State*, 349.
42. Timms, "Zwischen Symbiotik und Holocaustismus," 25.

Bibliography

Abusch, Alexander. *Der Deckname: Memoiren.* Berlin: Dietz, 1981.

———. *Mit offenem Visier: Memoiren.* Berlin: Dietz, 1986.

Adler, H. G. *The Jews in Germany: From the Enlightenment to National Socialism.* Notre Dame IN: University of Notre Dame Press, 1969.

Adler-Rudel, S. *Jüdische Selbsthilfe unter dem Naziregime, 1933–1939: Im Spiegel der Berichte der Reichsvertretung der Juden in Deutschland.* Tübingen: J. C. B. Mohr, 1974.

———. *Ostjuden in Deutschland, 1880–1940: Zugleich eine Geschichte der Organisation die sie betreuten.* Tübingen: J. C. B. Mohr, 1969.

Adriaansen, Robbert-Jan. *The Rhythm of Eternity: The German Youth Movement and the Experience of the Past, 1900–1933.* New York: Berghahn, 2015.

AG Antica, Uni Halle. *Trotz und wegen Auschwitz: Antisemitismus und nationale Identität nach 1945.* Münster: Unrast, 2004.

Ahlheim, Klaus. *Die unbequeme Vergangenheit: NS-Vergangenheit, Holocaust und die Schwierigkeiten des Erinnern.* Schwalbach/Ts: Wochenschau, 2002.

Alexander, Edgar. *Jews against Themselves.* New Brunswick NJ: Transaction, 2015.

Amery, Jean. *At the Mind's Limits: Contemplations by a Survivor on Auschwitz and its Realities.* Bloomington: Indiana University Press, 1980.

Angress, Werner T. *Between Fear and Hope: Jewish Youth in the Third Reich.* Translated by Werner T. Angress and Christine Granger. New York: Columbia University Press, 1988.

———. "The German Army's 'Judenzählung' of 1916: Genesis-Consequences-Significance." *Leo Baeck Institute Yearbook* 23 (1978): 117–37.

———. "Prussia's Army and the Jewish Reserve Officer Controversy before WWI." *Leo Baeck Institute Yearbook* 17 (1972): 19–42.

Arendt, Hannah. *Eichmann in Jerusalem: A Report on the Banality of Evil*. New York: Viking, 1963.

Ascher, Abraham. *Stalin: A Beginner's Guide*. London: One World, 2017.

Aschheim, Steven E. *Brothers and Strangers: The East European Jew in German and German-Jewish Consciousness, 1800–1923*. Madison: University of Wisconsin Press, 1982.

———. *In Times of Crisis: Essays on European Culture, Germans, and Jews*. Madison: University of Wisconsin Press, 2001.

———. *Scholerm, Arendt, Klemperer: Intimate Chronicles in Turbulent Times*. Bloomington: Indiana University Press, 2011.

———, and Vivian Liska, eds. *The German-Jewish Experience Revisited*. Berlin: Walter de Gruyter, 2015.

Axen, Hermann. *Ich war Diener der Partei: Autobiographische Gespräche mit Harald Neubert*. Berlin: Edition Ost, 1996.

Azadovskii, Konstantin, and Boris Egorov. "From Anti-Westernism to Anti-Semitism: Stalin and the Impact of the 'Anti-Cosmopolitan' Campaign on Soviet Culture." *Journal of Cold War Studies* 4 (2002): 66–80.

Baker, Leonhard. *Days of Sorrow and Pain: Leo Baeck and the Berlin Jews*. New York: Oxford University Press, 1978.

Bamberger, Fritz. *Leo Baeck: The Man and the Idea*. New York: Leo Baeck Institute, 1958.

Bankier, David. *Probing the Depth of German Antisemitism: German Society and the Persecution of the Jews*. New York: Berghahn, 2000.

Barkai, Avraham. *"Wehr dich!" Der Centralverein deutscher Staatsbürger jüdischen Glaubens (C.V.), 1893–1938*. Munich: C. H. Beck, 2002.

———, and Paul Mendes-Flohr. *Deutsch-Jüdische Geschichte der Neuzeit*. Vol. 4: *Aufbruch und Zerstörung 1918–1945*. Munich: C. H. Beck, 1997.

Barnouw, Dagmar. *Visible Spaces: Hannah Arendt and the German-Jewish Experience*. Baltimore: Johns Hopkins University Press, 1990.

Bauer, Yehuda. "'German-Jewish Symbiosis' Against the Background of the 30s." Shoah Resource Center, www.yadvashem.org (accessed December 19, 2019).

Bauman, Zygmunt. *Modernity and Ambivalence*. Oxford: Polity, 1991.

Becker, Jurek. *My Father, the Germans, and I: Essays, Lectures, Interviews*. London: Seagull, 2010.

Beckhardt, Lorenz S. *Der Jude mit dem Hakenkreuz: Meine deutsche Familie*. Berlin: Aufbau, 2014.

Bein, Alex. "The Jewish Parasite: Notes on the Semantics of the Jewish Problem, with Special Reference to Germany." *Leo Baeck Institute Yearbook* 9 (1964): 3–40.

Benz, Wolfgang. "Jewish Existence in Germany from the Perspective of the Non-Jewish Majority: Daily Life between Anti-Semitism and Philo-Semitism." In *Unlikely History: The Changing German-Jewish Symbiosis, 1945–2000*, edited by Leslie Morris and Jack Zipes, 101–17. New York: Palgrave, 2002.

———. "The Legend of the German-Jewish Symbiosis." *Leo Baeck Institute Yearbook* 37 (1992): 95–102.

———. "The November Progrom of 1938: Participation, Applause, Disapproval." In *Exclusionary Violence: Antisemitic Riots in Modern German History*, edited by Christhard Hoffmann, Werner Bergmann, and Helmut Walser, 141–59. Ann Arbor: University of Michigan Press, 2002.

———, ed. *Antisemitismus in Deutchland: Zur Aktualität eines Vorurteils*. Munich: Deutscher Taschenbuch Verlag, 1995.

———. *Das Exil der kleinen Leute: Alltagserfahrungen deutscher Juden in der Emigration*. Munich: C. H. Beck, 1991.

———. *Die Juden in Deutschland 1933–1945: Leben unter nationalsozialistischer Herrschaft*. Munich: C. H. Beck, 1988.

Berding, Helmut. *Moderner Antisemitismus in Deutchland*. Frankfurt/M: Suhrkamp, 1988.

Bergbauer, Knut. "Jüdische Jugendbewegung in Breslau, 1912–1938." n.p., 2011.

———. *"Wir sind jung, die Welt is offen": Eine jüdische Jugendtruppe im 20. Jahrhundert*. Berlin: Haus der Wannsee Konferenz, 2002.

Berghahn, Klaus L., ed. *The German-Jewish Dialogue Reexamined: A Symposium in Honor of George L. Mosse*. New York: Peter Land, 1996.

Bergmann, Werner, and Rainer Erb. *Anti-Semitism in Germany: The Post Nazi Epoch Since 1945*. Translated by Belinda Cooper and Allison Brown. New Brunswick NJ: Transaction, 1997.

———. "Wie antisemitisch sind die Deutschen? Meinungsumfragen 1945–1994." In *Antisemitismus in Deutschland*, edited by Wolfgang Benz, 47–63. Munich: Deutscher Taschenbuch Verlag, 1995.

———, and Julian Wetzel. "'Der Mitlebende weiss nichts': Alltagsantisemitismus als zeitgenössische Erfahrung und spätere Erinnerung (1919–1933)." In *Jüdisches Leben in der Weimarer Republik*, edited by Wolfgang Benz et al., 173–96. Tübingen: Mohr, 1998.

Bering, Dietz. *Der Name als Stigma: Antisemitismus im deutschen Alltag 1817–1933*. Stuttgart: Klett-Cotta, 1987.

Biale, David. "Gerschom Scholem between German and Jewish Nationalism." In *The German-Jewish Dialogue Reexamined: A Symposium in Honor of George L. Mosse*, edited by Klaus L. Berghahn, 177–88. New York: Peter Land, 1996.

———. *Gerschom Scholem: Master of the Kabbalah*. New Haven CT: Yale University Press, 2018.

Bieber, Hans-Joachim. "Antisemitism as a Reflection of Social, Economic and Political Tension in Germany, 1880–1933." In *Jews and Germans from 1860 to 1933*, edited by David Bronson, 33–77. Heidelberg: Carl Winter, 1979.

Birnbaum, Pierre, and Ira Katznelson, eds. *Paths of Emancipation: Jews, States and Citizenship*, edited by Pierre Birnbaum and Ira Katznelson. Princeton NJ: Princeton University Press, 1995.

Blasius, Dirk, and Dan Diner, eds., *Zerbrochene Geschichte: Leben und Selbstverständnis der Juden in Deutschland*. Frankfurt/M: Fischer, 1991.

Blüher, Hans. *Secessio Judaica: Philosophische Grundlegung der historischen Situation des Judentums and der antisemitischen Bewegung*. Berlin: Der Weisse Ritter, 1922.

Blumenthal, W. Michael. *The Invisible Wall: Germans and Jews, a Personal Exploration*. Washington DC: Counterpoint, 1999.

Boas, Jacob. "German-Jewish Internal Politics under Hitler, 1933–1938." *Leo Baeck Institute Yearbook* 29 (1984): 3–25.

Bodemann, Y. Michal, ed. *Jews, Germans, Memory: Reconstructions of Jewish Life in Germany*. Ann Arbor: University of Michigan Press, 1996.

Bolkosky, Sidney M. *The Distorted Image: German-Jewish Perceptions of Germans and Germany, 1919–1935*. New York: Elsevier, 1975.

Borinski, Fritz, and Werner Milch. *Jugendbewegung: The Story of German Youth, 1896–1933*. London: German Educational Reconstruction, 1945.

Borneman, John, and Jeffrey Pick, eds., *Sojourners: The Return of German Jews and the Question of Identity*. Lincoln: University of Nebraska Press, 1995.

Borries, Achim von, ed. *Selbsterzeugnis des deutschen Judentums, 1870–1945*. Frankfurt/M: Fischer, 1962.

Brenner, Michael. *After the Holocaust: Rebuilding Jewish Lives in Postwar Germany*. Translated by Barbara Harshav. Princeton NJ: Princeton University Press, 1997.

———. *The Renaissance of Jewish Culture in Weimar Germany*. New Haven CT: Yale University Press, 1996.
———. "The Transformation of the German-Jewish Community." In *Unlikely History: The Changing German-Jewish Symbiosis, 1945–2000*, edited by Leslie Morris and Jack Zipes, 49–61. New York: Palgrave, 2002.
———, ed. *Geschichte der Juden in Deutschland von 1945 bis zur Gegenwart: Politik, Kultur und Gesellschaft*. Munich: C. H. Beck, 2012.
Broder, Henryk. *A Jew in the New Germany*. Translated by Broder Translators' Collective. Urbana: University of Illinois Press, 2004.
———. "Ein moderner Antisemit." In *"Es muss doch in diesem Lande wieder möglich sein . . .": Der neue Antisemitismus-Streit*, edited by Michael Naumann, 92–95. Munich: Ullstein, 2002.
Broder, Michael, and Michel R. Lang, eds., *Fremd im eignen Land: Juden in der Bundesrepublik*. Frankfurt/M: Fischer, 1979.
Bronson, David, ed. *Jews and Germans from 1860 to 1933*. Heidelberg: Carl Winter, 1979.
Brumlik, Micha. *Jüdisches Leben in Deutschland seit 1945*. Frankfurt-t/M: Athenäum, 1986.
———. *Kein Weg als Deutscher und Jude: Eine bundesrepublikanische Erfahrung*. Munich: Luchterhand, 1996.
Buber, Martin. *Der Jude und sein Judentum: Gesammelte Aufsätze und Reden*. Cologne: Lambert Schneider, 1993.
Bubis, Ignatz. *Juden in Deutschland*. Berlin: Aufbau, 1996.
Bundesministerium des Innern. *Antisemitismus in Deutschland: Erscheinungsformen, Bedingungen, Präventionsansätze*. Berlin: Eigenverlag des BMI, 2011.
Burgauer, Erica. *Zwischen Erinnerung und Verdrängung: Juden in Deutschland nach 1945*. Reinbek bei Hamburg: Rowohlt, 1993.
Cohen, Hermann. *Deutschtum und Judentum*. Giessen: Alfred Töppelmann, 1915.
Cohn, Willy. *No Justice in Germany: The Breslau Diaries, 1933–1941*. Translated by Kenneth Kronenberg. Stanford CA: Stanford University Press, 2012.
Deak, Istvan. *Weimar's Left-Wing Intellectuals: A Political History of the Weltbühne and its Circle*. Berkeley: University of California Press, 1968.
Dennis, Mike, and Norman La Porte. *State and Minorities in Communist East Germany*. New York: Berghahn, 2011.
Dershowitz, Alan M. "'Alle lieben toten Juden . . .': '. . . aber wenn Israel sich wehrt, hat die Welt ein Problem damit.'" In *"Es muss doch in*

diesem Lande wieder möglich sein . . .": Der neue Antisemitismus-Streit, edited by Michael Naumann. 131–37. Munich: Ullstein, 2002.
Deutscher, Isaac. *The Non-Jewish Jew and other Essays*. London: Oxford University Press, 1968.
Deutscher Vortrupp. In *Wille und Weg des deutschen Judentums*. Berlin: Vortrupp Verlag, 1935.
Diamant, Adolf. *Geschändete Friedhöfe in Deutschland: 1945–1999*. Potsdam: Berlin-Brandenburg, 2000.
"Die Schicksalsstunde des deutschen Judentums." *Jüdische Rundschau* 28, no. 46 (November 9, 1923): 557.
Diner, Dan. "Negative Symbiosis: Germans and Jews after Auschwitz." *Babylon* 1 (1986): 251–61.
Dippel, John V. H. *Bound upon a Wheel of Fire: Why So Many German Jews Made the Tragic Decision to Remain in Nazi Germany*. New York: Basic Books, 1996.
Dohm, Christian Wilhelm von. *Concerning the Amelioration of the Civil Status of the Jews*. Translated by Helen Lederer. Cincinnati OH: Hebrew Jewish College, 1957.
Dunker, Ulrich. *Der Reichsbund jüdischer Frontsoldaten, 1919–1938: Geschichte eines jüdischen Abwehrvereins*. Düsseldorf: Droste, 1977.
Elbogen, Ismar, and Eleonore Sterling. *Die Geschichte der Juden in Deutschland*. Frankfurt/M: Europäische Verlagsanstalt, 1966.
Elon, Amos. *The Pity of It All: A Portrait of the German-Jewish Epoch, 1743–1933*. New York: Henry Holt, 2002.
Engel, Amir. *Gerschom Scholem: An Intellectual Biography*. Chicago: University of Chicago Press, 2017.
Eschwege, Helmut. *Fremd unter meinesgleichen: Erinnerungen eines Dresdner Juden*. Berlin: Ch. Links, 1991.
———. *Geschichte der Juden im Territorium der ehemaligen DDR*. Dresden: Selbstverlag, 1991.
Evans, Stephen. "Kristallnacht 75 Years Ago: How Strong Is Anti-Semitism in Germany?" BBC, November, 8, 2013.
Faber, Richard. *Deutschbewusstes Judentum und jüdischbewusstes Deutschtum: Der historische und politische Theolog Hans-Joachim Schoeps*. Würzburg: Königshausen und Neumann, 2008.
Fink, Carole, Isabel V. Hull, and MacGregor Knox, eds. *German Nationalism and the European Response, 1890–1945*. Norman: University of Oklahoma Press, 1985.

Fischer, Joshka. "Deutschland, deine Juden: Wider die Sprachlosgkeit im deutsch-jüdischen Verhältnis." In *"Es muss doch in diesem Lande möglich sein. . . ,"* edited by Michael Naumann. Munich: Ullstein, 2002.

Fleischmann, Lea. *Dies ist nicht mein Land: Eine Jüdin verlässt die Bundesrepublik*. Hamburg: Hoffmann & Campe, 1980.

Foerder, Ludwig. *Die Stellung des Centralvereins zu den innerjüdischen Fragen in den Jahren 1919–1926: Eine Denkschrift für die Vereinsmitglieder*. Berlin: Volkswacht Buchdruckerei, n.d.

Fox, Thomas C. "Stefan Heym and the Negotiation of Socialist-Jewish Identity." In *Stefan Heym: Socialist, Dissenter, Jew*, edited by Peter Hutchinson and Reinhard K. Zachau, 145–60. Oxford: Peter Lang, 2003.

Fuchs, Eugen. *Um Deutschtum und Judentum: Gesammelte Reden und Aufsätze (1894–1919)*. Frankfurt/M: J. Kaufmann, 1919.

Gay, Peter. *The Berlin-Jewish Spirit: A Dogma in Search of Some Doubts*. New York: Leo Baeck Institute, 1972.

———. *Freud, Jews, and Other Germans: Masters and Victims in Modernist Culture*. New York: Oxford University Press, 1978.

———. *Weimar Culture: The Outsider as Insider*. New York: Harper & Row, 1968.

Gay, Ruth. *The Jews of Germany: A Historical Portrait*. New Haven CT: Yale University Press, 1992.

———. *Safe among the Germans: Liberated Jews after World War II*. New Haven CT: Yale University Press, 2002

Genin, Salomea. *Ich folgte den falschen Göttern: Eine australische Jüdin in der DDR*. Berlin: VBB, 2009.

———. "Rückkehr? Wie ich in der DDR aus einer Kommunistin zu einer Jüdin wurde." In *Das Exil der kleinen Leute*, edited by Wolfgang Benz, 309–26. Munich: C. H. Beck, 1991.

Gerber, Jan. "Sieger der Geschichte: Auschwitz im Spiegel der Geschichtswissenschaft und Geschichtspolitik der DDR." In *Trotz und wegen Auschwitz: Antisemitismus und nationale Identitä nach 1945*, edited by AG Antifa and Uni Halle, 29–47. Münster: Unrast, 2004.

Gerson, Hermann. *Werkleute: Ein Weg jüdischer Jugend*. Berlin: Kommissionsverlag, 1935.

Gilman, Sander L. "German Reunification and the Jews." *New German Critique* 52 (1991): 173–91.

———. "Negative Symbiosis: The Reemergence of Jewish Culture in Germany after the Fall of the Wall." In *The German-Jewish Dialogue*

Reconsidered: A Symposium in Honor of George L. Mosse, edited by Klaus L. Berghahn, 207–32. New York: Peter Lang, 1996.

Ginsburg, Hans Jakob. “Politik danach: Jüdische Interessenvertretung in der Bundesrepublik.” In *Jüdisches Leben in Deutschland seit 1945*, edited by Micha Brumlik, 108–18. Frankfurt/M: Athenäum, 1986.

Giordano, Ralph. “Das Problem—der ‘hässliche Deutsche.’” In *Fremd im eignen Land: Juden in der Bundesrepublik*, edited by Henryk Broder and Michel R. Lang, 168–89. Frankfurt/M: Fischer, 1979.

Goldschmidt, Hermann Levin. *The Legacy of German Jewry*. Translated by David Suchoff. New York: Fordham University Press. 2007

Goldstein, Moritz. “ German Jewry’s Dilemma: The Story of a Provocative Essay.” *Leo Baeck Institute Yearbook* 2 (1957): 236–54.

Goran, Morris. *The Story of Fritz Haber*. Norman: University of Oklahoma Press, 1967.

Grab, Walter. *Der deutsche Weg der Judenemanzipation, 1789–1938*. Munich: Piper, 1991.

———. *Jüdische Integration und Identität in Deutschland und Österreich, 1848–1918*. Tel Aviv: University of Tel Aviv, 1984.

———, and Hans-Joachim Schoeps, eds. *Juden in der Weimarer Republik: Skizzen und Portraits*. Darmstadt: Primus, 1998.

Grady, Tim. “Fighting a Lost Battle: The *Reichsbund jüdischer Frontsoldaten* and the Rise of National Socialism.” *German History* 28 (2010): 1–20.

———. *The German-Jewish Soldiers of the First World War in History and Memory*. Liverpool: Liverpool University Press, 2011.

Grieder, Peter. *The East-German Leadership 1946–73: Conflict and Crisis*. New York: Manchester University Press, 1999.

Groehler, Olaf. “Der Holocaust in der Geschichtsschreibung der DDR.” In *Erinnerung: Zur Gegenwart des Holocaust in Deutschland-West und Deutschland-Ost*, edited by Bernhard Moltmann, 47–65. Frankfurt/M: Haag & Herchen, 1993.

Grossmann, Atina. “Where Did All ‘Our’ Jews Go? Germans and Jews in Post-Nazi Germany.” In *The Germans and the Holocaust: Popular Response to the Persecution and the Murder of the Jews*, edited by Susanna Strafstetter and Alan E. Steinweiss, 131–54. New York: Berghahn, 2016.

Grunfeld, Frederich V. *Prophets without Honor: A Background to Freud, Kafka, Einstein, and Their World*. New York: Holt, Reinhard & Winston, 1979.

Hambrock, Matthias. *Die Etablierung der Aussenseiter: Der Verband nationaldeutscher Juden, 1921–1935*. Cologne: Böhlau, 2003.

Hartewig, Karin. *Zurückgekehrt: Die Geschichte der jüdischen Kommunisten in der DDR*. Cologne: Böhlau, 2000.

Hayman, Ronald. *Thomas Mann: A Biography*. New York: Scribner, 1995.

Hecht, Cornelia. *Deutsche Juden und Antisemitismus in der Weimarer Republik*. Bonn: J. H. W. Dietz, 2003.

Heitzer, Enrico, ed. *Nach Auschwitz: Schwieriges Erbe der DDR*. Frankfurt/M: Wochenschauverlag, 2018.

Heller, Otto. *Der Untergang des Judentums: Die Judenfrage, ihre Kritik, ihre Lösung durch den Sozialismus*. 2nd rev. ed. Vienna: Verlag für Literatur & Politik, 1933.

Herf, Jeffrey. "Antisemitismus in der SED: Geheime Dokumente zum Fall Paul Merker aus SED und MdS Akten." *Vierteljahrshefte für Zeitgschichte* 42 (1994): 635–67.

———. *Divided Memory: The Nazi Past in the Two Germanys*. Cambridge MA: Harvard University Press, 1997.

———. "East Germany Communists and the Jewish Question: The Case of Paul Merker." *Journal of Contemporary History* 29 (1994): 627–61.

———. "Im Krieg mit Israel: Antizionismus in Ostdeutschland seit den 1960er Jahren bis zum Mauerfall." In *Nach Auschwitz: Schwieriges Erbe der DDR*, edited by Enrico Heitzer, 125–45. Frankfurt/M: Wochenschauverlag, 2018.

———. *Undeclared War with Israel: East Germany and the West German Far Left, 1967–1989*. New York: Cambridge University Press, 2016.

Hermand, Jost. "Juden in der Kultur der Weimarer Republik." In *Juden in der Weimarer Republik: Skizzen und Portraits*, edited by Walter Grab and Hans-Joachim Schoeps, 9–37. Darmstadt: Primus, 1998.

———. *Judentum und deutsche Kultur: Beispiele einer schmerzhaften Symbiose*. Cologne: Böhlau 1996.

———. *Jüdische Intelligenz in Deutschland*. Hamburg: Argument, 1988.

Hermann, Georg. "Zur Frage der Westjuden." *Neue Jüdische Monatshefte* 3 (1919): 399–405.

Herrmann, Klaus J. *Das Dritte Reich und die deutsch-jüdischen Organisationen 1933/34*. Cologne: Carl Heymann, 1969.

Hertz, Deborah. *How Jews Became Germans: The History of Conversion and Assimilation in Berlin*. New Haven CT: Yale University Press, 2007.

Herzfeld, Hans. "Der Geist eines neuen Emanzipationskampfes." *Der Schild*, July 13, 1933, 96–98.

Hetkamp, Jutta. *Die jüdische Jugendbewegung in Deutschland von 1913–1933*. Münster: LIT, 1994.

Heym, Stefan. *Auf Sand gebaut: Sieben Geschichten aus der unmittelbaren Vergangenheit*. Munich: C. Bertelsmann, 1990.

———. *Nachruf*. Munich: C. Bertelsmann, 1988.

Heyworth, Peter. *Otto Klemperer*. Cambridge: Cambridge University Press, 1996.

Hirschberg, Alfred. "Der Centralverein deutscher Staatsbürger jüdischen Glaubens." In *Wille und Weg des deutschen Judentums*, edited by Deutscher Vortrupp, 12–29. Berlin: Vortrupp Verlag, 1935.

Hoffmann, Christhard, Werner Bergmann, and Helmut Walser, eds. *Exclusionary Violence: Antisemitic Riots in Modern German History*. Ann Arbor: University of Michigan Press, 2002.

Holzmann, Günter. *Und es beginnt ein neuer Tag: Autobiographie*. Zurich: Rotpunktverlag, 2001.

Honigmann, Barbara. *Damals, Dann, und Danach*. Munich: Carl Hauser, 1999.

———. *Ein Kapitel aus meinem Leben*. Munich: Carl Hauser, 2004.

Honigmann, Peter. *Die Austritte aus der jüdischen Gemeinde Berlin, 1873–1941: Statistische Auswertung und historische Interpretation*. Frankfurt/M: Peter Lang, 1987.

———. "Gibt es in der DDR Antisemitismus?" *Civis* 2 (1986): 4–12.

Horch, Hans Otto, and Charlotte Wardi, eds. *Jüdische Selbstwahrnehmung*. Tübingen: Max Niemeyer, 1997.

Huhn, Klaus. *Der Fall Rudolf Herrnstadt*. Berlin: Das neue Berlin, 2008.

Hutchinson, Peter, and Reinhard K. Zachau, eds. *Stefan Heym: Socialist, Dissenter, Jew*. Oxford: Peter Lang, 2003.

Illichmann, Jutta. *Die DDR und die Juden: Die deutschlandpolitische Instrumentalisierung von Juden und Judentum durch Partei und Staatsführung der SBZ /DDR von 1945 bis 1990*. Frankfurt/M: Peter Lang, 1997.

Ilsar, Yehiel. "Zum Problem der Symbiose: Prolegomena zur deutsch-jüdischen Symbiose." *Bulletin des Leo Baeck Instituts* 14 (1975): 122–65.

Isaacson, Walter. *Einstein: His Life and Universe*. New York: Simon & Schuster, 2007.

Jacobs, Jack. *The Frankfurt School, Jewish Lives, and Anti-Semitism.* New York: Cambridge University Press, 2015.

Jander, Martin. "Antifaschismus ohne Juden: Der Kollaps der DDR und die linke DDR-Opposition." In *Nach Auschwitz: Schwieriges Erbe der DDR*, edited by Enrico Heitzer. 206–22. Frankfurt/M: Wochenschauverlag, 2018.

Jochmann, Werner. *Gesellschaftskrise und Judenfeindschaft in Deutschland, 1870–1945.* Hamburg: Christians, 1988.

Johannsen, Ernst. *Klärung: 12 Autoren, Politiker über die Judenfrage.* Berlin: Tradition Wilhelm Kolk, 1932.

Joseph, Detlef. *Die DDR und die Juden: Eine kritische Untersuchung.* Berlin: Das neue Berlin, 2010.

Kahane, Anetta. *Ich sehe was, was du nicht siehst: Meine deutschen Geschichten.* Berlin: Rowohlt, 2004.

———. "Wirkung eines Tabus: Juden und Antisemitismus in der DDR." In *Nach Auschwitz: Schwieriges Erbe der DDR*, edited by Enrico Heitzer, 39–47. Frankfurt/M: Wochenschauverlag, 2018.

Kahler, Erich von. "Deutsche und Juden." In *Auf gespaltenen Pfad*, edited by Manfred Schlösser, 159–85. Darmstadt: Erato Presse, 1964.

Kampmann, Wanda. *Deutsche und Juden: Die Geschichte der Juden in Deutschland vom Mittelalter bis zum Beginn des ersten Weltkrieges.* Frankfurt/M: Fischer, 1979.

Kantorowicz, Alfred. *Deutsche Schicksale: Intellektuelle unter Hitler und Stalin.* Vienna: Europa, 1964.

———. *Deutsches Tagebuch.* 2 vols. Munich: Kindler, 1959–61.

Käppner, Joachim. *Erstarrte Geschichte: Faschismus und Holocaust im Spiegel der Geschichtswissenschaft und Geschichtspropaganda der DDR.* Hamburg: Ergebnisse, 1999.

Katz, Jacob. "Berthold Auerbach's Anticipation of the German-Jewish Tragedy." *Hebrew Union College Annual* 53 (1982): 215–40.

———. *Out of the Ghetto: The Social Background of Jewish Emancipation, 1770–1870.* Cambridge MA: Harvard University Press, 1973.

Kaznelson, Siegmund, ed. *Juden im deutschen Kulturbereich: Ein Sam-* ... Berlin: Jüdischer Verlag, 1959.

... Persecution of Jews and German Popular Opinion ... ch." *Leo Baeck Institute Yearbook* 17 (1981): 261–89.

Kessler, Mario. *Die SED und die Juden zwischen Repression und Toleranz: Politische Entwicklungen bis 1967*. Berlin: Akademischer Verlag, 1995.

———. "Verdrängung der Geschichte: Antisemitismus in der SED 1952/53." In *Zwischen Politik und Kultur: Juden in der DDR*, edited by Moshe Zuckermann, 34–47. Göttingen: Wallstein, 2002.

Kindt, Werner. *Grundschriften der Deutschen Jugendbewegung*. Düsseldorf: Eugen Diederich, 1963.

Klein, Thomas. *Für die Einheit und Reinheit der Partei: Die innerpartlichen Kontrollorgane der SED in der Ära Ullbricht*. Cologne: Böhlau, 2002.

———. *Visionen: Repression und Opposition in der SED (1949–1989)*. 2 vols. Frankfurt/Oder: Editionen, 1996.

Klemperer, Victor. *Curriculum Vitae: Erinnerungen, 1881–1918*. Edited by Walter Nowojski. Berlin: Aufbau, 1996.

———. *I Will Bear Witness: A Diary of the Nazi Years*. Translated by Martin Chalmers. New York: Random House, 1998.

Klönne, Irmgard: *Deutsch, Jüdisch, Bündisch: Erinnerungen*. Witzenhausen: Südmarktverlag, 1993

Kneip, Rudolf. *Jugend der Weimarer Zeit: Handbuch der Jugendverbände, 1919–1938*. Frankfurt/M: Dipa, 1974.

Knott, Marie Luise, ed. *The Correspondence of Hannah Arendt and Gerschom Scholem*. Translated by Anthony David. Chicago: University of Chicago Press, 2017.

Koehler, John O. *Stasi: The Untold Story of the East German Secret Police*. Boulder CO: Westview, 2010.

Korn, Salomon. *Die fragile Grundlage: Auf der Suche nach der deutsch-jüdischen Normalität*. 2nd rev. ed. Berlin: Philo, 2004.

Krämer, Herbert. *"Der Hase und der Igel: Oder Vom Kampf des Zensors mit dem Abweichler": Zur Zensurgeschichte von Stefan Heym's Die Schmähschrift und Der König-David Bericht*. In *Stefan Heym: Socialist, Dissenter, Jew*, edited by Peter Hutchinson and Reinhard K. Zachau, 79–95. Oxford: Peter Lang, 2003.

Kreisler, Georg. "Misstrauen." In *Fremd im eignen Land: Juden in der Bundesrepublik*, edited by Michael Broder and Michel R. Lang, 242–44. Frankfurt/M: Fischer, 1979.

Krojanker, Gustav. *Zum Problem des neuen deutschen Nationalismus: Eine zionistische Orientierung gegenüber der nationalistischen Strömungen unserer Zeit*. Berlin: Verlag der Jüdischen Rundschau, 1932.

Krüger, Horst, ed. *Das Ende einer Utopie: Hingabe und Selbstbefreiung früherer Kommunisten*. Olten: Walter, 1963.

Kuczynski, Jürgen. *Dialog mit meinem Urenkel: Neunzehn Briefe und ein Tagebuch*. Berlin: Aufbau, 1983.

———. *Memoiren: Die Erziehung des Jürgen Kuczynski zum Kommunisten und Wissenschaftler*. Cologne: Pahl-Rugenstein, 1983.

———. "Wo wäre das anders gewesen?" *Konkret*, no. 8 (1992): 44–46.

Kurthen, Hermann, Werner Bergmann, and Rainer Erb, eds. *Antisemitism and Xenophobia in Germany after Unification*. New York: Oxford University Press, 1997.

Kwiet, Konrad, and Helmut Eschwege. *Selbstbehauptung und Widerstand: Deutsche Juden im Kampf um Existenz und Menschenwürde, 1933–1945*. Hamburg: Christians, 1984.

Landauer, Gustav. *Dichter, Ketzer, Aussenseiter: Essays und Reden zu Literatur, Philosophie, Judentum*. Edited by Hanna Delf. Berlin: Akademischer Verlag, 1997.

Laqueur, Walter. *Young Germany: A History of the German Youth Movement*. London: Routledge & Kegan Paul, 1962.

Large, David Clay. "'Out with the Ostjuden': The Scheunenviertel Riots in Berlin, November 1923." In *Exclusionary Violence: Antisemitic Riots in Modern German History*, edited by Christhard Hoffmann, Werner Bergmann, and Helmut Walser, 123–40. Ann Arbor: University of Michigan Press, 2002.

Legge, Jerome S., Jr. *Jews, Turks, and Other Strangers: The Roots of Prejudice in Modern Germany*. Madison: University of Wisconsin Press, 2003.

Leschnitzer, Adolf. *The Magic Background of Modern Anti-Semitism: An Analysis of the German-Jewish Relationship*. New York: Universities Press, 1956.

Lessing, Theodor. *Der jüdische Selbsthass*. Munich: Matthes & Leitz, 1984.

Levine, Herbert S. "The Jewish Leadership in Germany and the Nazi Threat in 1933." In *German Nationalism and the European Response, 1890–1945*, edited by Carole Fink, Isabel V. Hull, and MacGregor Knox, 181–206. Norman: University of Oklahoma Press, 1985.

Levy, Richard S. *Antisemitism in the Modern World: An Anthology of Texts*. Lexington MA: D. C. Heath, 1991.

Lewy, Guenter. *Perpetrators: The World of the Holocaust Killers*. New York: Oxford University Press, 2017.

Liebmann, Irina. *Wäre es schön? Es wäre schön! Mein Vater Rudolf Herrnstadt*. Berlin: Berlin Verlag, 2008.

Limberg, Margarete, and Hubert Rübsaat, eds. *Germans No More: Accounts of Jewish Everyday Life, 1933–1938*. New York: Berghahn, 2006.

Liptzin, Solomon. *Germany: Stepchildren*. Philadelphia: Jewish Publication Society, 1944.

Loewenberg, Peter. *Walter Rathenau and Henry Kissinger: The Jewish Modern Statesmen in Two Political Cultures*. New York: Leo Baeck Institute, 1980.

Löwenfeld, Raphael. *Schutzjuden oder Staatsbürger? Von einem jüdischen Staatsbürger*. Berlin: Schweitzer & Mohr, 1893.

Löwenstein, Leo. "Die Linie des Reichsbundes jüdischer Frontsoldaten." In *Wille und Weg des deutschen Judentums*, 7–11. Berlin: Vortrupp, 1935.

Maoz, Eliyahu. "The Werkleute." *Leo Baeck Institute Yearbook* 4 (1959): 165–82.

Marx, Jakob. *Das deutsche Judentum und seine jüdischen Gegner*. Berlin: Philo, 1925.

Marx, Karl. *A World Without Jews*. 4th rev. ed. New York: Philosophical Library, 1959.

Maser, Peter. "Juden und jüdische Gemeinden in der DDR bis in das Jahr 1988." *Tel Aviv Jahrbuch für jüdische Geschichte* 20 (1991): 393–426.

Matthäus, Jürgen. *Jewish Responses to Persecution*. Vol. 1. Lanham MD: Altamira, 2010.

Maurer, Trude. *Ostjuden in Deutschland, 1918–1933*. Hamburg: Hans Christians, 1986.

Maybaum, Ignaz. "Absage an den RJF." *Jüdische Rundschau*, no. 48 (June 16, 1933): 259–61.

Mayer, Hans. "Das Gedächtnis und die Geschichte: Gedanken beim Aufschreiben von Erinnerungen." In *Juden in der deutschen Literatur: Ein deutsch-israelitisches Sympsium*, edited by Stephane Moses and Albrecht Schöne, 13–24. Frankfurt/M: Suhrkamp, 1986.

———. *Der Widerruf: Über Deutsche und Juden*. Frankfurt/M: Suhrkamp, 1994.

Meier-Cronemeyer, Hermann. "Jüdische Jugendbewegung." *Germania Judaica* 8 (1969): 1–122.

Meining, Stefan. *Kommunistische Judenpolitik: Die DDR, die Juden and Israel*. Münster: LIT, 2002.

Meiring, Kerstin. *Die christlich-jüdische Mischehe in Deutschland, 1840–1933*. Hamburg: Dölling & Galitz, 1998.

Melzer, Abraham, ed. *Deutsche und Juden: Ein unlösbares Problem. Reden zum jüdischen Weltkongress 1966*. Düsseldorf: Kontakte, 1966.

Mendes-Flohr, Paul. "Between Germanism and Judaism, Christians and Jews: The Outsiders as Insiders." In *German-Jewish History in Modern Times*, edited by Michael A. Meyer, 157–94. New York: Columbia University Press, 1998.

———. *German Jews: A Dual Identity*. New Haven CT: Yale University Press, 1999.

———. *Gershom Scholem: The Man and His Work*. Albany: State University of New York Press, 1994.

———. "The *Kriegserlebnis* and Jewish Consciousness." In *Jüdisches Leben in der Weimarer Republik / Jews in the Weimar Republic*, edited by Wolfgang Benz, Arnold Paucker, and Peter Pulzer, 225–37. Tübingen: Mohr, 1998.

Mertens, Lothar. *Davidstern unter Hamner und Sichel: Die jüdischen Gemeinden in der SBZ/DDR und ihre Behandlung durch Partei und Staat, 1945–1990*. Hildesheim: Georg Olms, 1997.

Messerschmidt, Manfred. *Die Wehrmacht im NS-Staat: Zeit der Indoktrination*. Hamburg: R. v. Decker, 1969.

Meyer, Beate. "The Mixed Marriage: A Guarantee of Survival or a Reflection of German Society during the Nazi Regime?" In *Probing the Depth of German Antisemitism: German Society and the Persecution of the Jews, 1933–1941*, edited by David Bankier, 54–77. New York: Berghahn, 2000.

Meyer, Michael A., ed. *German-Jewish History in Modern Times*. New York: Columbia University Press, 1998.

Moltmann, Bernhard, ed. *Erinnerung: Zur Gegenwart des Holocaust in Deutschland-West und Deutschland-Ost*. Frankfurt/M: Haag und Herchen, 1993.

Morris, Leslie, and Jack Zipes, eds. *Unlikely History: The Changing German-Jewish Symbiosis, 1945–2000*. New York: Palgrave, 2002.

Moses, Stephane, and Albrecht Schön, eds. *Juden in der deutschen Literatur: Ein deutsch-israelitisches Symposium*. Frankfurt/M: Suhrkamp, 1986.

Mosse, George L. *German Jews beyond Judaism*. Bloomington: Indiana University Press, 1985.

———. "The Influence of the *Völkische* Idea on German Jewry." *Studies of the Leo Baeck Institute*, edited by Max Kreutzberger, 83–114. New York: F. Ungar, 1967.

Mosse, Werner E. "From 'Schutzjude' to 'Deutscher Staatsbürger jüdischen Glaubens': The Long and Bumpy Road of Jewish Emancipation in Germany." In *Paths of Emancipation: Jews, States, and Citizenship*, edited by Pierre Birnbaum and Ira Katznelson, 59–93. Princeton NJ: Princeton University Press, 1995.

———. *Deutsches Judentum in Krieg und Revolution, 1916–1923*. Tübingen: J. C. B. Mohr, 1971.

Mounk, Yasha. *Stranger in My Own Country: A Jewish Family in Modern Germany*. New York: Farrar, Strauss & Giroux, 2014.

Müller, Volker. "Die Dichterwitwe Lotte Fürnberg erinnert sich ihrer Lebensjahre mit Lorie Fürnberg: Es ist so viel Blut umsonst geflossen." *Berliner Zeitung*, January 26, 2001.

Müller-Enberges, Helmut. *Der Fall Rudolf Herrnstadt: Tauwetterpolitik vor dem 17. Juni*. Berlin: Links-Druck, 1991.

Munk, Elie. *Juden und Umwelt: Sechs Vorträge*. Frankfurt/M: Israelit & Herman, 1930.

Naumann, Max. *Vom nationaldeutschen Juden*. Berlin: Albert Goldschmidt, 1920.

———. *Von Zionisten und Jüdischnationalen*. Berlin: Deutsche Verlagsanstalt für Politik & Geschichte, 1921.

Naumann, Michael, ed. *"Es muss doch in diesem Lande wieder möglich sein . . .": Der neue Antisemitismus*. Munich: Ullstein, 2002.

Necker, Gerold, Elke Morlok, and Matthias Morgenstern, eds. *Gerschom Scholem in Deutschland: Zwischen Seelenverwandschaft und Sprachlosigkeit*. Tübingen: Mohr Siebeck, 2014.

Neimark, Anne E. *One Man's Valor: Leo Baeck and the Holocaust*. New York: E. P. Dutton, 1986.

Nicosia, Francis R. "The End of Emancipation and the Illusion of Preferential Treatment: German Zionists, 1933–1938." *Leo Baeck Institute Yearbook* 36 (1991): 243–65.

———. "Revisionist Zionism in Germany II: Georg Kareski and the Staatszionistische Organisation, 1933–1938." *Leo Baeck Institute Yearbook* 32 (1987): 231–71.

Niether, Hendrik. *Leipziger Juden und die DDR: Eine Existenzerfahrung im Kalten Krieg*. Göttingen: Vandenhoeck & Ruprecht, 2015.

Niewyk, Donald L. *Jews in Weimar Germany*. New Brunswick NJ: Transaction, 1980.
———. "Solving the 'Jewish Problem': Continuity and Change in German Antisemitism, 1871–1945." *Leo Baeck Institute Yearbook* 35 (1990): 335–70.
Norden, Albert. *Ereignisse und Erlebtes*. Berlin: Dietz, 1981.
O'Doherty, Paul. "The GDR in the Center of Stalinist Show Trials and Anti-Semitism in Eastern Europe, 1948–54." *German History* 3 (1992): 302–17.
Otto, Wilfriede. *Die SED im Juni 1953: Interne Dokumente*. Berlin: Karl Dietz, 2003.
Paucker, Arnold. *Deutsche Juden im Kampf um Recht und Freiheit: Studien zu Abwehr, Selbstbehauptung und Widerstand der deutschen Juden seit Ende des 19. Jahrhunderts*. Teetz: Hentrich & Hentrich, 2003.
———. *Die Juden im nationalsozialistischen Deutschland/Jews in Nazi Germany, 1933–1943*. Tübingen: J. C. B. Mohr, 1986.
———. *Der jüdische Abwehrkampf gegen Antisemitismus und Nationalsozialismus in den letzten Jahren der Weimarer Republik*. Hamburg: Leibnitz, 1968.
———. "Zum Selbstverständnis jüdischer Jugend in der Weimarer Republik und unter nationalsozialistischer Diktatur." In *Jüdische Selbstwahrnehmung*, edited by Hans Otto Horch and Charlotte Wardi, 111–28. Tübingen: Max Niemeyer, 1997.
Pauker, Arnold, and Peter Pulzer, eds. *Jüdisches Leben in der Weimarer Republik: Jews in the Weimar Republic*. Tübingen: Mohr, 1998.
Peck, Jeffrey. *Being Jewish in the New Germany*. New Brunswick NJ: Rutgers University Press, 2006.
Peyser, Alfred. *Nationaldeutsche Juden und ihre Lästerer: Eine Streitschrift*. Berlin: Alfred Goldschmidt, n.d.
Pierson, Ruth. "Embattled Veterans: The Reichsbund jüdischer Frontsoldaten." *Leo Baeck Institute Yearbook* 19 (1974): 139–54.
Podewin, Norbert. *Albert Norden, der Rabbinersohn im Politbureau: Stationen eines ungewöhnlichen Lebens*. 2nd rev. ed. Berlin: Edition Ost, 2003.
Poor, Harold. *Kurt Tucholsky and the Ordeal of Germany, 1914–1935*. New York: Charles Scribner's Sons, 1968.
Prinz, Joachim. *Rebellious Rabbi: An Autobiography*. Bloomington: Indiana University Press, 2008.
———. *Wir Juden*. Berlin: Erich Reiss, 1934.

Prochnik, George. *Stranger in a Strange Land: Searching for Gerschom Scholem and Jerusalem*. New York: Other Press, 2016.

Pulzer, Peter. "Between Hope and Fear: Jews and the Weimar Republic." In *Jüdisches Leben in der Weimarer Republik/Jews in the Weimar Republic*, edited by Wolfgang Benz, Arnold Paucker, and Peter Pulzer, 271–79. Tübingen: Mohr, 1998.

———. *Jews and the German State: The Political History of a Minority, 1848–1933*. Detroit: Wayne State University Press, 2003.

———. *The Rise of Political Anti-Semitism in Germany and Austria*. New York: John Wiley, 1964.

Rabinbach, Anson. *Germans and Jews Since the Holocaust: The Changing Situation in West Germany*. New York: Holmes & Meier, 1986.

Rahden, Till van. "History in the House of the Hangman: How Postwar Germany Became a Key Site for the Study of Jewish History." In *The German-Jewish Experience Revisited*, edited by Steven E. Aschheim and Vivian Liska, 171–92. Berlin: Walter de Gruyter, 2015.

Rapaport, Lynn. *Jews in Germany: Memory, Identity, and German-Jewish Relations*. Cambridge: Cambridge University Press, 1997.

Rathenau, Walther. *Schriften*. Edited by Arnold Harttung, Günther Jenne, and Golo Mann. Berlin: Berlin Veerlag, 1965.

———. "Staat und Judentum." *Gesammelte Schriften*. Vol. 1. Berlin: S. Fischer, 1925.

Reich-Ranicki, Marcel. *Mein Leben*. Stuttgart: Deutsche Verlags-Anstalt, 1999

———. *Ohne Rabatt: Über Literatur aus der DDR*. Stuttgart: Deutche Verlags-Anstalt, 1991.

———. *Über Ruhestörer: Juden in der deutschen Literatur*. Munich: Piper, 1973.

Reichmann, Eva. "Der Bewusstseinwandel der deutschen Juden." In *Deutsches Judentum in Krieg und Revolution, 1916–1923*, edited by Werner E. Mosse, 511–612. Tübingen: J. C. B. Mohr, 1971.

———. *Grösse und Verhängnis deutsch-jüdischer Existenz: Zeugnisse einer tragischen Begegnung*. Heidelberg: Schneider, 1974.

Reinharz, Jehuda. *Fatherland as Promised Land: The Dilemma of the German Jew, 1893–1914*. Ann Arbor: University of Michigan Press, 1975.

———. "Hashomer Hatzair in Nazi Germany." In *Die Juden im nationalsozialistischen Deutschland/Jews in Nazi Germany, 1933–*

1943, edited by Arnold Paucker, 317–50. Tübingen: J. C. B. Mohr, 1986.

———. "The Zionist Response to Antisemitism in Germany." *Leo Baeck Institute Yearbook* 30 (1985): 105–40.

Rensmann, Lars, and Julius H. Schoeps, eds. *Politics and Resentment: Antisemitism and Counter-Cosmopolitanism in the European Union*. Leiden: Brill, 2011.

Rheins, Carl. J. "Deutscher Vortrupp: Gefolgschaft deutscher Juden, 1933–1935." *Leo Baeck Institute Yearbook* 26 (1981): 207–29.

———. "The Schwarzes Fähnlein, Jungenschaft, 1932–1934." *Leo Baeck Institute Yearbook* 23 (1978): 173–97.

———. "Der Verband nationaldeutscher Juden, 1921–1933." *Leo Baeck Institute Yearbook* 25 (1980): 243–68.

Richarz, Monika, ed. *Jewish Life in Germany: Memoirs from Three Centuries*. Translated by Stella P. and Sidney Rosenfeld. Bloomington: Indiana University Press, 1991.

———. "Juden in der Bundesrepublik Deutschland und in der Demokratischen Republick seit 1945." In *Jüdisches Leben in Deutschland seit 1945*, edited by Micha Brumlik, 13–30. Frankfurt/M: Athenäum, 1986.

Riesser, Gabriel. *Eine Auswahl aus seinen Schriften und Briefen*. 2nd rev. ed. Frankfurt/M: J. Kaufmann, 1918.

Rinott, Chanoch. "Major Trends in Jewish Youth Movements in Germany." *Leo Baeck Institute Yearbook* 19 (1974): 77–95.

Robertson, Ritchie. *The "Jewish Question" in German Literature, 1749–1939*. Oxford: Oxford University Press, 1999.

Roemer, Nils. *Jewish Scholarship and Culture in Nineteenth Century Germany: Between History and Faith*. Madison: University of Wisconsin Press, 2005.

Rohrbacher, Stefan. *Gewalt im Biedermeier: Antijüdische Ausschreitungen in Vormärz und Revolution (1815–1948/49)*. Frankfurt/M: Campus, 1993.

Rosenstock, Werner. "Exodus 1933–1939: A Survey of Jewish Emigration from Germany." *Leo Baeck Institute Yearbook* 1 (1956): 373–90.

Rotenstreich, Nathan. "Gerschom Scholem's Conception of Jewish Nationalism." In *Gerschom Scholem: The Man and His Work*, edited by Paul Mendes-Flohr, 104–19. Albany: State University of New York Press, 1994.

Rubin, Abraham. "Max Brod and Hans-Joachim Schoeps: Literarische Collaborators, Ideologische Rivalen." *Leo Baeck Institute Yearbook* 60 (2015): 5–24.

Ryding, Erik, and Rebecca Pechefsky, *Bruno Walter: A Word Elsewhere*. New Haven CT: Yale University Press, 2001.

Salamon, George. *Arnold Zweig*. Boston: Twayne, 1975.

Salzborn, Samuel. "Anti-Jewish Guilt Deflected and National Self-Victimization in Germany." In *Politics and Resentment: Antisemitism and Counter-Cosmopolitanism in the European Union*, edited by Lars Rensmann and Julius H. Schoeps, 397–423. Leiden: Brill, 2011.

Schatzker, Chaim. "The Jewish Youth Movement in Germany in the Holocaust Period." *Leo Baeck Institute Yearbook* 32 (1987): 157–181; 33 (1988): 301–25.

Schay, Rudolf. *Juden in der deutschen Politik*. Berlin: Welt-Verlag, 1929.

Schleunes, Karl. A. *The Twisted Road to Auschwitz: Nazi Policy toward German Jews, 1933–39*. Urbana: University of Illinois Press, 1990

Schlösser, Manfred, ed. *Auf gespaltenem Pfad*. Darmstadt: Erato, 1964.

Schmidt, Holger J. *Antizionismus, Israelkritik und "Judenhass": Antisemitismus in der deutschen Linken nach 1945*. Bonn: Bouvier, 2010.

Schneider, Richard Chaim. *Zwischenwelten: Ein jüdisches Leben im heutigen Deutschland*. Munich: Kindler, 1994.

Schnitzler, Arthur. *The Road into the Open (Der Weg ins Freie)*. Translated by Roger Byers. Berkeley: University of California Press, 1992.

Schoeps, Hans-Joachim. *"Bereit für Deutschland": Der Patriotismus der deutschen Juden und der Nationalsozialismus*. Berlin: Haude & Spenerische Verlagsbuchhandlung, 1970.

———. *Ja, Nein, und Trotzdem: Erinnerungen, Begegnungen, Erfahrungen*. Zurich: Hase & Koehler, 1974.

Schoeps, Julius H. *Deutsch-jüdische Symbiose oder die Missglückte Emanzipation*. Berlin: Philo, 1996.

———. *Das Gewaltsyndrom: Verformungen und Brüche im deutsch-jüdischen Verhältnis*. Berlin: Argon, 1998.

———. *Mein Weg als deutscher Jude: Autobiographische Notizen*. Zurich: Pendo, 2003.

Scholem, Gershom. *From Berlin to Jerusalem: Memoirs of My Youth*. Translated by Harry Zohn. New York: Schocken, 1980.

———. "Jews and Germans." *Commentary* 42 (November 1966): 31–38.

———. *On Jews and Judaism in Crisis: Selected Essays*. New York: Schocken, 1976.

Schubarth, Wilfried. “Xenophobia among East German Youth.” In *Antisemitism and Xenophobia in Germany after Unification*, edited by Hermann Kurthen, 143–58. New York: Oxford University Press, 1997.

Schulin, Ernst. “Walther Rathenau und sein Integrationsversuch als ‘Deutsch-Jüdischen Stammes.’” In *Jüdische Integration und Identität in Deutschland und Österreich, 1848–1918*, edited by Walter Grab, 13–38. Tel Aviv: University of Tel Aviv, 1984.

Schulte, Christoph. *Deutschtum und Judentum: Ein Disput under Juden aus Deutschland*. Stuttgart: Philipp Reclam, 1993.

Schwarzschild, Steven S. “‘Germanism and Judaism’: Hermann Cohen’s Normativer Paradigm and the German-Jewish Symbiosis.” In *Jews and Germans from 1860 to 1933*, edited by David Bronson, 129–72. Heidelberg: Carl Winter, 1979.

Seligmann, Rafael. *Mit beschränkter Hoffnung: Juden, Deutsche, Israelis*, Hamburg: Hoffmann & Campe, 1991.

Shapira, Shahak. *Das wird man ja wohl noch schreiben dürfen: Wie ich der deutscheste Jude der Welt wurde*. Reinbek bei Hamburg: Rohwolt, 2016.

Sinn, Andrea. “Going Public: Jewish Life in Postwar Germany.” *Journal of Modern Jewish Studies* 13 (2014): 23–36.

Sorkin, David. “‘Emancipation and Assimilation’: Two Concepts and their Application to German-Jewish History.” *Leo Baeck Institute Yearbook* 35 (1990): 17–33.

Spalek, John M. *Lion Feuchtwanger: The Man, His Ideas, His Work*. Los Angeles: Hennessey & Ingalls, 1972.

Stachura, Peter D. *The German Youth Movement, 1900–1945: An Interpretation and Documentary History*. London: Macmillan, 1981.

Stapel, Wilhelm. “Antigermanismus.” *Deutsches Volkstum*, no. 6 (1927): 417–26.

Stern, Frank. *The Whitewashing of the Yellow Badge: Antisemitism and Philosemitism in Postwar Germany*. Translated by William Templer. Oxford: Pergamon, 1992.

Stern, Fritz. *Dreams and Delusions: The Drama of German History*. New York: Alfred A. Knopf, 1987.

———. *Gold and Iron: Bismarck, Bleichröder, and the Building of the German Empire*. New York: Alfred A. Knopf, 1977.

Stern, Heinemann. *Warum hassen sie uns eigentlich? Jüdisches Leben zwischen den Kriegen*. Edited by Hans Ch. Meyer. Düsseldorf: Droste, 1970.

———. *Warum sind wir Deutsche? Sechs Aufsätze für die deutsch-jüdische Jugend*. Berlin: Philo, 1926.

Sternburg, Wilhelm von. *Arnold Zweig*. Frankfurt/M: Anton Hain, 1990.

Stolzfus, Nathan. *Resistance of the Heart: Intermarriage and the Rosenstrasse Protest in Nazi Germany*. New York: W. W. Norton, 1996.

Strafstetter, Susanna. "Submergence into Illegality: Hidden Jews in Munich, 1941–45." In *The Germans and the Holocaust: Popular Responses to the Persecution and the Murder of the Jews*, edited by Susanna Strafstetter and Alan E, Steinweiss, 107–28. New York: Berghahn, 2016.

Stulz-Herrnstadt, Nadja. *The Herrnstadt Dokument: Das Politbureau der SED und die Geschichte des 17. Januar 1953*. Reinbek bei Hamburg: Rohwolt, 1991.

Suchy, Barbara. "The Verein zur Abwehr des Antisemitismus (I): From its Beginnings to the First World War." *Leo Baeck Institute Yearbook* 28 (1983): 205–39.

Temme, Marc. "Heyms Kritik am falschen Sozialismus." In *Stefan Heym: Socialist, Dissenter, Jew*, edited by Peter Hutchinson and Reinhard K. Zachau, 127–43. Oxford: Peter Lang, 2003.

Timm, Angelika. "Ein ambivalentes Verhaältnis: Juden in der DDR und der Staat Israel." In *Zwischen Politik ud Kultur: Juden in der DDR*, edited by Moshe Zuckermann, 17–33. Göttingen: Wallstein, 2002.

———. *Jewish Claims against East Germany: Moral Obligation and Pragmatic Policy*. Budapest: Central European University Press, 1997.

Timms, Edward. "Zwischen Symbiotis and Holocaustismus: Neue Ansätze in der deutsch-jüdischen Geschichtsforschung." *Menora* 7 (1996): 25–40.

Toller, Ernst. *I Was a German: The Autobiography of Ernst Toller*. Translated by Edward Crankshaw. New York: William Morrow, 1991

Toury, Jacob. "Gab es ein Krisenbewusstsein unter den Juden während der 'Guten Jahre' der Weimarer Republic, 1924–1929." *Tel Aviv Journal für deutsche Geschichte* 17 (1988): 145–68.

Trachtenberg, Jakow. *Die Greuelpropaganda ist eine Lügenpropaganda sagen die deutschen Juden selbst*. Berlin: Jakow Trachtenberg, 1933.

Traverso, Enzo. *The Jews and Germany: From the "Judeo-German Symbiosis" to the Memory of Auschwitz*. Translated by Daniel Weissbort. Lincoln: University of Nebraska Press, 1995.

———. *The Marxists and the Jewish Question: The History of a Debate (1843–1943)*. Translated by Bernard Gibbons. Atlantic Highlands NJ: Humanities, 1994.

Trefz, Bernhard. *Jugendbewegung und Juden in Deutschland: Eine historische Untersuchung mit besonderer Berücksichtigung des Deutsch-Jüdischen Wanderbundes "Kameraden."* Frankfurt/M: Peter Lang, 1999.

Vogel, Rolf. *Ein Stück von uns: Deutsche Juden in deutschen Armeen, 1813–1976: Eine Dokumentation.* Mainz: Von Hase & Koehler, 1977.

Voigts, Manfred. *Die deutsch-jüdische Symbiose: Zwischen deutschem Sonderweg und Idee Europa.* Tübingen: Niemeyer, 2006.

———. *Zwischen Antisemitismus und deutsch-jüdischer Symbiose.* Würzburg: Königshausen und Neumann, 2013.

Volkov, Shulamit. *German Jews and Antisemites: Trials in Emancipation.* Cambridge: Cambridge University Press, 2006.

———. "Reflections on German-Jewish Historiography: A Dead End or a New Beginning." *Leo Baeck Institute Yearbook* 41 (1996): 309–20

Wagner, Heike. *Hilde Banjamin und die Stalinisierung der DDR Justiz.* Aachen: Shaker, 1999.

Wallach, Kerry. *Passing Illusions: Jewish Visibility in Weimar Germany.* Ann Arbor: University of Michigan Press, 2017.

Wassermann, Jakob. *My Life as German and Jew.* Translated by S. N. Brainin. New York: Coward McCann, 1933.

Weltsch, Robert. *Die deutsche Judenfrage: Ein kritischer Rückblick.* Königstein: Jüdischer Verlag, 1981.

———. *Deutsches Judentum, Aufstieg, und Krise: Gestalten, Ideen, Werke.* Stuttgart: Deutsche Verlagsanstalt, 1963.

Wiegel, Gerd, and Johannses Klotz. *Geistige Brandstiftung: Die Walser-Bubis Debatte.* Cologne: Pappy Rossa, 1999.

Wildt, Michael. "Violence against Jews in Germany: 1933–1939." In *Probing the Depth of German Antisemitism: German Society and the Persecution of the Jews*, edited by David Bankier, 181–209. New York: Berghahn, 2000.

Wistrich, Robert. *From Ambivalence to Betrayal: The Left, the Jews, and Israel.* Lincoln: University of Nebraska Press, 2012.

———. *Socialism and the Jews: The Dilemma of Assimilation in Germany and Austro-Hungary.* East Brunswick NJ: Fairleigh Dickinson University Press, 1982.

Wiznitzer, Manuel. *Arnold Zweig: Das Leben eines deutsch-jüdischen Schriftstellers.* Frankfurt/M: Fischer, 1987.

Wolf, Markus. *The Man without a Face: The Autobiography of Communism's Greatest Spymaster*. New York: Random House, 1997.
Wolffsohn, Michael. *Die Deutschland-Akte: Juden und Deutsche in Ost und West. Tatsachen und Legenden*. Munich: Edition Ferenczy, 1995.
———. *Meine Juden—Eure Juden*. Munich: Piper, 1997.
———. *Verwirrtes Deutschland? Provokative Zwischenberufe eines deutsch-jüdischen Patrioten*. Munich: Bruckmann, 1993.
Wroblesky, Vincent von. *Eine unheimliche Liebe: Juden in der DDR*. Berlin: Philo, 2001.
Zadoff, Noam. *Gerschom Scholem: From Berlin to Jerusalem and Back*. Translated by Jeffrey Green. Waltham MA: Brandeis University Press, 2018.
———. "Der Menschentanz: Gerschom Scholem, Hannah Arendt und der Eichmann Prozess." In *Gerschom Scholem in Deutschland: Zwischen Seelenverwandschaft und Sprachlosigkeit*, edited by Gerold Necker, Elke Morlok, and Matthias Morgenstern, 145–66. Tübingen: Mohr Siebeck, 2014.
Zimmermann, Moshe. *Dei deutschen Juden, 1914–1945*. Translated by Matthias Schmidt. Munich: R. Oldenbourg, 1997.
Zipes, Jack. "The Critical Embracement of Germany: Hans Mayer and Marcel Reich-Ranicki." In *Unlikely History: The Changing German-Jewish Symbiosis, 1945–2000*, edited by Morris Leslie and Jack Zipes, 183–201. New York: Palgrave Macmillan, 2002.
———. "The Cultural Operations of Germans and Jews as Reflected in Recent German Fiction." In *Jews, Germans, Memory: Reconstructions of Jewish Life in Germany*, edited by Michal Y. Bodemann, 163–78. Ann Arbor: University of Michigan Press, 1996.
Zuckermann, Moshe, ed. *Zwischen Politik und Kultur: Juden in der DDR*. Göttingen: Wallstein, 2002.
Zweig, Stefan. *The World of Yesterday*. Lincoln: University of Nebraska Press, 1964.

Index

Photographs are indicated by P *with a numeral; all appear following page 76*